S0-BAL-113

# A Colorful Introduction to the Anatomy of the Human Brain

## A Brain and Psychology Coloring Book

*John P.J. Pinel*
*Department of Psychology*
*University of British Columbia*

*with*

**Maggie Edwards**
*Gnosis Consulting Corporation*
*Vancouver, British Columbia*

Allyn and Bacon
Boston London Toronto Sydney Tokyo Singapore

Copyright © 1998 by Allyn & Bacon
A Viacom Company
160 Gould Street
Needham Heights, MA 02194

Internet: www.abacon.com
America Online: keyword: College Online

All rights reserved.  No part of the material protected by this copyright notice may
be reproduced or utilized in any form or by any means, electronic or mechanical,
including photocopying, recording, or by any information storage and retrieval
system, without written permission from the copyright holder.

ISBN 0-205-16299-1

Printed in the United States of America

10 9 8 7 6 5 4 3 2    02 01 00 99 98

# Contents

**Preface** *vii*

**To the Reader** *xi*

**How to Use This Book** *xii*

***Part 1: Basic Neuroanatomy 1***

**Chapter 1: Organization of the Human Nervous System**

Introduction *3*
1.1 Divisions of the Nervous System *4*
1.2 Divisions of the Central Nervous System *6*
1.3 Divisions of the Peripheral Nervous System *8*
1.4 Organization of the Spinal Cord *10*
1.5 Divisions of the Autonomic Nervous System *12*
1.6 The Endocrine System *14*
Review Exercises *16*

**Chapter 2: Planes and Directions in the Human Nervous System**

Introduction *21*
2.1 Planes in the Human Brain *22*
2.2 Directions in the Human Nervous System *24*
2.3 Sides of the Human Nervous System *26*
Review Exercises *28*

**Chapter 3: Cells of the Nervous System**

Introduction *31*
3.1 The Neuron: Its Major Regions *32*
3.2 The Neuron: Structures of the Cell Body *34*
3.3 The Neuron: Structures of the Terminal Buttons *36*
3.4 Neural Conduction Through Dendrites and Cell Body *38*
3.5 Axonal Conduction and Synaptic Transmission *40*
3.6 Glial Cells and Saltatory Conduction *42*
3.7 The Neuron Cell Membrane and Receptors *44*
Review Exercises *46*

**Chapter 4: Early Development of the Human Nervous System**

Introduction 51
4.1 Development of the Neural Tube *52*
4.2 Six Processes of Early Neural Development *54*
4.3 Early Development of the Brain's Three Major Divisions *56*
4.4 Early Development of the Brain's Five Divisions *58*
4.5 Axon Growth: Correctly Wiring the Nervous System *60*
Review Exercises *62*

**Chapter 5: Gross Anatomy of the Human Brain**
Introduction   67
5.1   Cerebral Hemispheres and Brain Stem   68
5.2   The Five Divisions of the Mature Brain   70
5.3   The Meninges   72
5.4   The Cerebral Ventricles   74
5.5   Tracts and Nuclei   76
5.6   The Cerebral Commissures   78
5.7   The Cranial Nerves   80
Review Exercises   82 ⟶ 5.2/5.3

**Chapter 6: Major Structures of the Brain Stem**
Introduction   87
6.1   Major Structures of the Myelencephalon   88
6.2   Major Structures of the Metencephalon   90
6.3   Major Structures of the Mesencephalon   92
6.4   Diencephalon: The Thalamus   94
6.5   Diencephalon: The Hypothalamus   96
6.6   The Hypothalamus and Pituitary   98
Review Exercises   100

**Chapter 7: Major Structures of the Cerebral Hemispheres**
Introduction   105
7.1   Major Fissures of the Cerebral Hemispheres   106
7.2   Lobes of the Cerebral Hemispheres   108
7.3   Major Gyri of the Cerebral Hemispheres   110
7.4   The Cerebral Cortex   112
7.5   Divisions of the Cerebral Cortex   114
7.6   Primary Sensory and Motor Areas   116
7.7   Subcortical Structures: The Limbic System   118
7.8   Subcortical Structures: The Basal Ganglia   120
Review Exercises   122

**Part 2: Functional Neuroanatomy   129**

**Chapter 8: Sensory Systems of the Central Nervous System**
Introduction   129
8.1   Visual System: From Eye to Cortex   130
8.2   Cortical Visual Areas   132
8.3   Auditory System: From Ear to Cortex   134
8.4   Cortical Auditory Areas   136
8.5   Somatosensory System: From Receptors to Cortex   138
8.6   Cortical Somatosensory Areas   140
8.7   The Descending Analgesia Circuit   142
Review Exercises   144

## Chapter 9: Sensorimotor Pathways of the Central Nervous System

Introduction  *149*

9.1  Sensorimotor Cortical Pathways  *150*
9.2  Primary Motor Cortex  *152*
9.3  The Descending Dorsolateral Motor Pathways  *154*
9.4  The Descending Ventromedial Motor Pathways  *156*
9.5  The Cerebellum and Basal Ganglia  *158*
9.6  Parkinson's Disease and the Nigrostriatal Pathway  *160*
Review Exercises  *162*

## Chapter 10: Brain Structures and Memory

Introduction  *167*

10.1  Hippocampal Formation and Memory: The Case of H.M.  *168*
10.2  Rhinal Cortex and Memory  *170*
10.3  Hippocampus and Spatial Memory  *172*
10.4  Medial Diencephalon and Memory: Korsakoff's Amnesia  *174*
10.5  Basal Forebrain and Memory: Alzheimer's Amnesia  *176*
Review Exercises  *180*

179: 1,4,7,15,18

## Chapter 11: Motivational Systems of the Brain

Introduction  *183*

11.1  Hypothalamus and Eating  *184*
11.2  Subfornical Organ and Deprivation-Induced Thirst  *186*
11.3  Mesotelencephalic Dopamine System and Pleasure  *188*
11.4  Neural Mechanisms of Fear and Anxiety  *190*
11.5  Reticular Formation and Sleep  *192*
11.6  Suprachiasmatic Nucleus and Circadian Rhythms  *194*
11.7  Brain Stem Sex Circuits  *196*
Review Exercises  *199*

199: 1,2,4,5,7

## Chapter 12: Cortical Localization of Language and Thinking

Introduction  *203*

12.1  The Wernicke-Geschwind Model of Language  *204*
12.2  Cortical Areas Involved in Reading: Mapped by PET  *206*
12.3  Cortical Areas Involved in Naming Objects: Mapped by Stimulation  *208*
12.4  Cortical Areas Involved in Thinking: Mapped by Blood Flow Measurement  *210*
12.5  Cognitive, Social, and Emotional Effects of Prefrontal Cortex Lesions  *212*
Review Exercises  *214*

**Answers to Review Exercises**  *219*

**Index**  *223*

# Preface

Neuroscience is currently one of the most active and exciting fields of scientific research. In official recognition of this fact, the U.S. Congress has declared this to be *The Decade of the Brain.*

### The Purpose of this Book

Although important advances are currently being made in all areas of brain research, it is the study of the brain's psychological functions that has truly captured peoples' imaginations. How does the brain see, think, remember, speak, love, fear, and so forth? And what goes wrong with the brain in various psychological disorders? The purpose of this book is to make the fascinating world of brain-and-psychology research more accessible to people who have little or no background in neuroscience.

Unfortunately, before you can learn about the brain's psychological functions, it is necessary to understand its overall organization and to know the names and locations of its major parts. In my experience, this neuroanatomical imperative is a barrier that keeps many people from pursuing their interest in the brain's psychological functions—their initial interest is all too often squelched by their first serious encounter with ponderous neuroanatomical terminology. This book is a simple, effective, and enjoyable introduction to brain anatomy for these people.

### Who Is This Book For?

It's simplicity, clarity, and effective pedagogical features make this book suitable as a text in any course in which students with little or no background in neuroscience are being introduced to human neuroanatomy—it assumes no prior knowledge. The list of such courses has increased rapidly in recent years as knowledge of the brain's psychological functions has increased. Today, discussion of the human brain is an integral part of most courses that deal with human behavior: This includes courses in psychology, medicine, nursing, law, zoology, anthropology, physiology, education, athletics, pharmacology, and physiotherapy.

One consequence of the current explosion of knowledge about the human brain is that coverage of the brain in many introductory texts is often inadequate, and as a result, first- and second-year students have difficulty delving into relevant areas of modern brain research in their senior years. Accordingly, this book can be used effectively as a supplemental text in introductory courses to flesh out texts that do not provide adequate coverage of human brain anatomy, or it can be used in senior courses to provide students with the systematic introduction to human neuroanatomy that they may have missed in their introductory courses.

In addition to its use as a text, this book is particularly well suited to the needs of educated lay people, and of health and education professionals who are following independent programs of reading and self-improvement. It assumes no prior knowledge; it actively involves its readers by requiring that they color the structures that they are learning about; and it includes review exercises that strengthen retention and enable readers to gauge their own progress.

**Organization of This Book**

This book is composed of 72 learning units. On the average, each learning unit focuses on four or five key neuroanatomical structures. Each learning unit has three major components: (1) a brief introduction to the neural structures that are the focus of the unit, (2) a list of these structures with a brief definition of each, and (3) a labeled line drawing that illustrates their location. The reader learns by coloring each of the designated structures.

The 72 learning units are organized into 12 chapters. The first 7 chapters constitute Part I of the book, *Basic Neuroanatomy*; they provide an overview of the human brain's structure and organization, and the names and locations of its major structures. The 5 chapters of Part II, *Functional Neuroanatomy*, revisit many of the same structures introduced in Part I, but they include more information and they focus on each structure's psychological function. Each chapter ends with a series of review exercises that help the reader review the chapter and assess her or his own progress.

**How Does This Book Differ From Other Neuroanatomy Texts?**

Most of the differences between this book and other introductions to neuroanatomy stem from the fact that this book is specifically designed for novices. There are several excellent introductions to human neuroanatomy that are appropriate for neuroanatomy majors and others with strong backgrounds in the neurosciences. In contrast, this book is designed for students, lay people, and health and education professionals who lack such a background and who require just enough neuroanatomical detail—no more, no less—to allow them to pursue their interests in the brain's psychological functions.

The need for this book was recently driven home to me by one of my students. His interest in the brain had been piqued by an introductory psychology course that I was teaching, but he was having difficulty getting a sense of the brain's overall structure from the superficial coverage in the text. He asked me if I could recommend a more effective introduction to brain anatomy, so I selected a book from my shelves that I thought might be appropriate for him. I knew that it was a highly respected neuroanatomy text, and its preface stated emphatically that it was suitable for novices—so I lent it to him. A few days later, he returned the book. When I asked him if it was useful, he picked up the book and flipped to the index. "Look at this," he said, "close to 20 pages of index terms with three columns on each page. There must be over 3,000 technical terms in this book." I got his point, and I have kept it constantly in mind during the preparation of this book.

## This Book's Pedagogical Features

Because the primary purpose of this book is to provide an introduction to neuroanatomy that is suitable for beginners, its pedagogical features are key.

*Less Is More.* This book is based on the premise that, when it comes to teaching introductory neuroanatomy to novices "less is often more." Introductions to neuroanatomy that try to do too much often leave students intimidated, confused, and with little appetite for further study. This book attempts to establish a strong foundation for further study of the brain by limiting itself to key neuroanatomical concepts and structures.

*Looking From Two Perspectives.* Many of the brain structures that are introduced in this book are examined from two perspectives: structural and functional. In Part I, they are introduced, defined, and their location is illustrated; in Part II, their psychological functions and their positions in functioning circuits are discussed. Covering structures twice, particularly when it is from two different perspectives, increases comprehension and facilitates retention.

*The Psychological Focus.* Many people who are attracted to the study of human neuroanatomy are initially motivated by an interest in the brain's psychological functions. Accordingly, the psychological focus of this book helps hold the readers' interest.

*Learning Through Coloring.* The effectiveness of coloring in the teaching of anatomy is well established. It actively involves readers in the learning process, it encourages them to pay close attention to structural details, and it facilitates review. In addition, the aesthetic qualities of some readers' creations provide them with a sense of satisfaction.

*The Cover Flap.* In each learning unit, the anatomical illustration appears on the right-hand page, and the key labels appear in its right margin. Accordingly, students can use the cover flap on the last page of the book to conceal the labels while they are reviewing the illustrations.

***Review Exercises.*** Each chapter ends with a series of review exercises. Their primary purpose is to improve retention, but they also help each reader assess her or his own progress. Readers who do not perform almost perfectly on review exercises are encouraged to work through the chapter again.

***Organization, Consistency, and Repetition.*** Each learning unit comprises two pages, left and right, and each contains the same elements, presented in the same format, in the same locations. For example, all key neuroanatomical terms first appear in bold face in the opening introduction in the left column of the left page; they are listed with their definitions in the right column of the same page; and finally, they appear next to the illustration in the right margin of the right page. This organization, consistency, and repetition facilitates acquisition.

***Illustrations.*** Each illustration is specifically designed to illustrate the concepts and structures of its unit—detail is often sacrificed for the sake of simplicity and clarity.

# To the Reader

Many people find their introduction to neuroanatomy intimidating—I was one of them. In part, this intimidation stems from the complexity of the brain and the fact that early neuroanatomists had little consideration for subsequent generations of "non-Latin-speaking" students when it came to naming its structures. But much of it stems from the encyclopedic nature of conventional neuroanatomy text books. This book, A *Colorful Introduction to the Anatomy of the Human Brain*, is different.

Some of the uncommon features of this book are obvious—for example, it uses coloring to encourage you to pay close attention to neuroanatomical details and to get you actively involved, and it has a cover flap that you can use to conceal the names of brain structures while you are reviewing the illustrations. Less obvious, but more important, is the intention that guided all aspects of my writing. My main goal in writing this book was to provide you with just the right amount of detail: enough detail for you to be able to read magazine articles and watch television programs about the brain with ease and enjoyment, enough detail for you to be able to understand neuroscientific journal articles relevant to your professional goals, and enough detail to prepare you for more advanced study of the brain; but—and this is the really important part—not enough detail to be onerous, intimidating, or otherwise off-putting for beginning students of the brain. At every stage of the writing, I struggled against the chronic mental disorder that plagues virtually all professors: the chronic tendency to add just one more fact.

If my judgment has been sound, you will find this book to be a challenge, but not an unreasonable challenge, and you will finish it with a good working knowledge of human neuroanatomy, a feeling of accomplishment, and with a thirst for further knowledge of the brain and its psychological functions. I welcome your comments and suggestions. You can write to me at the Department of Psychology, University of British Columbia, Vancouver, B.C., Canada V6T 1Z4; e-mail me at jpinel@cortex.psych.ubc.ca; or FAX me at (604) 822-6923.

# How to Use This Book

There are 72 learning units in this book. Each one is laid out on two opposing pages like so. Begin by reading the introduction in the left column; it introduces the neuroanatomical terms that you will be focusing on in the unit, usually four or five. These neuroanatomical terms always appear in bold face; other noteworthy terms (e.g., terms that you have learned in previous units) appear in italics. Read the introduction several times, until you feel that you have a good grasp of it. Then, move on to the adjacent column, where you will find a list of the neuroanatomical terms that you have just been reading about, each with a definition. Study these terms and definitions until you are able to correctly recite the entire list of terms and definitions to yourself without referring to the text. The pronunciations of difficult-to-pronounce terms are also indicated in this column; say each term aloud until you can pronounce it with ease.

Next, move on to the right-hand page, the one with the illustration. Begin this page by coloring the bar under one of the anatomical terms in the right-hand margin—these are the same terms that were listed in bold face on the first page of the unit. Then, using the same color, color the structure on the illustration that corresponds to that term. Repeat this process until all the underlying bars and their associated structures have been colored. As you are coloring, pay close attention to the location, extent, and shape of each structure. In most cases, it will be obvious which part of an illustration should be colored; in cases where it is not, ambiguous boundaries are defined for you by dashed lines. Be careful to use coloring instruments that do not bleed through the paper. You will require four or five distinctive colors for most learning units—the maximum number required is nine. Use colors that you find aesthetically pleasing, but avoid those that are dark because they may obscure the drawing.

Once you have finished coloring the designated structures, use the cover flap on the last page of the book to conceal the terms in the right-hand margin; then, write the names of each of the colored structures on a scrap of paper, saying them aloud as you do. Repeat this exercise until you can do it without an error—not even a spelling or a pronunciation error. Now take a short break—say 5 minutes. When you return, repeat the preceding exercise. When you have achieved perfection for the second time, move on to the next learning unit.

When you have completed all of the learning units in a chapter, complete its review exercises. Then, check the accuracy of your answers—the correct answers are provided at the back of the book. Carefully, review material related to any errors that you make. If you make more than a few errors, review the entire chapter before proceeding to the next one.

If you follow these simple procedures, you will soon have a good working knowledge of basic neuroanatomy. I guarantee it.

# Part 1: Basic Neuroanatomy

This book has two parts. Part 1, *Basic Neuroanatomy*, comprises the first seven chapters. It provides you with an overview of the human brain's organization; it introduces you to the names and locations of the brain's major divisions and structures; and it explains how the brain interacts with other parts of the nervous system.

Part 2, *Functional Neuroanatomy*, revisits many of the same brain structures that you will have been introduced to in Part 1, but it does so from an entirely different perspective, from the perspective of psychological function. Rather than systematically surveying the structures in each part of the brain as does Part 1, Part 2 discusses in each of its chapters the structures involved in a particular psychological function, such as memory, hunger, speaking, vision and thinking.

The following are the seven chapters of Part 1—each is composed of several learning units:

1. **Organization of the Human Nervous System**
2. **Planes and Directions in the Human Nervous System**
3. **Cells of the Nervous System**
4. **Early Development of the Human Nervous System**
5. **Gross Anatomy of the Human Brain**
6. **Major Structures of the Brain Stem**
7. **Major Structures of the Cerebral Hemispheres**

# Chapter 1: Organization of the Human Nervous System

The appearance of the human brain is far from impressive. It is a squishy, wrinkled, walnut-shaped piece of tissue weighing about 1.3 kilograms—a bit less than 3 pounds. It looks more like something that you might find washed up on a beach than like one of the major wonders of nature—which it surely is.

Despite the human brain's unprepossessing appearance, it is capable of wondrous feats. It can feel the tenderness of a loving embrace, travel to the moon, create an artificial heart, and yes, even calculate the gross national product of Norway. You see, brains are us; everything that we see, feel, think, and do is a product of our brains' activities. In this chapter, your brain begins the process of understanding itself.

The human brain does not function in isolation; it is one component of the body's nervous system. In the learning units of this chapter, you will learn about the major divisions of the human nervous system and the relation of the brain to each of them.

The following are the six learning units of Chapter 1:

1.1   Divisions of the Nervous System

1.2   Divisions of the Central Nervous System

1.3   Divisions of the Peripheral Nervous System

1.4   Organization of the Spinal Cord

1.5   Divisions of the Autonomic Nervous System

1.6   The Endocrine System

# 1.1 Divisions of the Nervous System

The human nervous system, like the nervous systems of all *vertebrates* (i.e., animals with spines), has two major divisions: the **central nervous system** (CNS) and the **peripheral nervous system** (PNS). The central nervous system is the part of the vertebrate nervous system that is located within the spine and skull; the peripheral nervous system is the part of the vertebrate nervous system that is located outside the spine and skull. The primary function of the spine and skull is to protect the central nervous system from damage.

The PNS has two kinds of functions: *sensory* and *motor*. It conducts sensory signals to the CNS from sensory receptors in various parts of the body, and it conducts motor signals away from the CNS to muscles, glands and other *effector organs* (i.e., organs that are capable of action) in various parts of the body.

The functions of the CNS are more complex than those of the PNS. The CNS receives, stores, and analyzes the sensory signals conducted to it by the PNS, and on the basis of them, it generates the motor signals that are conducted by the PNS to the effector organs.

The spine is composed of 33 *vertebrae* (i.e., spinal bones). It is divided into four different regions: (1) the **cervical region** includes the vertebrae of the cervix or neck, (2) the **thoracic region** includes the vertebrae of the thorax or chest, the vertebrae to which the ribs are attached, (3) the **lumbar region** includes the vertebrae of the small of the back, and (4) the **sacral region** includes the vertebrae of the lower back, the vertebrae to which the bones of the pelvis are attached. In humans, the vertebrae of the sacral region fuse at about the age of 26 years and become known as the *sacrum*.

**Central nervous system (CNS)**
The part of the vertebrate nervous system that is located within the skull and spine.

**Peripheral nervous system (PNS)**
The part of the vertebrate nervous system that is located outside the skull and spine.

**Cervical region** (SIR vi cal)
The section of the spine that provides the flexible framework of the neck or cervix; it lies between the skull and the thoracic region.

**Thoracic region** (thor ASS ic)
The section of the spine to which the ribs are attached; it lies between the cervical and the lumbar regions.

**Lumbar region** (LUM bar)
The section of the spine that supports the small of the back; it lies between the thoracic region and the sacral region.

**Sacral region** (SAK rul)
The section of the spine to which the bones of the pelvis are attached; it lies adjacent to the lumbar region.

---

*Coloring notes*

*First, in the illustration of the human figure, color the central nervous system (brain and spinal cord) one color and all branches of the PNS, including those that are represented by single lines, another color. Then, in the illustration of the skull and spinal cord, color each region of the spine a different color.*

*In all learning units, color the bars under the terms in the right margin; use the same colors as you use for the structures to which they point.*

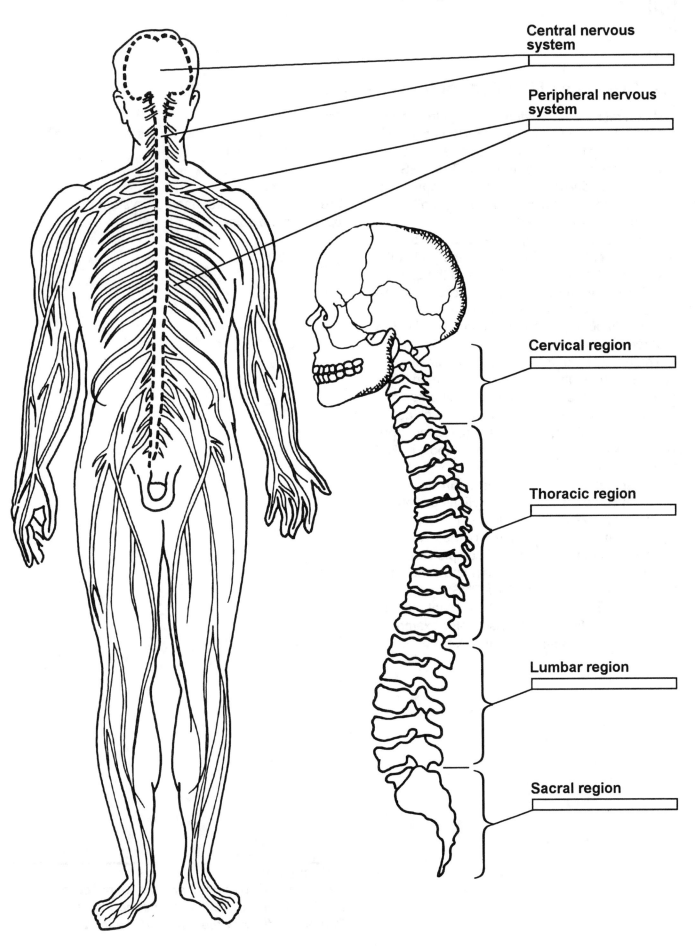

Central nervous
system

Peripheral nervous
system

Cervical region

Thoracic region

Lumbar region

Sacral region

## 1.2 Divisions of the Central Nervous System

The central nervous system (CNS) is the control center of the body. The CNS exerts its control over the body through its interactions with the peripheral nervous system (PNS). The CNS receives sensory information from receptors via the PNS and controls the muscles and other effector organs via the PNS

The CNS has two major divisions: the **brain** and the **spinal cord**. The brain is the part of the CNS that is located in the skull, and the spinal cord is the part of the CNS that is located in the spine. The spinal cord's four regions—*cervical*, *thoracic*, *lumbar*, and *sacral*—correspond to the four regions of the spine.

The functions of the brain are extremely complex. The highest levels of the human brain engage in processes of almost unfathomable complexity and flexibility: processes such as perceiving, thinking, remembering, feeling, and speaking—all of which you will learn about in Part 2 of this book.

The spinal cord performs three functions, which, in comparison to the functions performed by the brain, are relatively simple. It receives signals from the sensory fibers of the PNS and conducts them to the brain for complex analysis; it receives signals from the brain and conducts them to the motor fibers of the PNS; and it performs the simple rapid analyses that mediate many of our reflexive responses—for example, withdrawing a hand from a hot stove.

**Brain**
The part of the central nervous system that is located in the skull.

**Spinal cord**
The part of the central nervous system that is located in the spine.

*Coloring notes*
*Color the brain one color and the spinal cord a another color. Stay within the dashed lines. Remember to color the bars under each term.*

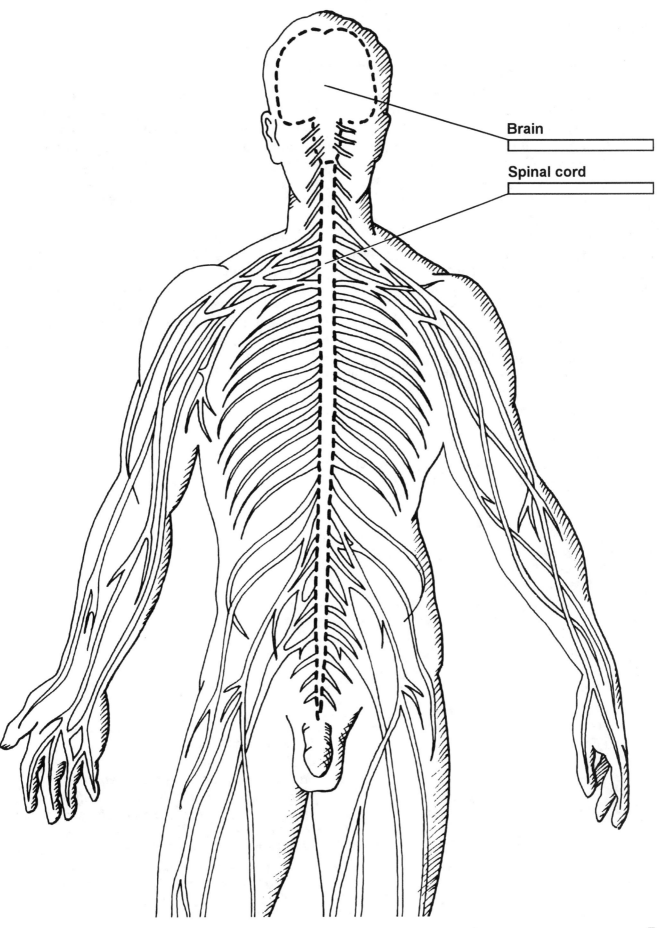

**Brain**

**Spinal cord**

## 1.3 Divisions of the Peripheral Nervous System

The peripheral nervous system (PNS) has two major divisions: the **somatic nervous system** and the **autonomic nervous system**. The somatic nervous system (SNS) is the division of the PNS that interacts with the external environment. It conducts signals to the CNS both from external sensory receptors (e.g., from eyes, ears, and touch receptors in the skin) and from sensory receptors in joints and *skeletal muscles* (i.e., the muscles of the skeleton, which control body movement), and it conducts motor signals from the CNS to skeletal muscles. In contrast, the autonomic nervous system (ANS) is the division of the PNS that participates in the regulation of the body's internal environment. It conducts signals from sensory receptors in internal organs (e.g., from receptors in the heart, liver, and stomach) to the CNS, and it conducts motor signals from the CNS back to many of the same internal organs.

From a psychological point of view, a major difference between the somatic nervous system and the autonomic nervous system has to do with consciousness. We are often conscious of signals carried by our somatic nervous systems, but rarely are we conscious of signals carried by our autonomic nervous systems. Important information about the external environment, that is carried to the CNS by our somatic nervous systems is almost always relayed to the highest levels of our brains for conscious consideration and voluntary reaction—even when immediate reflexive action is taken by the spinal cord. In contrast, the signals from our inner bodies are rarely conducted to the highest levels of our brains, and thus they rarely enter our consciousness and are not usually under our voluntary control.

**Somatic nervous system** (soe MA tik)
The division of the peripheral nervous system that interacts with the external environment; it conducts sensory signals to the CNS from external receptors and receptors in joints and skeletal muscles, and it conducts motor signals from the CNS to skeletal muscles.

**Autonomic nervous system** (aw tuh NOM mik)
The division of the peripheral nervous system that participates in the regulation of the body's internal environment; it conducts sensory signals to the CNS from receptors in internal organs, and motor signals from the CNS back to the same internal organs.

*Coloring notes*

*For clarity, the somatic nervous system and the autonomic nervous system are separately illustrated on different sides of the body— although in reality, somatic and autonomic fibers are intermingled. Color the somatic nervous system one color and the autonomic nervous system another by staying within the dashed lines. Use pale colors (e.g., yellow and pink) so as not to obliterate the detail beneath.*

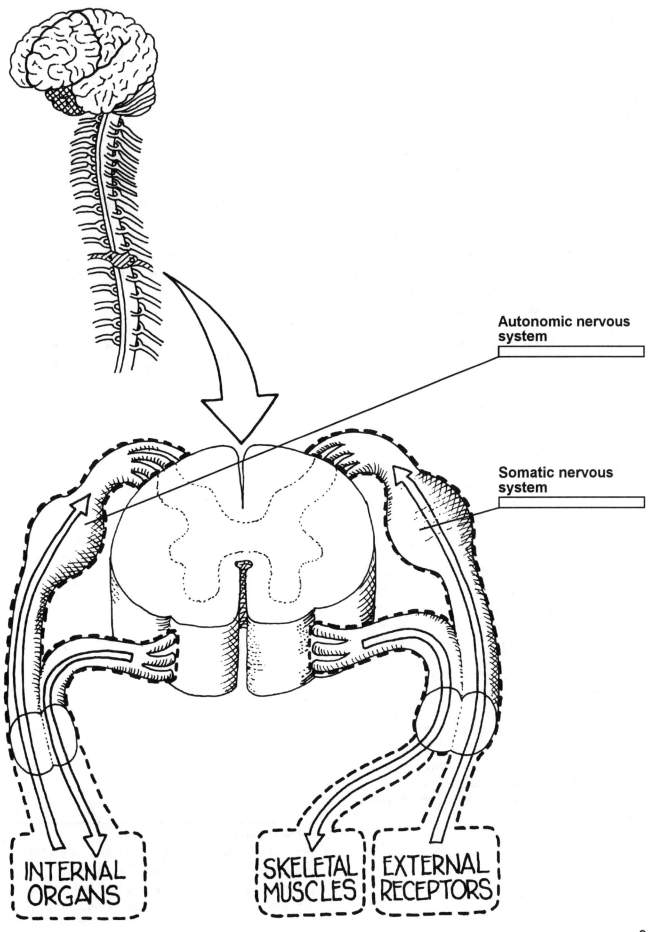

**Autonomic nervous system**

**Somatic nervous system**

INTERNAL ORGANS

SKELETAL MUSCLES

EXTERNAL RECEPTORS

## 1.4 Organization of the Spinal Cord

The spinal cord has two fundamentally different areas: an area of gray matter and an area of white matter. The **spinal gray matter** is the H-shaped area of gray tissue in the core of the spinal cord; the **spinal white matter** is the area of white tissue surrounding the spinal gray matter.

Four bundles of fibers emerge from the spinal cord at each of 31 different levels of the spinal cord. Two of each four are *sensory nerves*, that is, they are bundles of nerve fibers that conduct signals from sensory receptors to the CNS; the other two are *motor nerves*, that is, they are bundles of nerve fibers that conduct signals from the CNS to muscles, glands, and other effector organs. The two sensory nerves enter the back of the spinal cord, one from each side; the two motor nerves exit the front of the spinal cord, one from each side. Accordingly, the 31 pairs of sensory nerves are called the **dorsal roots** (*dorsal* means *toward the back*), and the 31 pairs of motor nerves are called the **ventral roots** (*ventral* means *toward the front*). Each of the 124 spinal nerves (4 x 31) contains both *autonomic nervous system* and *somatic nervous system* fibers.

Nerves that carry signals toward a structure are said to be *afferent* with respect to that structure, whereas nerves that carry signals away from a structure are said to be *efferent* with respect to that structure. The words *afferent* and *efferent* are most frequently used with respect to the CNS; accordingly, sensory nerves are often referred to as *afferent*, and motor nerves are often referred to as *efferent*. You will not get the terms *afferent* and *efferent* confused if you remember that many words that involve the idea of "going toward" begin with an "a" (e.g., advance, approach, and arrive) and that many words that involve the idea of "going away" start with an "e" (e.g., exit, emerge, and elope).

### Spinal gray matter
The H-shaped area of gray nervous tissue in the core of the spinal cord.

### Spinal white matter
The area of white nervous tissue in the spinal cord; it surrounds the spinal gray matter.

### Dorsal roots
The 31 pairs of sensory nerves that enter the spinal cord; they enter the spinal cord's dorsal surface.

### Ventral roots
The 31 pairs of motor nerves that exit the spinal cord; they project from the spinal cord's ventral surface.

***Coloring notes***

*First, color the spinal white matter and spinal gray matter. Then, color the four dorsal (sensory) and four ventral (motor) roots, which enter and exit, respectively, the spinal cord.*

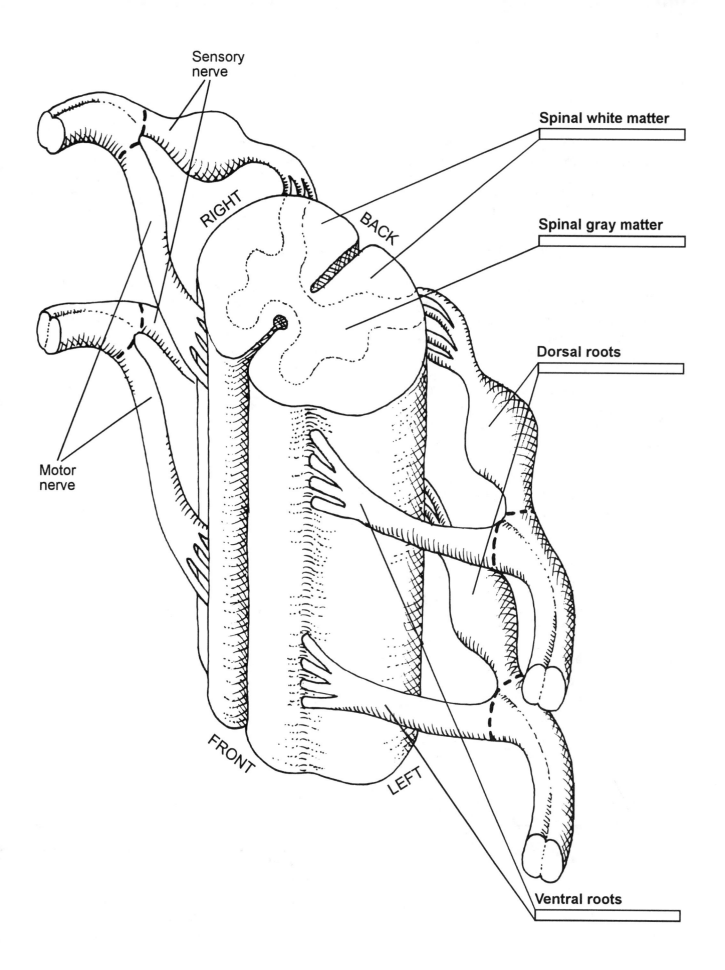

Sensory nerve

Spinal white matter

Spinal gray matter

Dorsal roots

RIGHT

BACK

Motor nerve

FRONT

LEFT

Ventral roots

## 1.5 Divisions of the Autonomic Nervous System

The motor component of the autonomic nervous system has two divisions: the **sympathetic nervous system** and the **parasympathetic nervous system**. Both the sympathetic and parasympathetic nervous systems carry motor signals from the CNS to the organs of the body. In general, the sympathetic nervous system carries signals that organize and mobilize energy resources during periods of threat, whereas the parasympathetic nervous system carries signals that act to conserve energy during periods of quiescence. Accordingly, the functioning of many of our bodies' organs is regulated by the relative levels of sympathetic and parasympathetic input that they are receiving at any point in time.

Sympathetic and parasympathetic nerves leave the CNS from different regions. The sympathetic nerves leave the CNS from the *thoracic* and *lumbar* regions of the spinal cord; the parasympathetic nerves leave the CNS from the *brain* and the *sacral* region of the spinal cord.

The following are some of the specific effects of sympathetic and parasympathetic activity.

**Sympathetic nervous system**
One of the two motor divisions of the autonomic nervous system; it tends to mobilize energy resources during periods of threat; sympathetic nerves project from the thoracic and lumbar regions of the spinal cord.

**Parasympathetic nervous system**
One of the two motor divisions of the autonomic nervous system, it tends to conserve energy during periods of quiescence; parasympathetic nerves project from the brain and from the sacral region of the spinal cord.

| Sympathetic | Parasympathetic |
| --- | --- |
| dilates pupils | constricts pupils |
| increases sweating | - |
| decreases salivation | increases salivation |
| increases heart rate | decreases heart rate |
| decreases digestion | increases digestion |
| erects hair | - |
| dilates lungs | constricts lungs |
| stimulates adrenaline release | - |
| dilates most blood vessels | constricts some blood vessels |

*Coloring notes*

*Color the autonomic nerves represented by solid lines (i.e., the sympathetic nervous system) one color and those represented by dashed lines (i.e., the parasympathetic nervous system) another.*

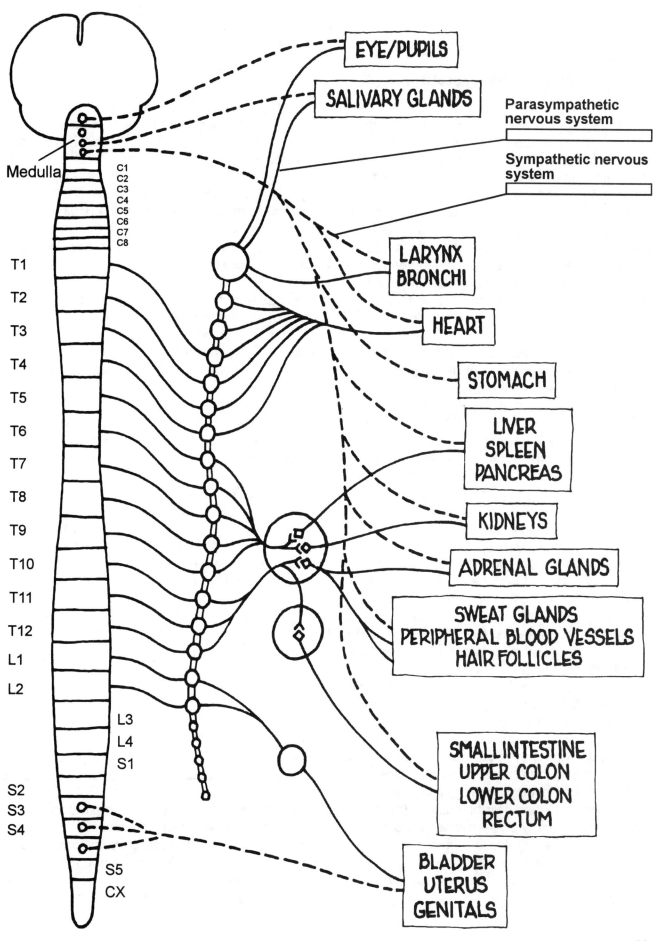

EYE/PUPILS

SALIVARY GLANDS

Parasympathetic nervous system

Sympathetic nervous system

Medulla

C1
C2
C3
C4
C5
C6
C7
C8

T1
T2
T3
T4
T5
T6
T7
T8
T9
T10
T11
T12
L1
L2
L3
L4
S1
S2
S3
S4
S5
CX

LARYNX BRONCHI

HEART

STOMACH

LIVER SPLEEN PANCREAS

KIDNEYS

ADRENAL GLANDS

SWEAT GLANDS PERIPHERAL BLOOD VESSELS HAIR FOLLICLES

SMALL INTESTINE UPPER COLON LOWER COLON RECTUM

BLADDER UTERUS GENITALS

## 1.6 The Endocrine System

Glands are effector organs of the body whose primary function is secretion. *Exocrine glands* are glands that secrete their products via ducts to the outside world (e.g., sweat glands); *endocrine glands* are glands without ducts that secrete their products, called *hormones,* into the blood stream, where they are carried to various parts of the body. The *endocrine system* is the body's second internal route of communication—the first is the nervous system. Each hormone acts on only those cells that contain *receptor molecules* for it (i.e., molecules to which the hormone can bind and, in so doing, influence the activities of the cell).

The following are some of the glands of the endocrine system. (1) The **pituitary gland** hangs by a stalk from the underneath surface of the brain; some of its hormones are *tropic hormones*, hormones whose primary function is to stimulate the release of hormones from other glands—that is why the pituitary gland is called the *master gland*. (2) The **hypothalamus** is part of the brain, but it also qualifies as a gland because it synthesizes and releases hormones. Some of its hormones are called *releasing factors* because they travel through the blood stream to the pituitary, where they trigger the release of pituitary hormones—the pituitary is suspended from the hypothalamus. (3) The *adrenal glands* are the glands that sit atop the kidneys (*renal* means *pertaining to the kidney*). Each adrenal gland is, in fact, two independent glands; its core is the **adrenal medulla**, and its outer layer is the **adrenal cortex** (*cortex* means *bark*). The adrenal medulla is activated by the sympathetic nervous system and releases hormones, such as *adrenaline*, whose effects mimic those of the sympathetic nervous system, but last longer; the adrenal cortex releases hormones that influence energy metabolism, mineral balance, and sexual function. (4) The **gonads** or "naughty bits"—*ovaries* in women and *testes* in men—release hormones that influence the development of female and male reproductive systems and the reproductive behavior of adults.

**Pituitary gland** (pi TUE i tair ee)
The gland that hangs from the hypothalamus; because it releases tropic hormones, it is often referred to as the *master gland*.

**Hypothalamus** (HIPE oh THAL a mus)
The brain structure from which the pituitary is suspended; it secretes releasing hormones, which stimulate the release of tropic hormones from the pituitary.

**Adrenal medulla** (a DREE null  me DULL la)
The core of the adrenal gland; it is activated by the sympathetic nervous system, and in turn it secretes hormones whose effects are similar to those of the sympathetic nervous system.

**Adrenal cortex**
The outer layer of the adrenal gland; it releases hormones that regulate energy metabolism, mineral balance, and reproductive behavior.

**Gonads** (GOE nads)
The sex glands (i.e., ovaries in women and testes in men); they release hormones that influence both the development of female and male reproductive systems and the reproductive behavior of adults.

---

***Coloring notes***

*First, color the hypothalamus and pituitary both in the brain and in the enlargement. Then, color the two parts of the adrenal glands: cortex and medulla. Finally, color both male and female gonads. Some of the other endocrine glands are shown in the illustration, but there is no need to color them.*

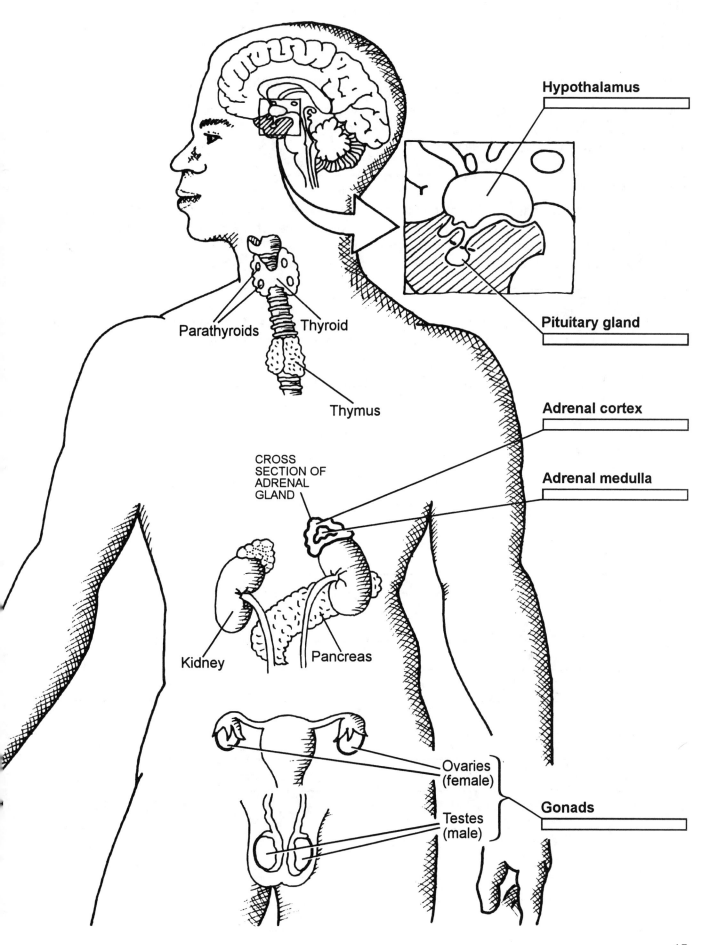

Hypothalamus

Pituitary gland

Adrenal cortex

Adrenal medulla

Parathyroids

Thyroid

Thymus

CROSS
SECTION OF
ADRENAL
GLAND

Kidney

Pancreas

Ovaries
(female)

Testes
(male)

Gonads

## Review Exercises: Organization of the Human Nervous System

Now it is time for you to pause and consolidate the terms and ideas that you have learned in the six learning units of Chapter 1. It is important that you overlearn them so that they do not quickly fade from your memory.

---

### Review Exercise 1.1

Turn to the illustrations in the six learning units of Chapter 1, and use the cover flap at the back of the book to cover the terms that run down the right-hand edge of each illustration page. Study the six illustrations until you can identify each labeled neuroanatomical structure. Once you have worked through each illustration twice without making an error, advance to Review Exercise 1.2.

---

### Review Exercise 1.2

Fill in the missing terms in the following illustration. The correct answers are provided at the back of the book. Carefully review the material related to your incorrect answers.

### DIVISIONS OF THE NERVOUS SYSTEM

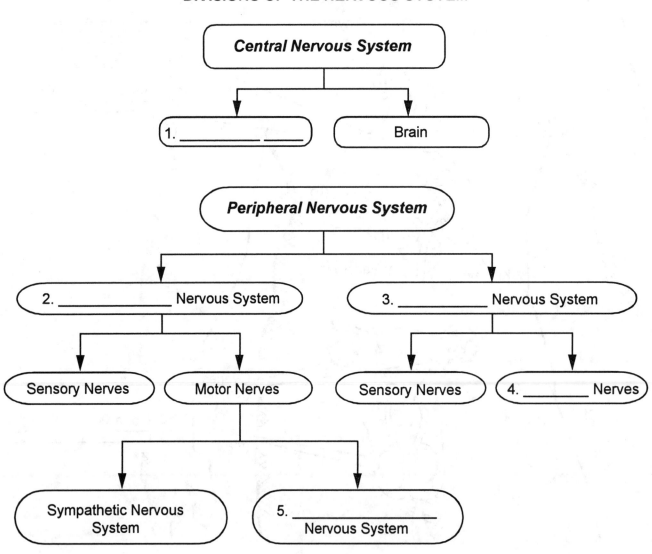

## Review Exercise 1.3

Without referring to Chapter 1, fill in each of the following blanks with the correct term from the chapter. The correct answers are provided at the back of the book. Carefully review the material related to your incorrect answers.

1. Together, the ovaries and testes are referred to as the "naughty bits" or _____.

2. In sequence, the four regions of the spine and spinal cord are, from head to bottom, the _____, _____, _____, and _____ regions.

3. The motor division of the autonomic nervous system that is active during periods of threat is the _____ nervous system.

4. The adrenal _____ releases hormones that influence energy metabolism, mineral balance, and reproductive behavior.

5. The _____ secretes releasing hormones.

6. The _____ nervous system is the major division of the peripheral nervous system that participates in the regulation of the body's internal environment.

7. The H-shaped area of tissue in the core of the spinal cord is referred to as the spinal _____ matter.

8. Nerves emerge from the spinal cord at 31 different levels; _____ motor nerves and _____ sensory nerves emerge from each level.

9. The _____ secretes tropic hormones.

10. Nerves that carry signals toward a structure are said to be _____ with respect to that structure.

11. The _____ nervous system increases heart rate, stimulates adrenaline secretion from the adrenal medulla, and decreases salivation.

12. The brain and spinal cord together compose the _____ nervous system.

13. The nerves of the _____ division of the ANS leave the CNS from the brain and the sacral region of the spinal cord.

14. Two important glands are visible on the underneath surface of the brain. The _____ is suspended by a stalk from the _____.

15. The two divisions of the peripheral nervous system are the autonomic nervous system and the _____ nervous system.

16. Sensory nerves enter the spinal cord via the _____ roots; motor nerves exit via the _____ roots.

17. All _____ glands release hormones into the blood stream.

18. Sympathetic nervous system activity causes the adrenal _____ to release hormones, such as adrenaline, which have effects similar to those of the sympathetic nervous system.

19. The _____ is the division of the CNS that mediates many of the rapid reflexive responses of our skeletal muscles, such as the reflexive withdrawal of a hand from a burning stove.

20. There are two kinds of fibers in the peripheral nervous system: sensory nerves and _____ nerves.

## Review Exercise 1.4

Below in alphabetical order is a list of all the terms and definitions that you learned in Chapter 1. Cover the definitions with a sheet of paper, and work your way down the list of terms, defining them to yourself as you go. Repeat this process until you have gone through the list twice without an error. Then, cover the terms and work your way down the list of definitions, providing the correct terms as you go. Repeat this second process until you have gone through the list twice without an

| | |
|---|---|
| Adrenal cortex | The outer layer of the adrenal gland; it releases hormones that regulate energy, metabolism, mineral balance, and reproductive behavior. |
| Adrenal medulla | The core of the adrenal gland; it is activated by the sympathetic nervous system, and in turn it secretes hormones whose effects are similar to those of the sympathetic nervous system. |
| Autonomic nervous system | The division of the peripheral nervous system that participates in the regulation of the body's internal environment; it conducts sensory signals to the CNS from receptors in internal organs, and motor signals from the CNS back to the same internal organs. |
| Brain | The part of the central nervous system that is located in the skull. |
| Central nervous system | The part of the vertebrate nervous system that is located within the skull and spine. |
| Cervical region | The section of the spine that provides the flexible framework of the neck or cervix. |
| Dorsal roots | The 31 pairs of sensory nerves that enter the spinal cord; they enter the spinal cord's dorsal surface. |
| Gonads | The sex glands (i.e., ovaries in women and testes in men); they release hormones that influence both the development of female and male reproductive systems and the reproductive behavior of adults. |
| Hypothalamus | The brain structure from which the pituitary is suspended; it secretes releasing hormones, which stimulate the release of tropic hormones from the pituitary. |
| Lumbar region | The section of the spine that supports the small of the back. |
| Parasympathetic nervous system | One of the two motor divisions of the autonomic nervous system; it tends to conserve energy during periods of quiescence; parasympathetic nerves project from the brain and from the sacral region of the spinal cord. |
| Peripheral nervous system | The part of the vertebrate nervous system that is located outside the skull and spine. |

| | | | |
|---|---|---|---|
| Pituitary gland | The gland that hangs from the hypothalamus; because it releases tropic hormones, it is often referred to as the master gland. | Ventral roots | The 31 pairs of motor nerves that exit the spinal cord; they project from the spinal cord's ventral surface. |
| Sacral region | The section of the spine to which the bones of the pelvis are attached. | | |
| Somatic nervous system | The division of the peripheral nervous system that interacts with the external environment; it conducts sensory signals to the CNS from external receptors and receptors in joints and skeletal muscles, and it conducts motor signals from the CNS to skeletal muscles. | | |
| Spinal cord | The part of the central nervous system that is located in the spine. | | |
| Spinal gray matter | The H-shaped area of gray nervous tissue in the core of the spinal cord. | | |
| Spinal white matter | The area of white nervous tissue in the spinal cord; it surrounds the spinal gray matter. | | |
| Sympathetic nervous system | One of the two motor divisions of the autonomic nervous system; it tends to mobilize energy resources during periods of threat; sympathetic nerves project from the thoracic and lumbar regions of the spinal cord. | | |
| Thoracic region | The section of the spine to which the ribs are attached. | | |

## Chapter 2: Planes and Directions in the Human Nervous System

Now that you have learned about the major divisions of the human nervous system, you are almost ready to learn about the specific neural structures that compose it—almost, but not quite. First, you need to understand the system that is used to describe the location of structures within the vertebrate body. You will learn this system of anatomical planes and directions in this chapter. It focuses on the human nervous system, but it is applicable to the entire body of any vertebrate.

Despite its brevity, this chapter is a critical one. Trying to study the anatomy of the human brain without understanding the system that is used to describe the location of structures in it is like trying to study geography without understanding east-west, north-south, and up-down.

The following are the three learning units of Chapter 2:

2.1 Planes in the Human Brain

2.2 Directions in the Human Nervous System

2.3 Sides of the Human Nervous System

## 2.1 Planes in the Human Brain

Neuroanatomists have built up a detailed knowledge of the human brain's three-dimensional structure by studying the details of two-dimensional slices or *sections*. As you can imagine, there is no limit to the number of different orientations or *planes* in which brain slices can be cut. However, most brain slices are cut in one of three different planes: the *horizontal plane*, the *sagittal plane*, or the *coronal plane* (also called the *frontal plane*). Each of these three planes is at right angles to the other two.

**Horizontal sections** are slices of the brain that are cut parallel to the horizon, assuming that the subject is in an upright position. **Sagittal sections** are slices of the brain that are cut parallel to the vertical plane that divides the brain into its left and right symmetrical halves—a sagittal section that is cut from the very center of the brain is called a **midsagittal section**. **Coronal sections** (also called *frontal sections*) are slices of the brain that are cut approximately parallel to the surface of the face.

**Cross sections** are slices that are cut at right angles to the long axis of any long, narrow structure, regardless of where that structure is located—for example, like right-angle slices of a cucumber. The anatomy of the spinal cord is almost always studied as a series of cross sections.

**Horizontal sections**
Slices of the brain that are cut in a horizontal plane, that is, cut parallel to the horizon when the subject is in an upright position.

**Sagittal sections** (SAJ i tull)
Slices of the brain that are cut in a sagittal plane, that is, cut parallel to the vertical plane that divides the brain into left and right halves.

**Midsagittal section**
A sagittal section that is cut from the very midline of the brain.

**Coronal sections** (KORE uh null)
Slices of the brain that are cut in a coronal or frontal plane, that is, cut approximately parallel to the surface of the face.

**Cross sections**
Sections that are cut at right angles to the long axis of any long narrow structure, for example, at right angles to the long axis of the spinal cord.

*Coloring notes*
*First, color the midsagittal section; then color the remaining sagittal sections a different shade of the same color. Finally, color the horizontal, coronal, and cross sections different colors. A reminder: In each learning unit, you should be coloring the bar underneath each term in the right-hand column the same color as the structure to which it points.*

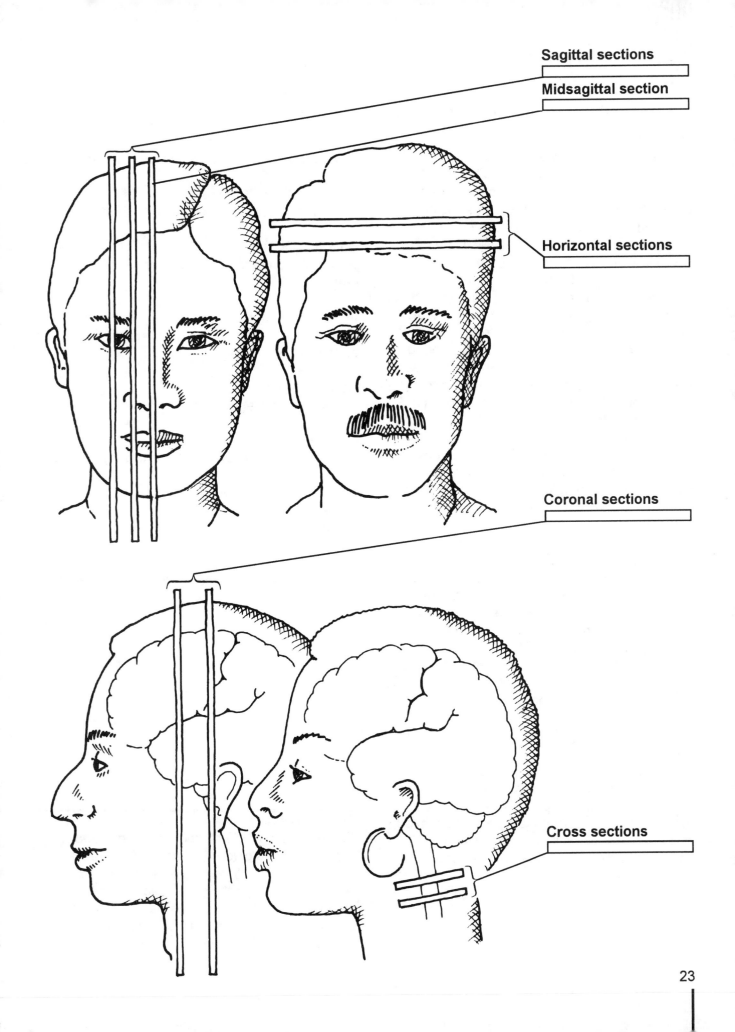

Sagittal sections

Midsagittal section

Horizontal sections

Coronal sections

Cross sections

## 2.2 Directions in the Human Nervous System

Locations in the nervous systems of all vertebrates are described in relation to the orientation of their spinal cords. The three-dimensional system of anatomical directions is straightforward for most vertebrates, which run about on four legs. First, the nose end is referred to as the **anterior** end (also known as the *rostral* end), and the tail end is referred to as the **posterior** end (also known as the *caudal* end). Second, above the spinal cord (i.e., toward the surface of the back) is referred to as **dorsal**, and below the spinal cord (i.e., toward the surface of the chest and stomach) is referred to as **ventral**. And third, toward the midline (i.e., toward the midsagittal plane) is referred to as **medial**, and toward the sides of the body (i.e., toward the left or right) is referred to as **lateral**.

We humans complicate this simple three-dimensional (anterior-posterior, dorsal-ventral, medial-lateral) system of neuroanatomical directions by insisting on walking about on our hind legs, thus changing the orientation of our brains in relation to our spinal cords. This creates a potential source of confusion when applying the *dorsal* and *ventral* labels to humans. In humans, as in four-legged vertebrates, the top of the head and the back are both referred to as *dorsal* although they are different directions in standing humans. Similarly, the stomach and the chin are both referred to as *ventral*. If you become confused by the fact that the dorsal-ventral axis is different in the body than in the head of standing humans, think of a human in the conventional vertebrate posture—on all fours looking straight ahead.

To reduce confusion with respect to the dorsal-ventral axis, in the brains of humans and other primates, **superior** is sometimes used instead of *dorsal* to refer to the top of the head, and **inferior** is sometimes used instead of *ventral* to refer to the bottom of the head.

**Anterior** (an TEER ee er)
Toward the nose end; also known as *rostral*.

**Posterior** (po STEER ee er)
Toward the tail end; also known as *caudal*.

**Dorsal** (DOR sul)
Toward the surface of the back or top of the head.

**Ventral** (VEN trul)
Toward the surface of the chest and stomach or bottom of the head.

**Medial** (MEED ee ul)
Toward the midsagittal plane.

**Lateral**
Away from the midsagittal plane; toward the left or right.

**Superior**
Toward the dorsal surface of the primate head.

**Inferior**
Toward the ventral surface of the primate head.

---

*Coloring notes*
*Color the arrows. First, color the dorsal and superior arrows different shades of the same color; then color the ventral and inferior arrows different shades of the same color. Finally, use different colors for the arrows associated with anterior and posterior and with medial and lateral.*

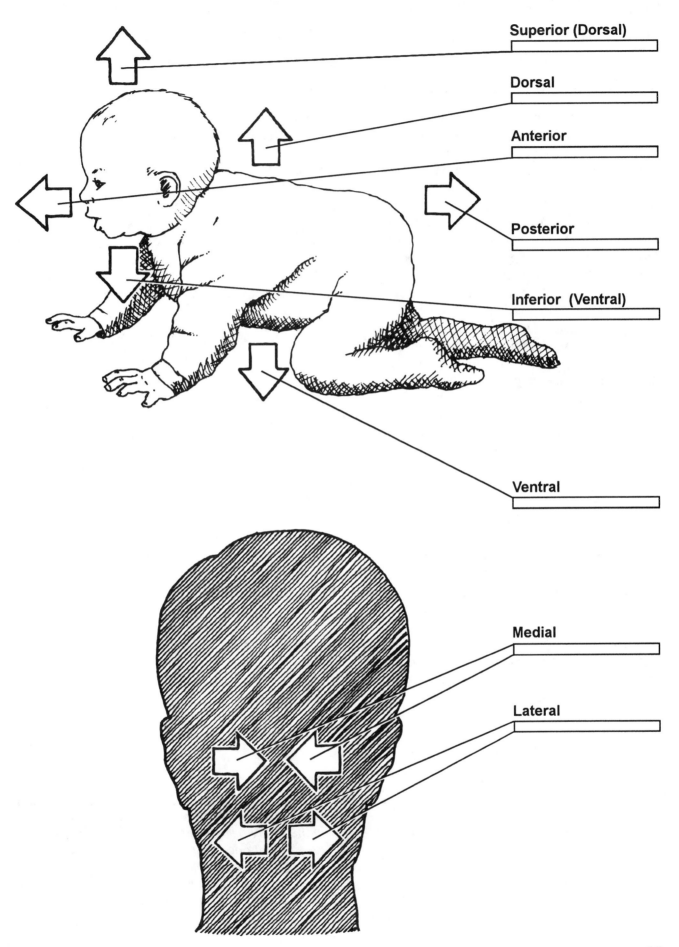

Superior (Dorsal)

Dorsal

Anterior

Posterior

Inferior (Ventral)

Ventral

Medial

Lateral

25

## 2.3  Sides of the Human Nervous System

Like all vertebrate nervous systems, the human nervous system has two sides: a left side and a right side. Although there are some subtle structural differences between the left side and the right side of the human brain, for the most part, the human nervous system is a bilaterally symmetrical structure. With the exception of those structures that lie right on the midline, all the structures of the nervous system come in pairs, one left and one right.

The term **unilateral** refers to things that are on only one side of the body; the term **bilateral** refers to things that are on both sides of the body. Accordingly, an area of brain damage (i.e., a brain *lesion*) is said to be unilateral if it is restricted to one side of the brain, and it is said to be bilateral if it involves both sides. Similarly, a structure is said to receive unilateral input if it receives signals from only one side of the body or to receive bilateral input if it receives signals from both sides of the body.

Neural signals from one side of the body are of two types: **ipsilateral** and **contralateral**. *Ipsilateral* means *same side*, and thus unilateral signals from one side of the body to a brain structure on the same side are said to be ipsilateral. Conversely, *contralateral* means *opposite side*, and thus unilateral signals from one side of the body to a brain structure on the opposite side are said to be contralateral. All contralateral fibers must *decussate*; that is, they must cross over from one side of the body to the other. The point at which they cross over is called a *decussation*.

**Unilateral**
On one side of the body.

**Bilateral**
On both sides of the body.

**Ipsilateral**
From or to the same side of the body.

**Contralateral**
From or to the opposite side of the body.

---

***Coloring notes***
*In the top two illustrations, color half the head on your left one color; then, using another color, color both sides of the head on the right hand side of the page. In the bottom two illustrations, color the two arrows in their entirety, each a different color.*

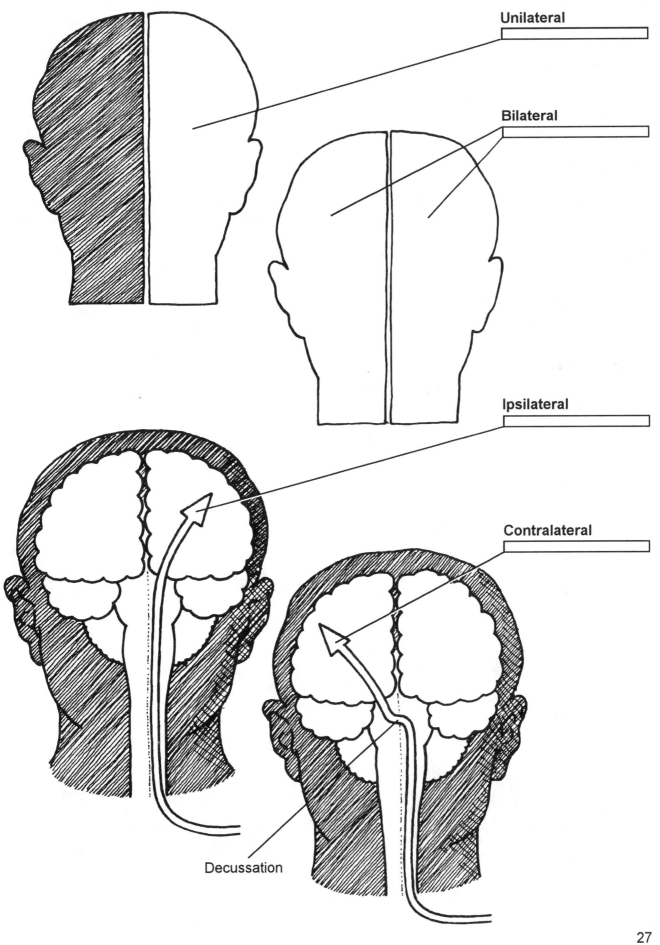

**Unilateral**

**Bilateral**

**Ipsilateral**

**Contralateral**

Decussation

# Review Exercises: Planes and Directions in the Human Nervous System

Now it is time for you to pause and consoilidate the terms and ideas that you have learned in the three learning units of Chapter 2. It is important that you overlearn them so that they do not quickly fade from your memory.

## Review Exercise 2.1

Turn to the illustrations in the three learning units of Chapter 2, and use the cover flap at the back of the book to cover the terms that run down the right-hand edge of each illustration page. Study the three illus- tration pages until you can identify each labeled neuroanatomical plane and direction. Once you have worked through all three illustrations twice without making an error, advance to Review Exercise 2.2.

## Review Exercise 2.2

Fill in the names of the sections (slices) in the fol- lowing illustrations. The correct answers are pro- vided at the back of the book. Carefully review the material related to your incorrect answers.

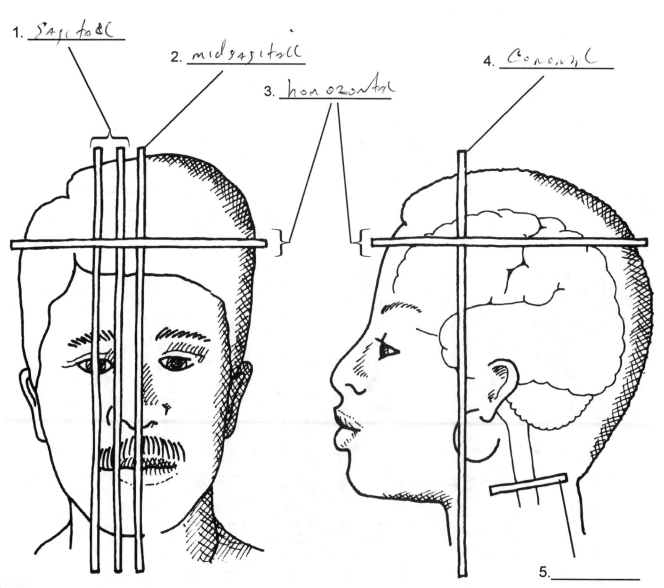

1. _Sagittal_

2. _midsagittal_

3. _horozontal_

4. _Coronal_

5. _____

## Review Exercise 2.3

Without referring to Chapter 2, fill in each of the following blanks with the correct term from the chapter. The correct answers are provided at the back of the book. Carefully review the material related to your incorrect answers.

1. Most brain slices are cut in one of three different _____, which are at right angles to each other.

2. Unilateral input to a brain structure is either contralateral or _____.

3. The _____ or frontal plane is perpendicular to both the horizontal and sagittal planes.

4. Any _____ section separates the anterior part of the brain from the posterior part.

5. Any _____ section separates the ventral part of the brain from the dorsal part.

6. Any _____ section of the brain separates the left ear from the right ear.

7. The anatomy of the spinal cord is usually studied in a series of _____ sections.

8. All contralateral fibers must _____.

9. In dogs, the direction toward the top of the head is referred to as _____.

10. In humans, the direction toward the back of the brain is referred to as _____.

11. In dogs, the direction toward the back of the brain is referred to as _____.

12. Toward the midsagittal plane is referred to as _____.

13. Away from the midsagittal plane is referred to as _____.

14. The nose is _____ to the back of the head in humans.

15. The nose is _____ to the back of the head in dogs.

16. In primates, ventral parts of the brain are often referred to as _____.

17. In humans, the tip of the nose is inferior, medial, and _____ to the eyes.

18. In primates, but not in other vertebrates, the direction toward the top of the head is often referred to as _____.

19. A section cut from the plane that divides the brain into equal left and right halves, is called a _____ section.

20. A lesion to both sides of the brain is said to be a _____ lesion.

21. A pathway from the right hand to the left side of the brain is said to be a _____ pathway.

22. Posterior is also known as _____.

23. Anterior is also known as _____.

## Review Exercise 2.4

Below in alphabetical order is a list of all the terms and definitions that you learned in Chapter 2. Cover the definitions with a sheet of paper, and work your way down the list of terms, defining them to yourself as you go. Repeat this process until you have gone through the list twice without an error. Then, cover the terms and work your way down the list of definitions, providing the correct terms as you go. Repeat this second process until you have gone through the list twice without an error.

| | |
|---|---|
| Anterior | Toward the nose end; also known as rostral. |
| Bilateral | On both sides of the body. |
| Contralateral | From or to the opposite side of the body. |
| Coronal sections | Slices of the brain that are cut in a coronal or frontal plane, that is, cut approximately parallel to the surface of the face. |
| Cross sections | Sections that are cut at right angles to the long axis of any long narrow structure, for example, at right angles to the long axis of the spinal cord. |
| Dorsal | Toward the surface of the back or top of the head. |
| Horizontal sections | Slices of the brain that are cut in a horizontal plane, that is, cut parallel to the horizon when the subject is in an upright position. |
| Inferior | Toward the ventral surface of the primate head. |
| Ipsilateral | From or to the same side of the body. |
| Lateral | Away from the midsagittal plane; toward the left or right. |
| Medial | Toward the midsagittal plane. |
| Midsagittal section | A sagittal section that is cut from the very midline of the brain. |
| Posterior | Toward the tail end; also known as caudal. |
| Sagittal sections | Slices of the brain that are cut in a sagittal plane, that is, cut parallel to the vertical plane that divides the brain into left and right halves. |
| Superior | Toward the dorsal surface of the primate head. |
| Unilateral | On one side of the body. |
| Ventral | Toward the surface of the chest and stomach or bottom of the head. |

## Chapter 3: Cells of the Nervous System

In Chapter 1, you were introduced to the structure of the vertebrate nervous system at its most general level—at the level of the major divisions that compose it. Then, in Chapter 2, you learned the system of neuroanatomical planes and directions that is used to define the location of neural structures. Now, you are prepared to take a closer look at the structure of the nervous system—a look at the cells that compose it.

The human nervous system is composed of several hundred billion cells—more than all the stars in the galaxy. In this chapter, you will learn that the cells of the nervous system are of two fundamentally different types, and you will be introduced to the fundamentals of their structure and function.

The following are the seven learning units of Chapter 3:

3.1   The Neuron: Its Major Regions

3.2   The Neuron: Structures of the Cell Body

3.3   The Neuron: Structures of the Terminal Buttons

3.4   Neural Conduction Through Dendrites and Cell Body

3.5   Axonal Conduction and Synaptic Transmission

3.6   Glial Cells and Saltatory Conduction

3.7   Neural Cell Membranes and Receptors

## 3.1 The Neuron: Its Major Regions

*Neurons* (nerve cells) are the functional units of the nervous system; they are cells that are specialized to receive, conduct, and transmit electrochemical signals. Like other cells, neurons are composed of a clear inner fluid, called **cytoplasm**, enclosed within a **cell membrane**. The cell membrane is semipermeable; that is, some molecules can pass through it, whereas others cannot.

Neurons come in a wide variety of sizes and shapes, but in most the following four regions are readily discernible. (1) The **cell body**, or *soma*, is the metabolic center of the neuron; it is the region of the neuron that coordinates the processes that are critical for the cell's survival. (2) The **dendrites** are the short bushy fibers that branch from the cell body; their primary function is to receive incoming signals from other neurons. (3) The **axon** is the single long fiber that extends from the cell body; its function is to conduct signals from the cell body to other sites in the nervous system. (4) The **buttons** are the button-like terminal endings of the *axon branches*; they are sites from which the neuron transmits most of its signals to other cells.

Typically, signals from other neurons are received by the dendrites; and, to some extent, the cell body. Then, they are conducted through the cell body, along the axon, and finally to the buttons, which transmit them to other cells.

**Cytoplasm** (SITE oh plazm)
The clear inner fluid of neurons and other cells.

**Cell membrane**
The semipermeable membrane that encloses the cytoplasm of neurons and other cells; the wall of the cell.

**Cell body**
The metabolic center of the neuron; also called the *soma* (pronounced SOE ma).

**Dendrites** (DEN drites)
The short bushy fibers that branch out from the cell body; they constitute the major signal-receiving area of the neuron.

**Axon**
The single long fiber that extends from a neuron's cell body; its function is to conduct neural signals from the cell body to other parts of the nervous system.

**Buttons**
The button-like terminal endings of the axon branches.

---

*Coloring notes*
*First, color all 10 dendrites including the dendrite branches, which are represented by lines. Next, color the 8 buttons—do not color over the dashed lines and into the axon branches. Finally, color the cell body, axon, cell membrane, and cytoplasm.*

# A NEURON

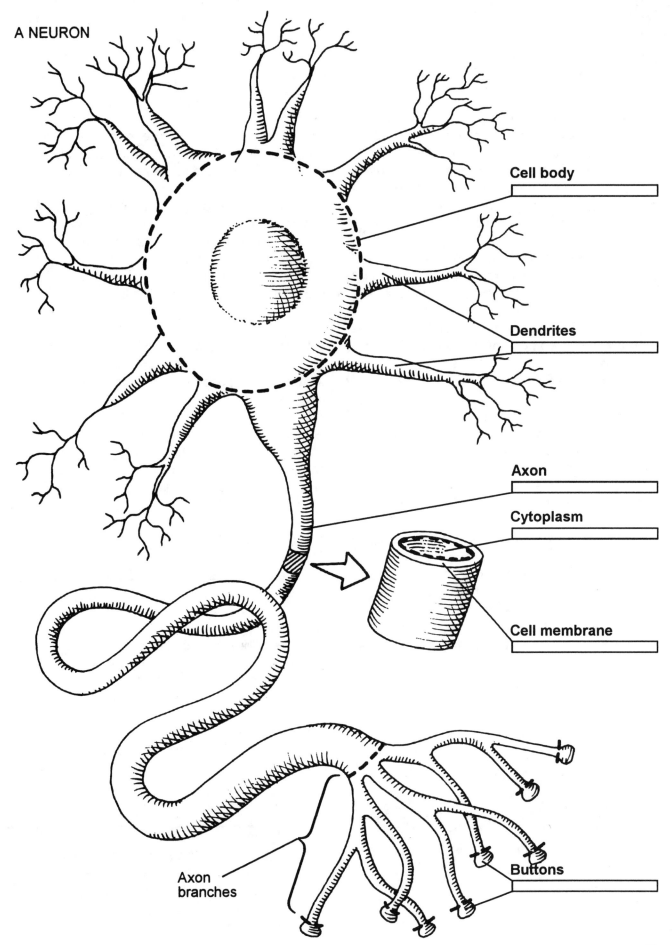

Cell body

Dendrites

Axon

Cytoplasm

Cell membrane

Axon branches

Buttons

## 3.2 The Neuron: Structures of the Cell Body

In the cytoplasm of all cells are structures that the cell needs to keep itself alive; in neurons, most of these structures are in the cell body. The most prominent structure of the cell body is the **nucleus**, the large spherical structure that contains the genetic material of the cell—the genetic material directs the synthesis of the cell's proteins.

Also prominent in the cell body are the **endoplasmic reticulum** and the **Golgi apparatus**. The endoplasmic reticulum is a system of plate-shaped membranous sacs— much of it has a rough appearance because it is dotted with **ribosomes**, the structures on which all the cell's proteins are synthesized. The Golgi apparatus is also a series of plate-shaped membranous sacs, but, unlike the endoplasmic reticulum, it lacks ribosomes. It is involved in packaging proteins and other molecules in membranes either for transport to other parts of the cell or for release from the cell.

**Mitochondria**, which play a role in cell respiration and energy consumption, are scattered throughout the neural cytoplasm, but they are particularly prevalent in the cell body and buttons. Also present throughout the neural cytoplasm are **neurofilaments** and **microtubules.** Neurofilaments provide skeleton-like support for the neuron, and microtubules play a role in the transport of substances within the neuron—at about 200 millimeters (8 inches) per day.

**Nucleus**
The large spherical structure in the cytoplasm of every cell; it contains the genetic material; in neurons, it is located in the cell body.

**Endoplasmic reticulum** (end oh PLAZ mik re TIK you lum)
The system of rough plate-shaped membranous sacs in the cytoplasm of cells; its rough appearance stems from the fact that it is covered with ribosomes; in neurons, it is located in the cell body.

**Ribosomes** (RIBE oh zohms)
The structures on which each cell's proteins are synthesized; ribosomes are attached to the rough endoplasmic reticulum.

**Golgi apparatus** (GOLE jee)
Systems of smooth plate-shaped membranous sacs in the cytoplasm of cells; they package proteins and other molecules in small membrane sacs.

**Mitochondria** (MITE oh KON dree a)
Structures of the cytoplasm that play a role in a cell's respiration and in its production and use of energy (singular: *mitochondrion*).

**Neurofilaments**
Fine thread-like structures that form a matrix in the cytoplasm; they provide support for the cell membrane and maintain the shape of the neuron.

**Microtubules** (MY kroe TUBE yules)
Fine tubes that course through the neural cytoplasm; they provide routes for the transport of molecules within neurons.

---

*Coloring notes*
*Because they are particularly small, first color every ribosome and every neurofilament in very bright colors. Then, color the endoplasmic reticulum, nucleus, Golgi apparatus, mitochondria, and microtubules.*

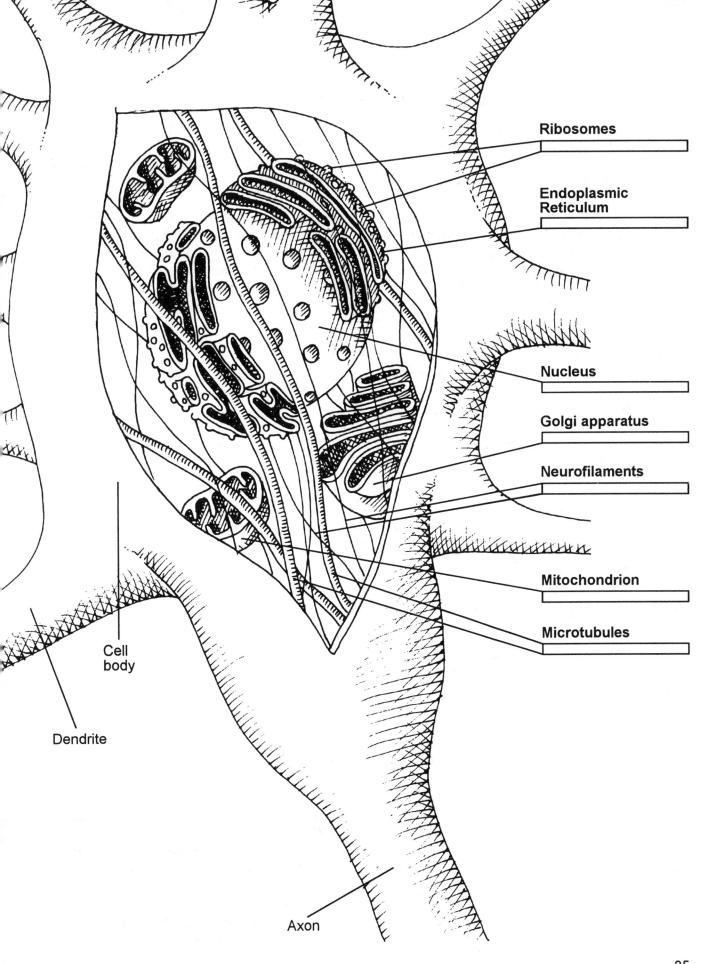

Ribosomes

Endoplasmic
Reticulum

Nucleus

Golgi apparatus

Neurofilaments

Mitochondrion

Microtubules

Cell
body

Dendrite

Axon

## 3.3 The Neuron: Structures of the Terminal Buttons

Prominent in the cytoplasm of the neuron's terminal buttons are *microtubules*, *neurofilaments*, and *mitochondria*, which you have already learned about. Microtubules serve as a network for the transportation of substances throughout the neuron; neurofilaments provide skeleton-like support for the neuron; and mitochondria play a critical role in the neuron's production and use of energy.

Also present in the cytoplasm of the neural buttons are **neurotransmitter molecules,** which are often contained in **synaptic vesicles**. Neurotransmitter molecules are molecules that are released from the terminal buttons of neurons and influence the activity of other cells. There are many different kinds of neurotransmitter molecules, but each neuron synthesizes and releases only one or two kinds. Some neurotransmitter molecules excite other cells, and some inhibit other cells. Synaptic vesicles are small membrane sacs that store neurotransmitter molecules ready for release from buttons. They are visible in clusters near the button membrane.

Some neurotransmitter molecules are complex fragments of proteins; these are synthesized in the cell body, packaged in vesicles by the *Golgi apparatus*, which you have already learned about, and then transported to the buttons via microtubules. Other, more simple, neurotransmitter molecules are present in the neural cytoplasm and are packaged in vesicles by a *Golgi apparatus* right in the terminal buttons. In the buttons, the Golgi apparatus manufactures vesicles from bits of the button cell membrane that break off and enter the button.

**Neurotransmitter molecules**
Molecules that are released from the buttons of active neurons and influence the activity of other cells.

**Synaptic vesicles** (si NAP tik  VESS i kls)
Membrane sacs that store neurotransmitter molecules ready for release near the presynaptic membrane; they are manufactured by the Golgi apparatus.

*Coloring notes*

*First, color each neurotransmitter molecule in each vesicle a bright color; then color the remainder of each vesicle a different light color. Note that the size of the neurotransmitter molecules and vesicles has been greatly exaggerated for illustrative purposes.*

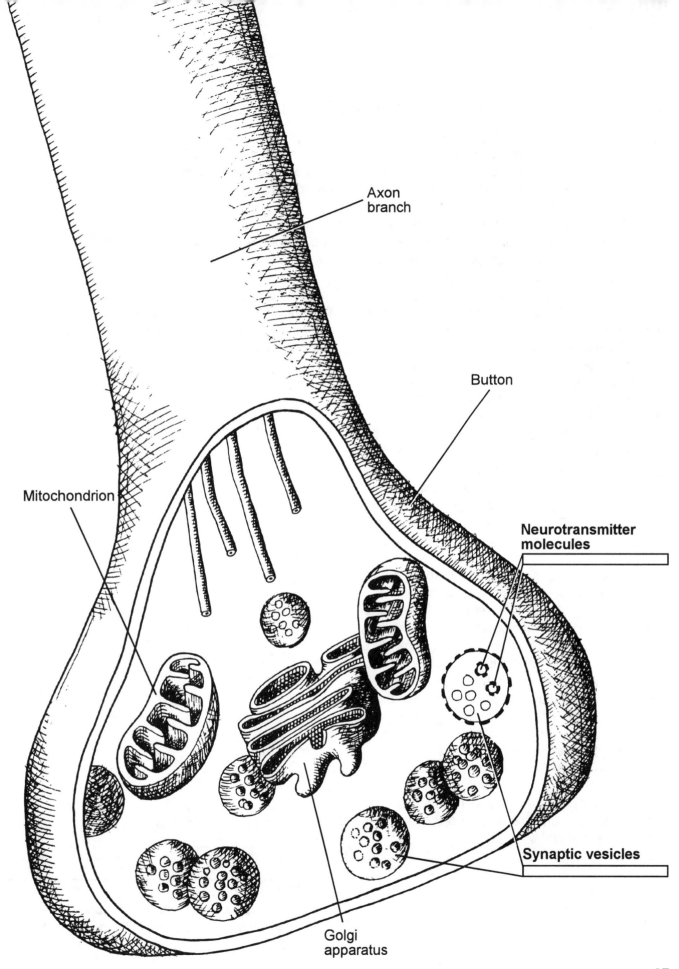

Axon
branch

Button

**Neurotransmitter
molecules**

Mitochondrion

**Synaptic vesicles**

Golgi
apparatus

## 3.4 Neural Conduction Through Dendrites and Cell Body

Together the dendrites and cell body are referred to as the **receptive area** of the neuron. This is because neurons typically receive most of their input from the thousands of buttons of other neurons that cover the dendrites and cell body. Between each button and the receptive membrane is a narrow gap called a **synapse**. Although synapses are most prevalent on the dendrites and cell body, there are some on other parts of the neuron as well.

The release of neurotransmitter molecules at some synapses produces small electrical charges that tend to excite the postsynaptic neuron; these charges are called *excitatory postsynaptic potentials* or *EPSPs*. Activity at other synapses produces small electrical charges that tend to inhibit the postsynaptic neuron; these charges are called *inhibitory postsynaptic potentials* or *IPSPs*. EPSPs and IPSPs are conducted *decrementally* through the postsynaptic neuron, that is, they get weaker as they go and die out before they get very far down the axon. Their function is to influence the production of other electrochemical signals that do not die out.

At any one time, many of the synapses on a neuron's receptive area are likely to be simultaneously active. The resulting EPSPs and/or IPSPs then travel decrementally, but instantly, to the axon hillock. The **axon hillock** is the cone-shaped region at the junction between the cell body and the axon; it is the neuron's trigger zone. The axon hillock adds together all of the EPSPs and IPSPs that are reaching it at any one time. Each time that the level of excitation at the axon hillock exceeds the amount of inhibition by a sufficient amount, an *action potential (AP)* is produced—this sufficient amount is called the *threshold of excitation*. Action potentials are then conducted down the axon to the terminal buttons.

**Receptive area**
The dendrites and cell body of a neuron; the area of a neuron that receives most of its synaptic input.

**Synapse** (SIN aps)
The narrow cleft between a terminal button of one neuron and the receptive membrane of another.

**Axon hillock** (HIL uk)
The cone-shaped junction between the cell body and axon; the part of the neuron that generates action potentials.

*Coloring notes*
*First, color the synapse and axon hillock by staying within the dashed lines. Then, color the receptive area (i.e., the dendrites and cell body).*

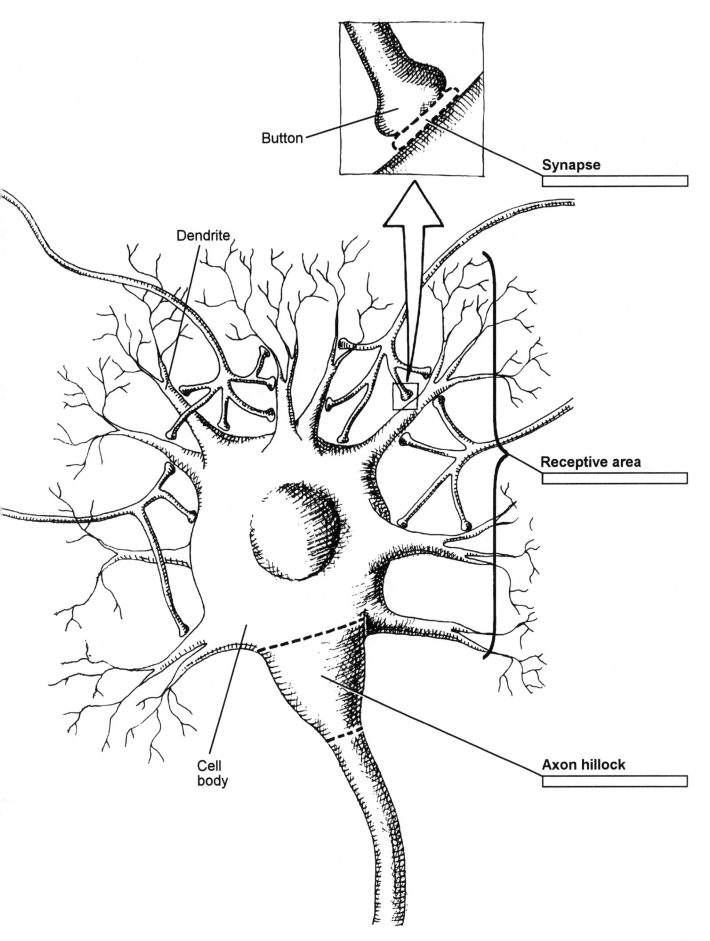

Button

Synapse

Dendrite

Receptive area

Cell body

Axon hillock

## 3.5 Axonal Conduction and Synaptic Transmission

*Action potentials* are generated at the *axon hillock* when the sum of the EPSPs and IPSPs that it receives at any given moment is sufficiently excitatory, that is, when it exceeds the *threshold of excitation*. Unlike EPSPs and IPSPs, which vary in strength, action potentials are *all-or-none* potentials, that is, they occur full blown or not at all. Through the active involvement of the axonal membrane, action potentials are conducted along the axon *nondecrementally*, that is, they do not grow weaker as they are conducted down the axon. Accordingly, each action potential is just as large when it reaches the terminal buttons as it was when it left the axon hillock.

When an action potential arrives at a terminal button, it triggers the release from the buttons of some of the *neurotransmitter molecules* that were stored in *synaptic vesicles* near the **presynaptic membrane**—the process of neurotransmitter release is called *exocytosis*. During exocytosis, the synaptic vesicles bind to the presynaptic membrane and then split open, thus releasing their contents into the synapse.

The neurotransmitter molecules travel across the synapse and bind in key-in-lock fashion to **receptors** in the **postsynaptic membrane**. There are specific receptors for each type of neurotransmitter molecule. In binding to its receptor, a neurotransmitter molecule usually induces either an EPSP or an IPSP in the postsynaptic neuron—a given synapse is either excitatory or inhibitory, not both.

**Presynaptic membrane**
The section of the button membrane that is adjacent to the synaptic cleft; the site from which neurotransmitter molecules are released into a synapse.

**Receptors**
Molecules in the neuron cell membrane to which neurotransmitter molecules bind in key-in-lock fashion and, in so doing, induce signals in the neuron.

**Postsynaptic membrane**
The section of the cell membrane of a postsynaptic neuron that is adjacent to the synaptic cleft; the postsynaptic membrane contains postsynaptic receptors.

---

*Coloring notes*

*First, color the presynaptic membrane, including the vesicle that is releasing its neurotransmitter molecules—once a vesicle becomes attached to the presynaptic membrane, it becomes part of it. Next, color the receptors and finally the postsynaptic membrane.*

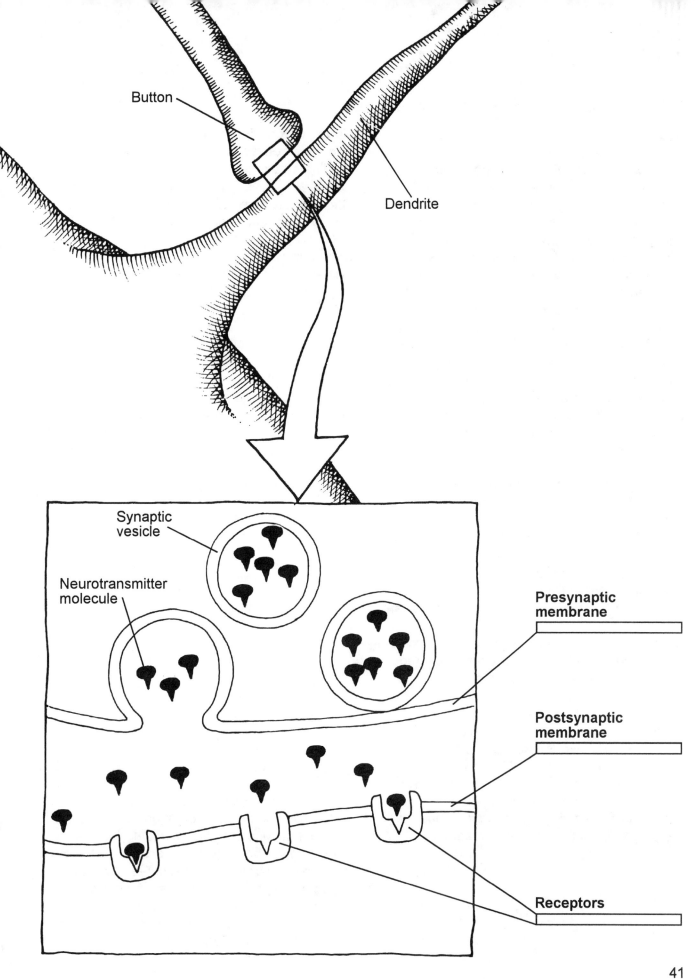

Button

Dendrite

Synaptic
vesicle

Neurotransmitter
molecule

**Presynaptic
membrane**

**Postsynaptic
membrane**

**Receptors**

## 3.6 Glial Cells and Saltatory Conduction

Neurons are not the only cells in the nervous system; the nervous system also contains many *glial cells*, or *neuroglia*. There are several different kinds of glial cells, each of which performs a different supportive or protective function. Some glial cells provide a physical framework to hold neurons in place (*neuroglia* means *nerve glue*); some remove debris and foreign material; and some regulate the passage of molecules from the blood to CNS neurons. Another important function of glial cells is the myelination of axons—*myelin* is a fatty substance that is produced in some glial cells. Glial cells myelinate axons by wrapping around them. There are gaps between the adjacent glial segments in each axon's myelin sheath; these gaps are called **nodes of Ranvier**.

Myelination increases the speed of axonal conduction. In myelinated axons, action potentials jump from node to node, rather than traveling at a constant speed along the axon. Conduction in myelinated axons is called *saltatory conduction* (*saltatory* means *jumping* or *skipping*). In large myelinated axons, action potentials are conducted along the axon at about 100 meters per second.

Myelin is white. Thus, areas of the nervous system that contain many myelinated axons are white and are referred to as *white matter*. In contrast, areas of the nervous system that contain few myelinated axons are gray and are referred to as *gray matter*—gray matter is largely composed of cell bodies, dendrites, unmyelinated axons.

**Oligodendrocytes** are the glial cells that myelinate CNS axons; **Schwann cells** are the glial cells that myelinate PNS axons. There are several major differences between them; the main one is that Schwann cells, but not oligodendrocytes, promote *axonal regeneration* (i.e., regrowth of axons after damage).

**Nodes of Ranvier** (rahn vee ay)
The gaps between adjacent glial segments on a myelinated axon.

**Oligodendrocytes** (O li go DEN dro sites)
Glial cells that myelinate CNS axons.

**Schwann cells**
Glial cells that myelinate PNS axons.

### Coloring notes

*First, color the Schwann cells—each Schwann cell myelinates one section of one axon. Then, color the oligodendrocyte (including the cell body, and the processes that extend from the cell and wrap around the axons)—each oligodendrocyte myelinates several sections of several axons. Finally, color the nodes of Ranvier (the short sections of axon that are not insulated by glial cells).*

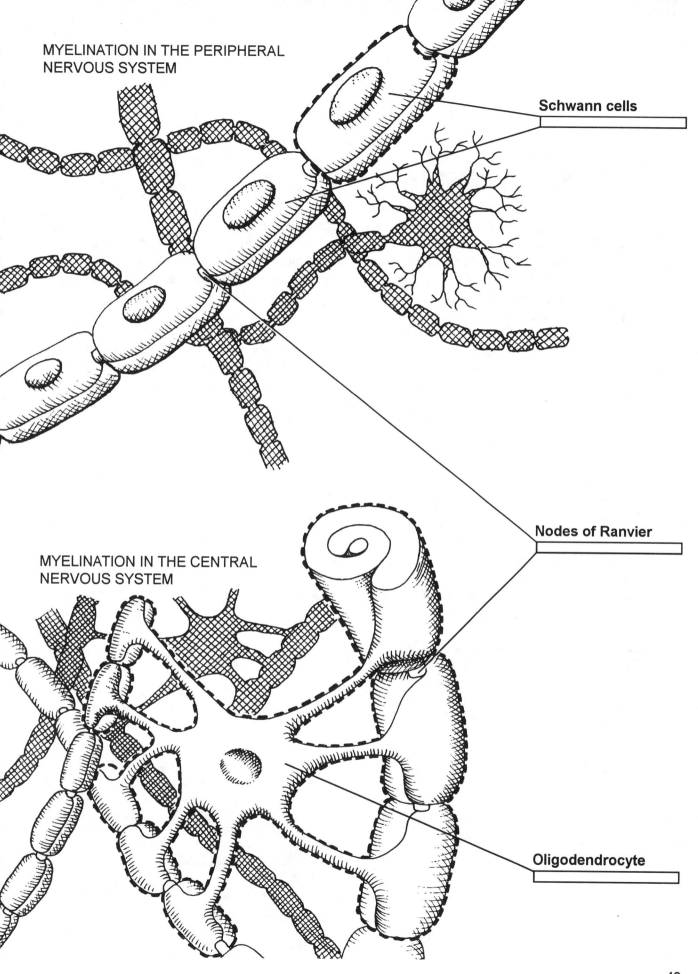

MYELINATION IN THE PERIPHERAL
NERVOUS SYSTEM

**Schwann cells**

**Nodes of Ranvier**

MYELINATION IN THE CENTRAL
NERVOUS SYSTEM

**Oligodendrocyte**

## 3.7 Neural Cell Membranes and Receptors

The ability of a neuron to conduct neural impulses is attributable to special properties of the *cell membrane*. The neural cell membrane is a lipid bilayer, two layers of fat molecules, in which are embedded two kinds of structures: **ion channels** and **signal proteins**.

Ion channels are specialized pores in the neuron cell membrane through which small, electrically charged particles, called *ions* (e.g., sodium, potassium, and chloride ions), can pass. It is the unequal distribution of charges between the inside and outside of the neuron that is the basis of all *postsynaptic potentials* and *action potentials*. Most of the ion channels of the dendrite and cell body membrane are *chemical-gated*, that is, they open or close in response to neurotransmitter chemicals. Most of the ion channels of the axon membrane are *voltage-gated*, that is, they open or close in response to changes in the voltage across the membrane.

Signal proteins are molecules that snake back and forth through the membrane seven times and are associated on the interior of the neuron with **G-proteins** (guanine-sensitive proteins). Activation of receptors on signal proteins by neurotransmitters activates the G-protein; the G-protein in turn initiates changes in the internal chemistry of neurons.

There are two kinds of receptor molecules. Some are **ionotropic receptors**; they are associated with ion channels, which are instantly and briefly opened or closed by the binding of a neurotransmitter molecule to its receptor. Other receptors are **metabotropic receptors**; they are associated with signal proteins and thus produce slower and longer-lasting effects.

### Ion channels
Specialized pores in the neuron cell membrane through which ions can pass; some are chemical-gated and some are voltage-gated.

### Signal proteins
Proteins that snake back and forth through the cell membrane seven times and conduct signals into the neuron when their associated receptors are activated.

### G-protein
A protein molecule that is activated inside a neuron when a neurotransmitter molecule binds to the receptor on its associated signal protein.

### Ionotropic receptors
Receptors that are associated with ion channels; when activated, they typically induce rapid, brief signals in the neuron by opening or closing the ion channel.

### Metabotropic receptors (meh TAB oh trope ik)
Receptors that are associated with signal proteins and G-proteins; when activated, they typically induce slow, long-lasting changes in the neuron by changing its internal chemistry.

***

### Coloring notes
First, color the ionotropic and metabotropic receptors by staying within the dashed lines. Then, color the ion channels, signal proteins, and G-protein.

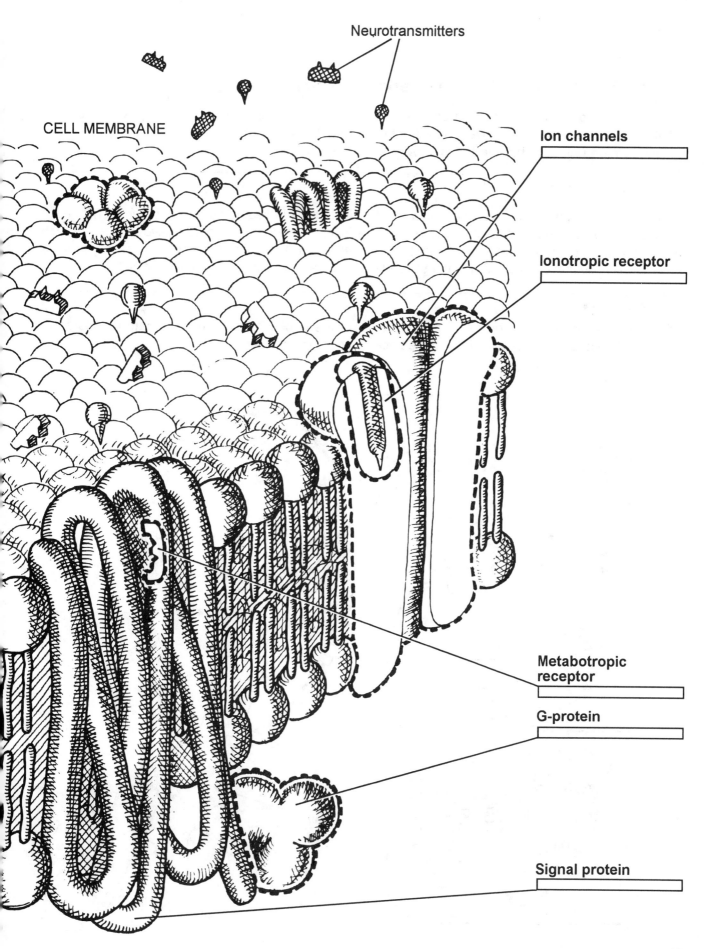

Neurotransmitters

CELL MEMBRANE

Ion channels

Ionotropic receptor

Metabotropic receptor

G-protein

Signal protein

# Review Exercises: Cells of the Nervous System

Now it is time for you to pause and consolidate the terms and ideas that you have learned in the seven learning units of Chapter 3. It is important that you overlearn them so that they do not quickly fade from your memory.

### Review Exercise 3.1

Turn to the illustrations in the seven learning units of Chapter 3, and use the cover flap at the back of the book to cover the terms that run down the right-hand edge of each illustration page. Study the seven illustrations in sequence until you can identify each labeled structure. Once you have worked through all seven illustrations twice without making a single error, advance to Review Exercise 3.2.

### Review Exercise 3.2

Fill in the missing terms in the following illustration. The correct answers are provided at the back of the book. Carefully review material related to your incorrect answers.

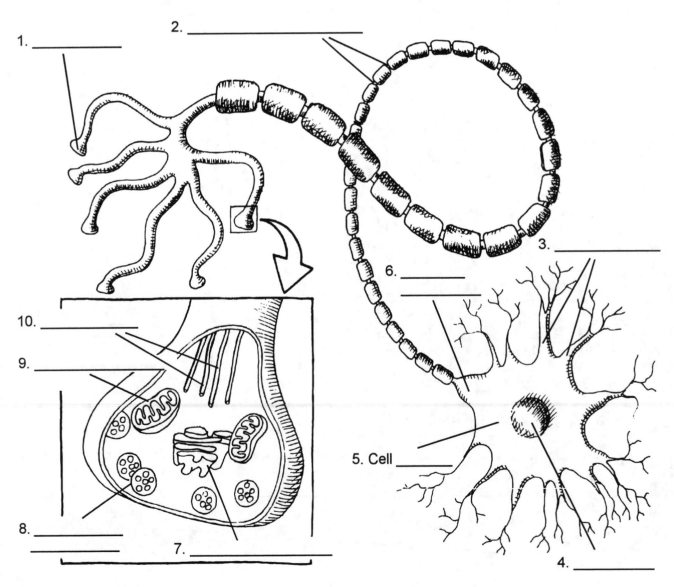

1. _____

2. _____

3. _____

4. _____

5. Cell _____

6. _____

7. _____

8. _____

9. _____

10. _____

## Review Exercise 3.3

Without referring to Chapter 3, fill in each of the following blanks with the correct term from the chapter. The correct answers are provided at the back of the book. Carefully review the material related to your incorrect answers.

1. APs are _____ potentials, that is, they occur full blown or not at all.

2. Two kinds of fibers extend from the somas of many neurons: one long _____ and many short bushy _____.

3. The tiny bulbous endings of axon branches are called _____.

4. The _____ of a neuron is the large spherical structure that contains its genetic material.

5. _____ potentials are conducted nondecrementally.

6. In the cell body, the _____ apparatus packages proteins in vesicles for transport to other parts of the neuron.

7. The process of neurotransmitter release is called _____.

8. Neurotransmitter molecules are often stored in synaptic _____ near the presynaptic membrane.

9. Together the dendrites and cell body are referred to as the _____ area of a neuron.

10. Action potentials are generated at the axon _____.

11. Each synapse is sandwiched between a _____ membrane and a _____ membrane.

12. Neurotransmitter molecules, once released, diffuse across the _____.

13. Prominent in the cytoplasm of the cell body is a system of plate-shaped membranous sacs, much of which has a rough appearance. This structure is called the _____ _____.

14. Neurotransmitter molecules bind in a key-in-lock fashion to postsynaptic _____.

15. The cone-shaped junction between cell body and the axon is the _____.

16. Proteins are synthesized on _____, which give the rough endoplasmic reticulum its rough appearance.

17. Unlike APs, EPSPs and IPSPs are conducted instantly and _____.

18. The _____ or soma is the metabolic center of a neuron.

19. Conduction in myelinated axons is called _____ conduction.

20. Gaps in the myelin of myelinated axons are called nodes of _____.

21. In the terminal buttons, the _____ manufactures synaptic vesicles from fragments of button membrane.

22. _____ myelinate CNS axons.

23. _____ receptors are associated with signal proteins and G-proteins.

24. _____, when open, permit the passage of ions through the cell membrane.

## Review Exercise 3.4

Below in alphabetical order is a list of all the terms and definitions that you learned in Chapter 3. Cover the definitions with a sheet of paper, and work your way down the list of terms, defining them to yourself as you go. Repeat this process until you have gone through the list twice without an error. Then, cover the terms and work your way down the list of definitions, providing the correct terms as you go. Repeat this second process until you have gone through the list twice without an error.

| Axon | The single long fiber that extends from a neuron's cell body; its function is to conduct neural signals from the cell body to other parts of the nervous system. |
|---|---|
| Axon hillock | The cone-shaped junction between the cell body and axon; the part of the neuron that generates action potentials. |
| Buttons | The button-like terminal endings of the axon branches. |
| Cell body | The metabolic center of the neuron; also called the *soma*. |
| Cell membrane | The semipermeable membrane that encloses the cytoplasm of neurons and other cells; the wall of the cell. |
| Cytoplasm | The clear inner fluid of neurons and other cells. |
| Dendrites | The short bushy fibers that branch out from the cell body; they constitute the major signal-receiving area of the neuron. |

| G-protein | A protein molecule that is activated inside a neuron when a neurotransmitter molecule binds to the receptor on its associated signal protein. |
|---|---|
| Golgi apparatus | Systems of smooth plate-shaped membranous sacs in the cytoplasm of cells; they package proteins and other molecules in small membrane sacs. |
| Ion channels | Specialized pores in the neuron cell membrane through which ions can pass; some are chemical-gated and some are voltage-gated. |
| Ionotropic receptors | Receptors that are associated with ion channels; when activated, they typically induce rapid, brief signals in the neuron by opening or closing the ion channel. |
| Metabotropic receptors | Receptors that are associated with signal proteins and G-proteins; when activated, they typically induce slow, long-lasting changes in the neuron by changing its internal chemistry. |
| Microtubules | Fine tubes that course through the neural cytoplasm; they provide routes for the transport of molecules within neurons. |
| Mitochondria | Structures of the cytoplasm that play a role in a cell's respiration and in its production and use of energy (singular: mitochondrion). |

| | | | |
|---|---|---|---|
| **Neurofilaments** | Fine thread-like structures that form a matrix in the cytoplasm; they provide support for the cell membrane and maintain the shape of the neuron. | **Receptors** | Molecules in the neuron cell membrane to which neurotransmitter molecules bind in key-in-lock fashion and, in so doing, induce signals in the neuron. |
| **Neurotransmitter molecules** | Molecules that are released from the buttons of active neurons and influence the activity of other cells. | **Ribosomes** | The structures on which each cell's proteins are synthesized; ribosomes are attached to the rough endoplasmic reticulum. |
| **Nodes of Ranvier** | The gaps between adjacent glial segments on a myelinated axon. | **Rough endoplasmic reticulum** | The system of rough plate-shaped membranous sacs in the cytoplasm of cells; its rough appearance stems from the fact that it is covered with ribosomes; in neurons, it is located in the cell body. |
| **Nucleus** | The large spherical structure in the cytoplasm of every cell; it contains the genetic material; in neurons, it is located in the cell body. | | |
| **Oligodendrocytes** | Glial cells that myelinate CNS axons. | **Schwann cells** | Glial cells that myelinate PNS axons. |
| **Postsynaptic membrane** | The section of the cell membrane of a postsynaptic neuron that is adjacent to the synaptic cleft; the postsynaptic membrane contains postsynaptic receptors. | **Signal proteins** | Proteins that snake back and forth through the cell membrane seven times and conduct signals into the neuron when their associated receptors are activated. |
| **Presynaptic membrane** | The section of the button membrane that is adjacent to the synaptic cleft; the site from which neurotransmitter molecules are released into a synapse. | **Synapse** | The narrow cleft between a terminal button of one neuron and the receptive membrane of another. |
| **Receptive area** | The dendrites and cell body of a neuron; the area of a neuron that receives most of its synaptic input. | **Synaptic vesicles** | Membrane sacs that store neurotransmitter molecules ready for release near the presynaptic membrane; they are manufactured by the Golgi apparatus. |

## Chapter 4: Early Development of the Human Nervous System

When the fleetest of your father's sperm cells penetrated your mother's egg, and his chromosomes were combined with hers, a truly astonishing process began—the developmental process that transformed that single fertilized egg cell into the current you. This chapter focuses on the early stages in the development of your brain.

Within a few hours of your conception, you divided and became 2 cells—then 4, then 8, then 16, and so on. At first, you were a shapeless clump of identical cells, but then different types of cells started to be produced, and they aligned themselves to form a hollow fluid-filled sphere, called an *embryo*. About 18 days after conception, your future nervous system first became visible as a patch of cells on the embryo's dorsal surface. This chapter begins with the development of this patch of cells, and then it describes how the five divisions of your brain developed from it.

The following are the five learning units of Chapter 4:

4.1   Development of the Neural Tube

4.2   Six Processes of Early Neural  Development

4.3   Early Development of the Brain's Three Major  Divisions

4.4   Early Development of the Brain's Five Divisions

4.5   Axon Growth: Correctly Wiring the Nervous System

# 4.1 Development of the Neural Tube

About 18 days after conception, cells that are destined to develop into the human nervous system become visible as a patch of cells on the dorsal surface of the human embryo. This patch of cells is called the **neural plate**. A day or two later, a large groove, called the **neural groove**, develops down the center of the neural plate. This groove grows deeper and deeper, and soon the two lips of the groove fuse to form a fluid-filled tube, called the **neural tube**.

Not all of the cells of the neural plate are incorporated into the neural tube. As the neural tube is being formed, cells from the edges of the neural plate break away, and they form a structure called the **neural crest**, which is situated just dorsal and lateral to the neural tube. The neural crest develops into the PNS, while the neural tube develops into the CNS. These early stages of nervous system development proceed in the same way in all vertebrates.

The development of the neural plate signals an important change in the cells that compose it. Prior to the development of the neural plate, the cells that will eventually constitute the neural plate are *totipotential*. That is, they have the potential to develop into any kind of human cell—if they are transplanted to another part of the embryo, they will develop into the type of cell that is appropriate for their new location (e.g., hair, muscle, skin, or liver cells). However, if they are transplanted after the neural plate appears, they will develop into nervous system cells regardless of their new location.

**Neural plate**
The patch of tissue on the dorsal surface of the vertebrate embryo that develops into the nervous system; in human embryos, it is first visible about 18 days following conception.

**Neural groove**
The groove that develops down the center of the neural plate.

**Neural tube**
The fluid-filled tube that is formed in the vertebrate embryo when the lips of the neural groove fuse; the neural tube develops into the CNS.

**Neural crest**
The vertebrate embryonic structure that is located just dorsal and lateral to the neural tube; it is formed from neural plate cells that break away as the neural tube is being formed; the neural crest develops into the PNS.

*Coloring notes*

*The three pairs of drawings illustrate the chronological development of the human embryonic nervous system between 18 and 24 days. Color your way backwards in time through these three coronal sections. First, color the neural crest and neural tube different colors in the bottom section. Then, using the same two colors, color the parts of the neural groove that eventually develop into the neural crest and neural tube. Finally, again using the same two colors, color the parts of the neural plate that eventually develop into the neural crest and neural tube.*

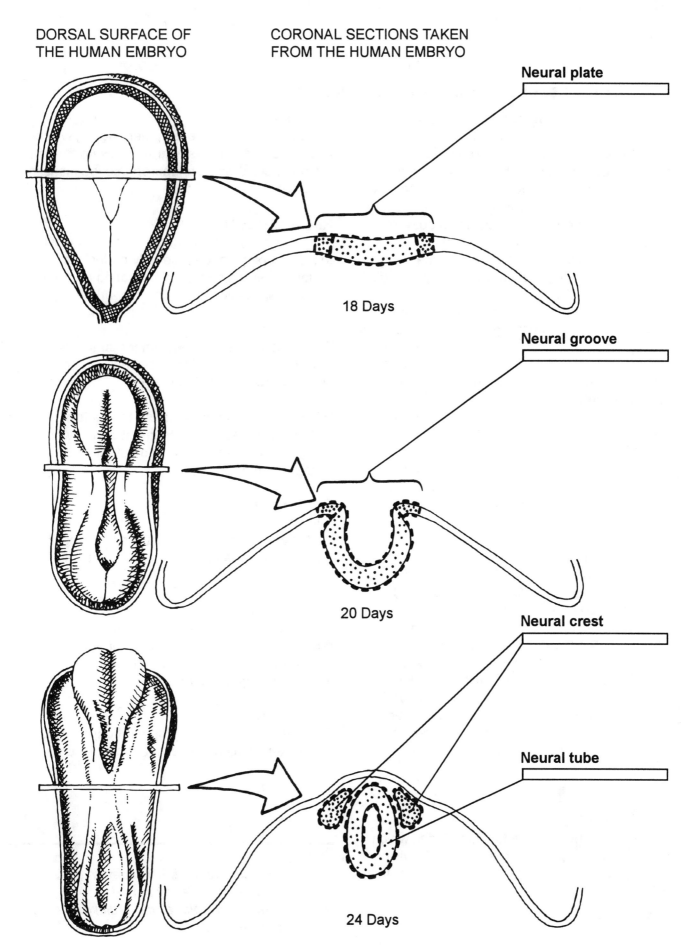

DORSAL SURFACE OF
THE HUMAN EMBRYO

CORONAL SECTIONS TAKEN
FROM THE HUMAN EMBRYO

**Neural plate**

18 Days

**Neural groove**

20 Days

**Neural crest**

**Neural tube**

24 Days

## 4.2  Six Processes of Early Neural Development

Once the neural tube has been formed, massive numbers of new neurons are created through cell division. This process, which is called **proliferation**, occurs in the region of the neural tube adjacent to its fluid-filled interior. The next developmental process is **migration**: Once new cells have been created, they travel outwards away from the region of cell division to appropriate locations in the neural tube. They travel along a temporary network of special glial cells, called **radial glial cells**.

Once neurons have reached their correct destinations, they must align themselves to form specific neural structures; this process of alignment is called **aggregation**. The next stage of neural development is **process growth and synapse formation**; during this stage, axons and dendrites grow out from the developing neurons and establish synaptic contacts. At the tip of each growing axon and dendrite is an ameba-like structure called a **growth cone**; the growth cones direct the growth of axons and dendrites to appropriate targets, sometimes over considerable distances.

The final two processes of early neural development are **neuron death** and **myelination**. By the end of the second trimester, the human brain has far more than the 100 billion neurons that it will be born with; then, many of them die—up to 85% in some parts of the brain. This neuron death is not random; the neurons that have not developed effective synaptic contacts are most likely to die. Finally, the axons of many of the surviving neurons become myelinated by glial cells. Different parts of the brain become myelinated at different times, and myelination is not complete until many months after birth.

### Migration
The stage of neural development during which newly created neurons migrate outward from the region of cell division to appropriate locations in the developing neural tube.

### Radial glial cells
The temporary network of glial cells that exists in the developing neural tube only during the period of neuron migration; migrating neurons travel outward along this glial network.

### Aggregation
The stage of neural development during which developing neurons align themselves to form the specific structures of the brain.

### Process growth and synapse formation
The stage of neural development during which axons and dendrites grow and establish synaptic contacts.

### Growth cone
The ameba-like structure at the growing tip of each axon and dendrite; growth cones direct the growth of axons and dendrites to appropriate targets.

### Neuron death
The stage of early nervous system development during which large numbers of neurons die, typically those that have not established effective synaptic contacts.

### Myelination
The stage of neuron development during which many axons become myelinated by glial cells.

### Proliferation
The stage of neural development during which many new neurons are created by cell division in the region of the neural tube adjacent to its fluid-filled inner canal.

---

*Coloring notes*

*Color the border around the illustration of each of the six processes of early neural development. Also, color all the radial glial cells and the growth cone.*

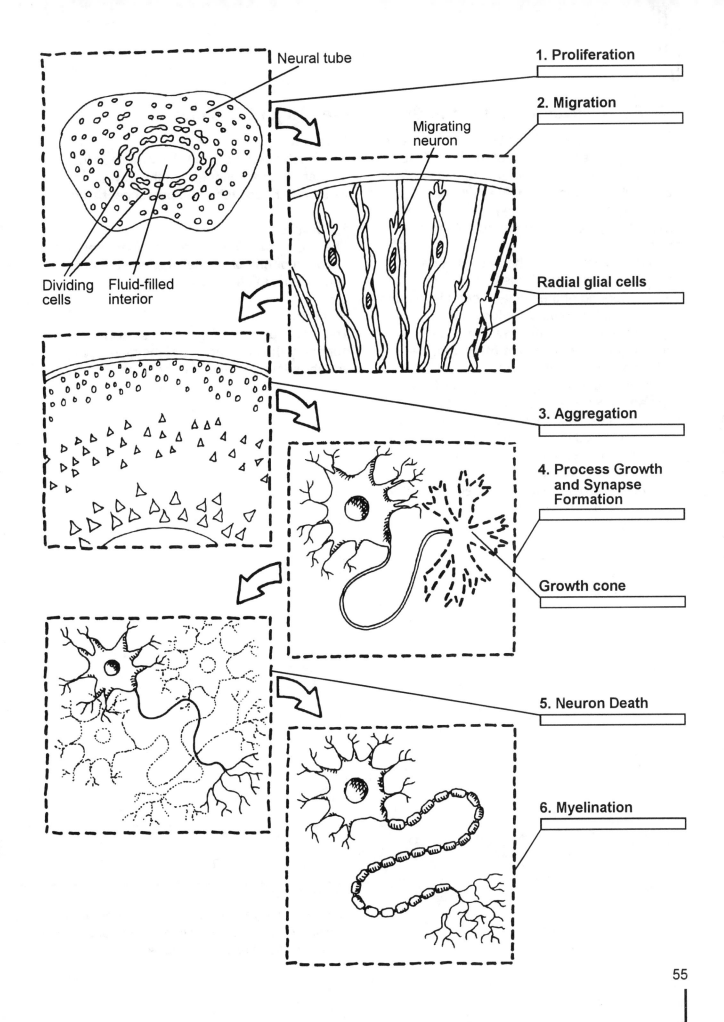

Neural tube

Migrating neuron

1. Proliferation

2. Migration

Radial glial cells

Dividing cells

Fluid-filled interior

3. Aggregation

4. Process Growth and Synapse Formation

Growth cone

5. Neuron Death

6. Myelination

55

## 4.3 Early Development of the Brain's Three Major Divisions

Neural proliferation does not occur at the same rate along the entire length of the neural tube. Cell division is particularly pronounced at the neural tube's anterior end, the end that eventually develops into the brain. The remainder of the neural tube develops into the spinal cord.

As a consequence of the pattern of neural proliferation, three swellings become visible at the anterior end of the human neural tube during the 4th week of *prenatal* (before birth) development. These three swellings are commonly referred to as the **forebrain,** the **midbrain**, and the **hindbrain.**

As their names imply, the forebrain is the most anterior of the three swellings, the hindbrain is the most posterior, and the midbrain is in the middle. However, if you are a fan of long words, you can refer to the forebrain, the midbrain, and the hindbrain as the *prosencephalon*, the *mesencephalon*, and the *rhombencephalon*, respectively.

### Forebrain
The most anterior of the three swellings that appear at the anterior end of the developing vertebrate neural tube; the prosencephalon.

### Midbrain
The middle swelling of the three that appear at the anterior end of the developing vertebrate neural tube; the mesencephalon.

### Hindbrain
The most posterior of the three swellings that appear at the anterior end of the developing vertebrate neural tube; the rhombencephalon.

*Coloring notes*

*Color the forebrain, midbrain, and hindbrain by staying within the dashed lines. Color both the walls and the interior of the tube.*

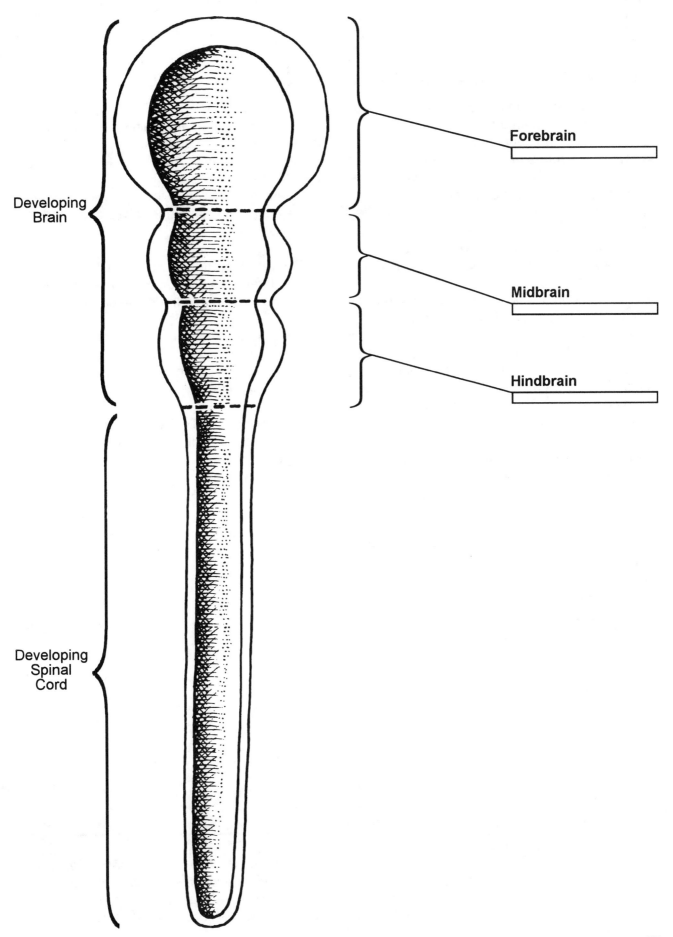

Developing
Brain

Developing
Spinal
Cord

**Forebrain**

**Midbrain**

**Hindbrain**

## 4.4 Early Development of the Brain's Five Divisions

You just learned that in the fourth prenatal week the developing human brain is visible at the anterior end of the neural tube as three swellings: the *forebrain*, the *midbrain*, and the *hindbrain*. In the fifth prenatal week, these three embryonic swellings develop into five swellings. These five swellings are important because they eventually develop into the five major divisions of the adult brain—in other words, it would be a good idea for you to put some extra effort into learning them.

The forebrain develops into two swellings: the **telencephalon** and the **diencephalon**. The telencephalon is the anterior division of the forebrain, and the diencephalon is its posterior division. The midbrain or mesencephalon remains itself, a single swelling just posterior to the diencephalon. The hindbrain develops into two swellings: the **metencephalon** and the **myelencephalon**. The metencephalon is the anterior division of the hindbrain, and the myelencephalon is its posterior division.

In summary, the five divisions of the brain from anterior to posterior are the telencephalon, the diencephalon, the mesencephalon, the metencephalon, and the myelencephalon. As a student, I found it useful to remember that the telencephalon is at the top of the human brain (telencephalon and top both begin with "t") and that the remaining four divisions are arranged below it in descending alphabetical order.

**Telencephalon** (TEL en SEF a lon)
The most anterior of the brain's five divisions; the anterior division of the forebrain.

**Diencephalon** (DYE en SEF a lon)
The posterior division of the forebrain; the area of the brain between the telencephalon and the mesencephalon.

**Mesencephalon** (MEEZ en SEF a lon)
The midbrain; the division of the brain between the diencephalon and the metencephalon.

**Metencephalon** (MET en SEF a lon)
The anterior division of the hindbrain; the area of the brain between the mesencephalon and the myelencephalon.

**Myelencephalon** (MY el en SEF a lon)
The most posterior of the brain's five divisions; the area of the brain between the metencephalon and the spinal cord.

*Coloring notes*

*Color each of the five divisions of the brain, shown here in a longitudinal section of the developing neural tube. Color both the walls and the fluid-filled interior of the neural tube.*

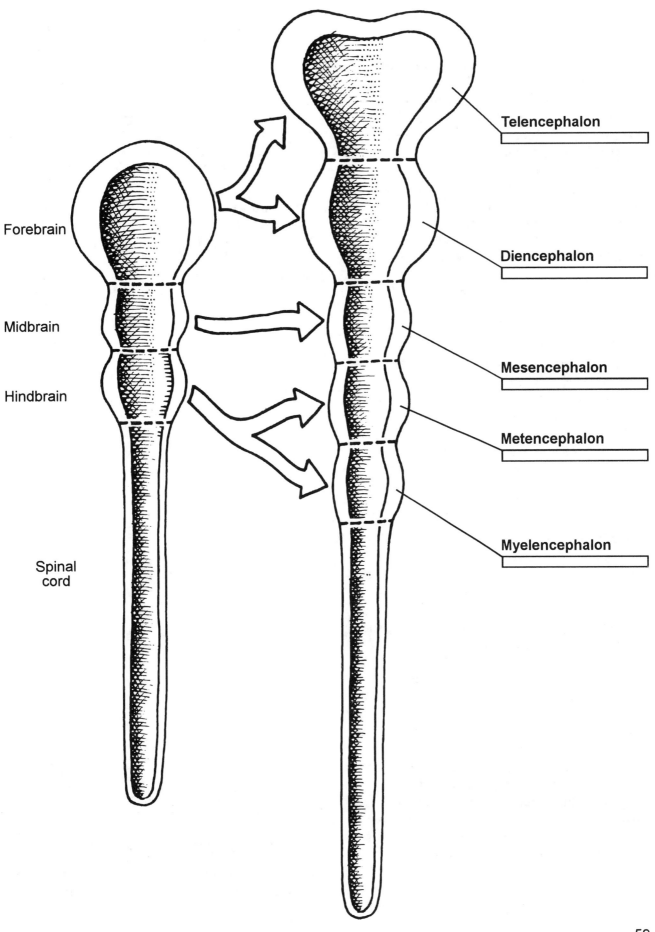

Forebrain

Midbrain

Hindbrain

Spinal
cord

**Telencephalon**

**Diencephalon**

**Mesencephalon**

**Metencephalon**

**Myelencephalon**

## 4.5 Axon Growth: Correctly Wiring the Nervous System

Once developing neurons have migrated to their correct locations and aligned themselves to form the various structures of the nervous system, the system "wires itself up." That is, axons and dendrites grow out from each neuron and establish synaptic contacts. This is an important phase of neural development because if inappropriate connections among neurons were formed, the nervous system could not function effectively. Imagine what would happen if axons from neurons in your eye grew out to the muscles of your leg: Every time the lights came on, you would fall over.

The question of how the *growth cone* at the growing tip of an axon finds its way to its destination has long puzzled neuroscientists. The following are two theories of how this occurs. The **chemoaffinity theory** is that each postsynaptic target releases a specific chemical label and that growing axons are programmed to follow a particular label to its source. The **blueprint theory** is that growing axons are programmed to follow particular trails (blood vessels, nerves, chemical trails, etc.) through the developing nervous system. In either case, only *pioneer growth cones* need to "know" the way. A pioneer growth cone is the first growth cone in a bundle of axons to reach the target—the growth cones of the other axons in the bundle can find their way by *fasciculation*, the tendency of growing axons to grow along the same path as their neighbors.

Which theory is correct, the chemoaffinity theory or the blueprint theory? Evidence suggests that both are. Each mechanism seems to direct the growth of some axons. In some experiments, axons have grown to their correct target cells even when the target cells have been transplanted to another part of the nervous system, thus suggesting a chemoaffinity mechanism; in other experiments, axons have grown to the correct location even after their correct target cells have been removed, thus suggesting a blueprint mechanism.

### Chemoaffinity theory
The theory that axons grow to their correct targets because they are programmed to follow to their source specific chemical signals released by their target cells.

### Blueprint theory
The theory that axons grow to their correct targets because they are programmed to follow specific trails through the developing nervous system.

*Coloring notes*

*The two illustrations show two major theories of accurate axon growth. Color just the borders of each.*

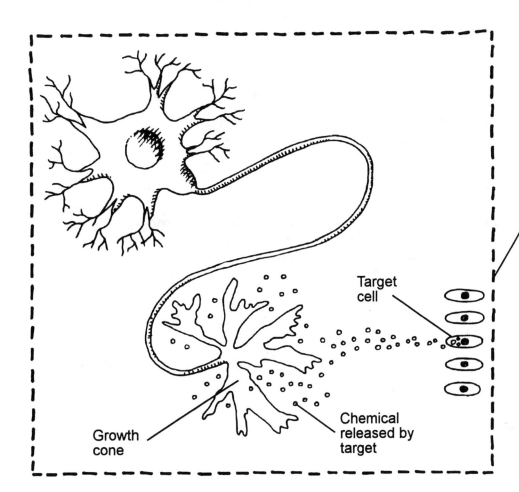

### Chemoaffinity theory

By growing towards high concentrations of the particular chemical that is released by the target cells.

Target cell

Growth cone

Chemical released by target

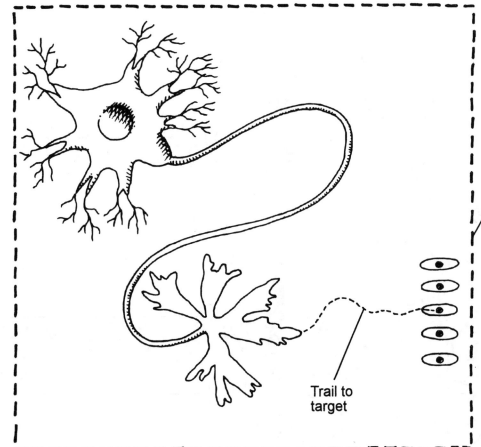

### Blueprint theory

By following specific trails (blood vessels, membranes, nerves etc.) through the substrate to the target cells.

Trail to target

## Review Exercises: Early Development of the Human Nervous System

Now it is time for you to pause and consolidate the terms and ideas that you have learned in the five learning units of Chapter 4. It is important that you overlearn them so that they do not quickly fade from your memory.

### Review Exercise 4.1

Turn to the illustrations in the five learning units of Chapter 4, and use the cover flap at the back of the book to cover the terms that run down the right-hand edge of each illustration page. Study the five illustrations in sequence until you can identify each labeled structure, process, and concept. Once you have worked through all five illustrations twice without making an error, advance to Review Exercise 4.2.

### Review Exercise 4.2

Fill in the missing terms in the following illustration. The correct answers are provided at the back of the book. Carefully review the material related to your incorrect answers.

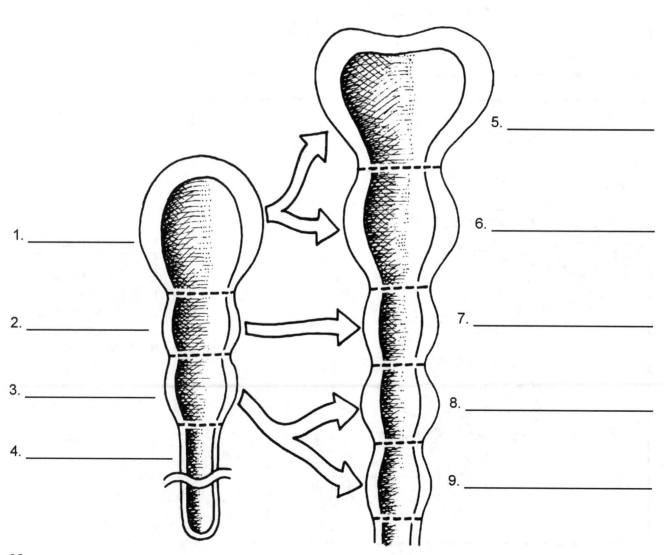

1. _____

2. _____

3. _____

4. _____

5. _____

6. _____

7. _____

8. _____

9. _____

## Review Exercise 4.3

Without referring to Chapter 4, fill in each of the following blanks with the correct term from the chapter. The correct answers are provided at the back of the book. Carefully review the material related to your incorrect answers.

1. The developing vertebrate nervous system first becomes visible as a patch of cells on the _____ surface of the embryo; this patch of cells is called the neural

   _____.

2. The rhombencephalon, the mesencephalon, and the prosencephalon are known more commonly as the _____, the _____, and the _____, respectively.

3. The lips of the neural _____ fuse to form the neural tube.

4. The alignment of developing neurons into the structures of the nervous system is called _____.

5. The telencephalon and the _____ compose the forebrain.

6. In humans, the human neural plate is first apparent about _____ days after conception.

7. The _____ and the myelencephalon compose the hindbrain.

8. Migration of neurons occurs along a temporary network of _____ glial cells.

9. The cells of the neural tube proliferate most rapidly at its _____ end.

10. At the tip of each growing axon is a _____.

11. Paradoxically, neuron _____ is an important phase of neural development; it reduces the number of neurons in some parts of the brain by up to 85%.

12. Many axons become _____ by _____ cells.

13. During the 4th week of prenatal development, swellings first become visible on the anterior end of the neural tube. At first, there are _____ of them.

14. The neural tube develops into the CNS; the neural _____ develops into the PNS.

15. Of the brain's five divisions, the most anterior is the _____, and the most posterior is the

    _____.

16. Prior to the development of the neural plate, the cells that will ultimately compose it are

    _____.

17. _____ occurs in the part of the neural tube adjacent to its fluid-filled interior.

18. The _____ lies between the diencephalon and the metencephalon.

19. Fasciculation results in later growth cones following the trail of the _____ growth cone.

20. The fact that some axons grow to their correct target cells, even when the target cells have been transplanted to a new location supports the _____ theory.

21. The fact that some axons grow to the location of their correct target cells, even when the target cells have been removed supports the _____ theory.

## Review Exercise 4.4

Below in alphabetical order is a list of all the terms and definitions that you encountered in Chapter 4. Cover the definitions with a sheet of paper, and then work your way down the list of terms, defining them to yourself as you go. Once you have gone through the list twice without an error, cover the terms and work your way down the list of definitions, providing the correct terms as you go. Repeat this process until you have worked through the list twice without an error.

Aggregation
The stage of neural development during which developing neurons align themselves to form the specific structures of the brain.

Blueprint theory
The theory that axons grow to their correct targets because they are programmed to follow specific trails through the developing nervous system.

Chemoaffinity theory
The theory that axons grow to their correct targets because they are programmed to follow to their source specific chemical signals released by their target cells.

Diencephalon
The posterior division of the forebrain; the area of the brain between the telencephalon and the mesencephalon.

Forebrain
The most anterior of the three swellings that appear at the anterior end of the developing vertebrate neural tube; the prosencephalon.

Growth cone
The ameba-like structure at the growing tip of each axon and dendrite; growth cones direct the growth of axons and dendrites to appropriate targets.

Hindbrain
The most posterior of the three swellings that appear at the anterior end of the developing vertebrate neural tube; the rhombencephalon.

Mesencephalon
The midbrain; the division of the brain between the diencephalon and the metencephalon.

Metencephalon
The anterior division of the hindbrain; the area of the brain between the mesencephalon and the myelencephalon.

Midbrain
The middle swelling of the three that appear at the anterior end of the developing vertebrate neural tube; the mesencephalon.

Migration
The stage of neural development during which newly created neurons migrate outward from the region of cell division to appropriate locations in the developing neural tube.

Myelencephalon
The most posterior of the brain's five divisions; the area of the brain between the metencephalon and the spinal cord.

| | | | |
|---|---|---|---|
| Myelination | The stage of neuron development during which many axons become myelinated by glial cells. | Proliferation | The stage of neural development during which many new neurons are created by cell division in the region of the neural tube adjacent to its fluid-filled inner canal. |
| Neural crest | The vertebrate embryonic structure that is located just dorsal and lateral to the neural tube; it is formed from neural plate cells that break away as the neural tube is being formed; the neural crest develops into the PNS. | Radial glial cells | The temporary network of glial cells that exists in the developing neural tube only during the period of neuron migration; migrating neurons travel outward along this glial network. |
| Neural groove | The groove that develops down the center of the neural plate. | Telencephalon | The most anterior of the brain's five divisions; the anterior division of the forebrain. |
| Neural plate | The patch of tissue on the dorsal surface of the vertebrate embryo that develops into the nervous system; in human embryos, it is first visible about 18 days following conception. | | |
| Neural tube | The fluid-filled tube that is formed in the vertebrate embryo when the lips of the neural groove fuse; the neural tube develops into the CNS. | | |
| Neuron death | The stage of early nervous system development during which large numbers of neurons die, typically those that have not established effective synaptic contacts. | | |
| Process growth and synapse formation | The stage of neural development during which axons and dendrites grow and establish synaptic contacts. | | |

# Chapter 5: Gross Anatomy of the Human Brain

The first four chapters have set the stage for this one. In the first four chapters, you learned about the divisions of the nervous system, about the system of anatomical planes and directions that is used to communicate location within the brain, about the cells that compose the brain, and about the brain's early development. Now, you are prepared to take your first look at the gross anatomy of the adult human brain. Because this is a major turning point in the book, it is a good time to pause to review what you have learned so far. Using the cover flap, review the illustrations in the learning units of each of the four preceding chapters.

This chapter will introduce you to the overall layout of the adult human brain and to its major divisions—you will be introduced to specific brain structures in subsequent chapters.

The following are the seven learning units of Chapter 5:

5.1    Cerebral Hemispheres and Brain Stem

5.2    The Five Divisions of the Mature Brain

5.3    The Meninges

5.4    The Cerebral Ventricles

5.5    Tracts and Nuclei

5.6    The Cerebral Commissures

5.7    The Cranial Nerves

## 5.1  Cerebral Hemispheres and Brain Stem

The human brain has three components: the two **cerebral hemispheres** and the **brain stem**. The two cerebral hemispheres sit atop the brain stem, which is an extension of the spinal cord.

In general, the structures of the human cerebral hemispheres mediate complex psychological processes such as memory, motivation, speaking, and thinking. In contrast, brain stem structures control simple bodily reflexes, many of which maintain the constancy of the body's internal environment—for example, brain stem structures regulate blood glucose and oxygen levels, heart rate, and body temperature.

During the course of vertebrate evolution, the cerebral hemispheres have undergone massive development. Virtually nonexistent in early vertebrates (i.e., in fish, amphibians, and reptiles), the cerebral hemispheres constitute the largest, most complex division of the primate brain. In contrast, the vertebrate brain stem has undergone little recent evolutionary development—there is little difference between the primate brain stem and the brain stems of early vertebrates.

**Cerebral hemispheres** (se REE brul   HEM iss feers)
The two large neural structures that sit atop the vertebrate brain stem, one on the left and one on the right; they mediate complex psychological processes.

**Brain stem**
The central neural stem on which the two cerebral hemispheres sit; many brain stem structures play key roles in the regulation of the body's inner environment.

---

*Coloring notes*

*Color the left hemisphere, right hemisphere, and brain stem different colors by staying within the dashed lines.*

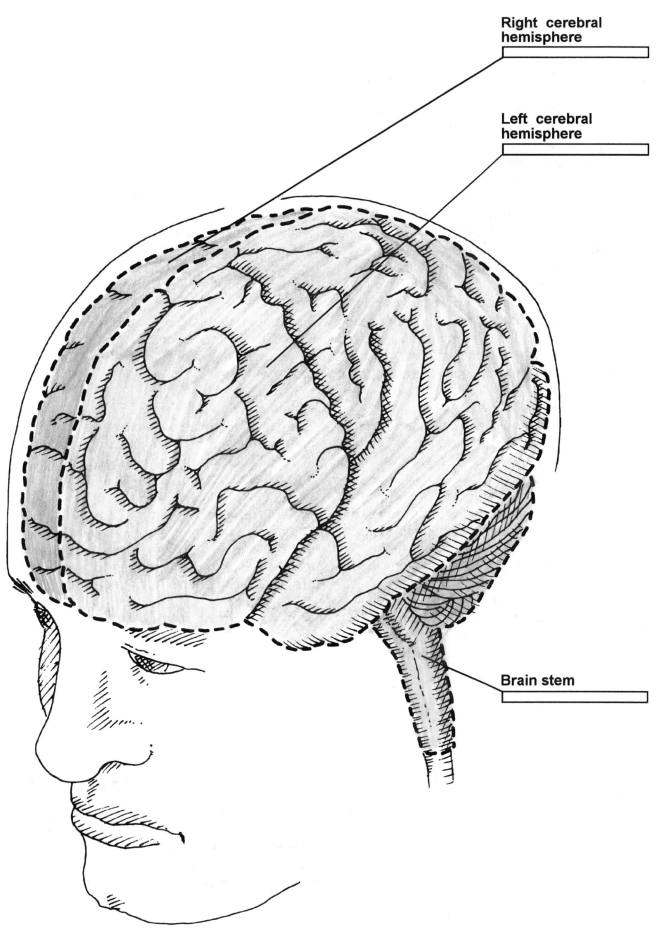

**Right cerebral hemisphere**

**Left cerebral hemisphere**

**Brain stem**

## 5.2 The Five Divisions of the Mature Brain

In Chapter 4, you learned how the *forebrain*, *midbrain*, and *hindbrain* divisions of the vertebrate brain first appear as swellings at the anterior end of the neural tube. Then, you learned how the forebrain develops into the **telencephalon** and **diencephalon**, the midbrain develops into the **mesencephalon**, and the hindbrain develops into the **metencephalon** and **myelencephalon**. Once formed, these five swellings in the neural tube undergo massive growth, and they ultimately develop into an adult brain. Accordingly, it is usual to consider adult brains as being composed of five divisions, each derived from one of the five embryologic swellings. In this learning unit, you are introduced to these five divisions of the mature human brain.

The adult human brain's five divisions are illustrated in a drawing of a midsagittal section; notice their locations and relative sizes. The brains of all vertebrates include these five divisions.

In the learning unit preceding this one, you learned that the human brain is composed of the two *cerebral hemispheres* and the *brain stem*. The two cerebral hemispheres compose the telencephalon, by far the largest division of the human brain. The brain stem comprises the brain's other four divisions; from anterior to posterior, the brain stem is composed of the diencephalon, the mesencephalon, the metencephalon, and the myelencephalon.

**Telencephalon** (TEL en SEF a lon)
The cerebral hemispheres; one of the two divisions of the forebrain (the other is the diencephalon).

**Diencephalon** (DYE en SEF a lon)
The region of the brain between the telencephalon and the mesencephalon; one of the two divisions of the forebrain (the other is the telencephalon); the most anterior region of the brain stem.

**Mesencephalon** (MEEZ en SEF a lon)
The midbrain; the region of the brain stem between the diencephalon and the metencephalon.

**Metencephalon** (MET en SEF a lon)
The region of the brain stem between the mesencephalon and the myelencephalon; one of the two divisions of the hindbrain (the other is the myelencephalon).

**Myelencephalon** (MY el en SEF a lon)
The most posterior region of the brain; the area of the brain stem between the metencephalon and the spinal cord; one of the two divisions of the hindbrain (the other is the metencephalon).

---

*Coloring notes*

*Start by coloring the inferior portions of the brain and then work upwards: Color in sequence the myelencephalon, metencephalon, mesencephalon, and diencephalon. Finally, color the remainder of the brain, which is the telencephalon. In your coloring, be sure to stay within dashed lines.*

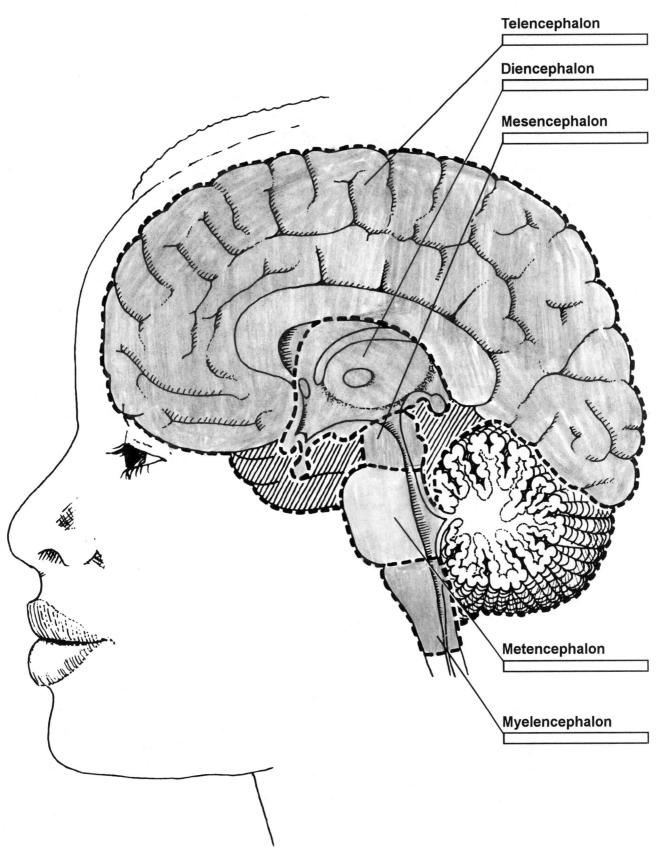

Telencephalon

Diencephalon

Mesencephalon

Metencephalon

Myelencephalon

71

## 5.3 The Meninges

The brain and spinal cord (i.e., the central nervous system) are covered by three membranes, called the *meninges* (meh NIN jees); the singular of *meninges* is, believe it or not, *menynx*. The outermost of the three meninges is the **dura mater**, which means *tough mother*. It is composed of tough fibrous connective tissue. The middle menynx is the **arachnoid membrane**, which means *spider membrane*. It is a delicate membrane that reminded early anatomists of a gauze-like spider web, thus its name. The innermost menynx is the **pia mater**, which means *delicate mother*. The pia mater, the most delicate of the three meninges, clings directly to the brain and spinal cord.

Between the pia mater and the main part of the arachnoid layer is a fluid-filled space called the **subarachnoid space**. It contains many blood vessels and the web-like processes of the arachnoid layer. Through it flows **cerebrospinal fluid** (CSF), which supports, nourishes, and cushions the brain. The hollow core of the brain and spinal cord is also filled with cerebrospinal fluid. People who have lost some of their cerebrospinal fluid—for example, during brain surgery—are well aware of the supporting and cushioning role of the cerebrospinal fluid; they experience severe stabbing pains each time they jerk their head.

**Dura mater** (DURE a  MATE er)
The outermost and toughest of the three meninges.

**Arachnoid membrane** (a RAK noyd)
The middle menynx; it has the texture of a gauze-like spider web.

**Pia mater** (PEE a  MATE er)
The innermost and most delicate of the three meninges; it adheres to the surface of the CNS.

**Subarachnoid space** (SUB a RAK noyd)
The space between the main part of the arachnoid membrane and the pia mater; it contains cerebrospinal fluid, the web-like processes of the arachnoid layer, and many blood vessels.

**Cerebrospinal fluid**
The fluid that fills both the subarachnoid space and the hollow core of the brain and spinal cord; it supports, nourishes, and cushions the central nervous system.

*Coloring notes*

*First, color the dura mater and pia mater; they are the easiest to color. Then, color the arachnoid membrane being sure to color its many spider-web-like processes. Finally, color the cerebrospinal-fluid-filled subarachnoid space, through which the processes of the arachnoid membrane pass.*

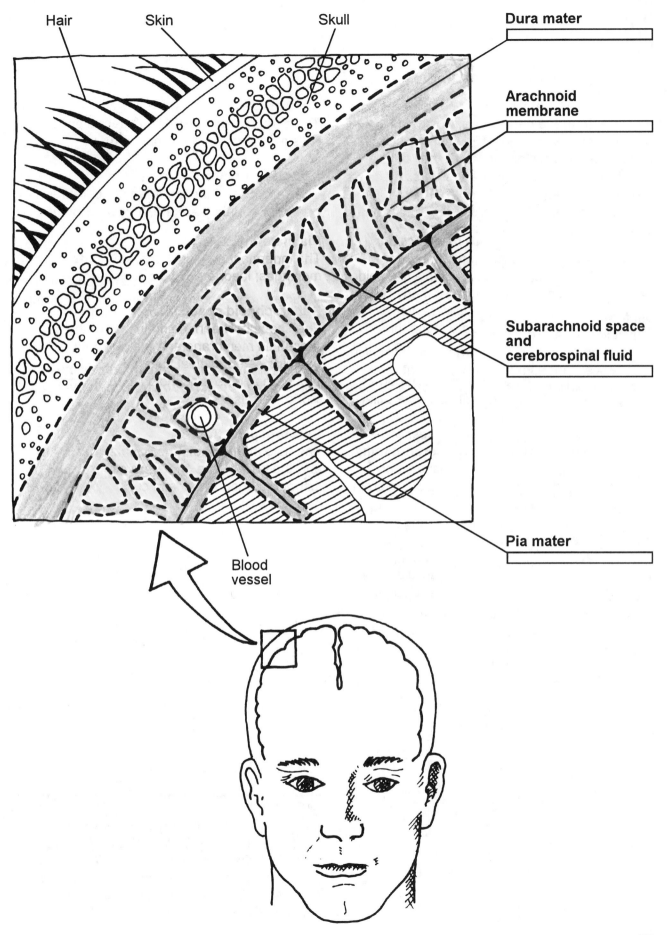

Hair   Skin   Skull

**Dura mater**

**Arachnoid membrane**

**Subarachnoid space and cerebrospinal fluid**

**Pia mater**

Blood vessel

## 5.4  The Cerebral Ventricles

You may recall that the central nervous system develops from the neural tube, which has a hollow cerebrospinal-fluid-filled core. As the central nervous system develops, this hollow core is maintained, but it changes in size and shape, particularly in the forebrain region.

The hollow fluid-filled core of the adult spinal cord is called the **central canal**—it is a long narrow space that runs the length of the cord. In the brain, the hollow fluid-filled core expands during development to form four large interconnected chambers; the four *cerebral ventricles*. There are two large **lateral ventricles**, one in each of the cerebral hemispheres; there is the **third ventricle**, which is a vertical sheet-shaped chamber that lies along the midline of the *diencephalon,* and there is the **fourth ventricle**, which is a small chamber in the *metencephalon*. The third and fourth ventricles are connected by the **cerebral aqueduct**, a narrow channel that runs through the *mesencephalon*.

The four cerebral ventricles are connected to the central canal of the spinal cord and to the *subarachnoid space. Cerebrospinal fluid* circulates continuously through this system. If the flow of cerebrospinal fluid from the brain is blocked by a tumor (e.g., by one near the cerebral aqueduct) in infants whose skull bones have yet to fuse, the skull expands to relieve the pressure, a condition called *hydrocephalus*, which means *water head*.

**Central canal**
The cerebrospinal-fluid-filled internal space that runs the length of the spinal cord.

**Lateral ventricles**
The ventricles of the left and right cerebral hemispheres; they are the largest of the four cerebral ventricles.

**Third ventricle**
The cerebral ventricle of the diencephalon; it is a vertical sheet-shaped chamber that lies along the midline.

**Fourth ventricle**
The cerebral ventricle of the metencephalon; it connects the cerebral aqueduct and the central canal.

**Cerebral aqueduct**
The narrow channel that connects the third and fourth ventricles; most of it is located in the mesencephalon.

---

***Coloring notes***

*First, color the two lateral ventricles. Then, in sequence, color the third ventricle, the cerebral aqueduct, the fourth ventricle, and the central canal. Note that much of the cerebral aqueduct is hidden from view in this illustration by the inferior arm of the left lateral ventricle.*

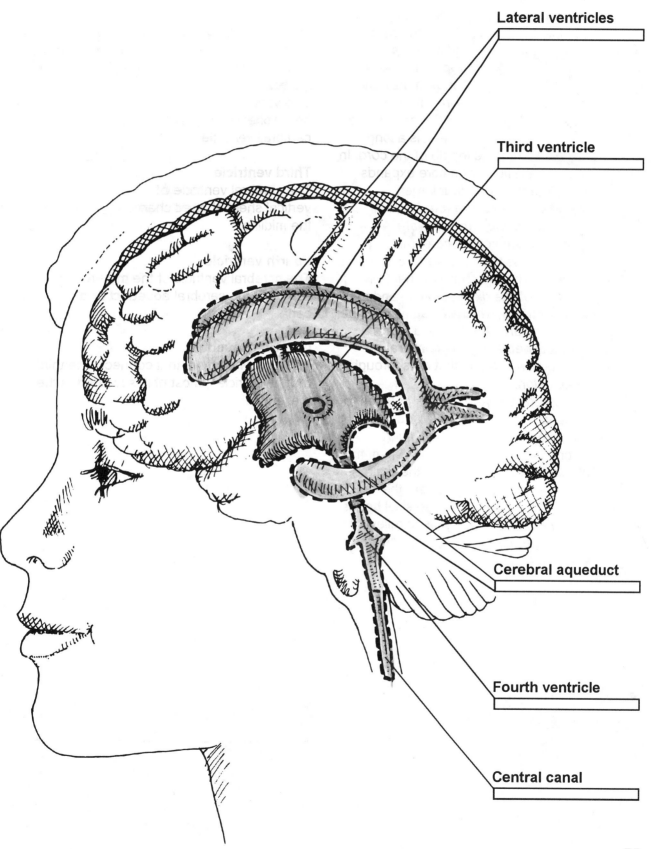

Lateral ventricles

Third ventricle

Cerebral aqueduct

Fourth ventricle

Central canal

## 5.5 Tracts and Nuclei

There are two fundamentally different kinds of structures in the nervous system: those that are largely composed of *cell bodies* and those that are largely composed of *axons*. The names of these structures depend on whether they are located in the central nervous system or in the peripheral nervous system. In the CNS, structures that are largely composed of cell bodies are called **nuclei** (singular: *nucleus*), and structures that are largely composed of axons are called **tracts.** Whereas, in the PNS, structures that are largely composed of cell bodies are called **ganglia** (singular: *ganglion*), and structures that are largely composed of axons are called **nerves**.

In general, the function of tracts and nerves is to conduct *action potentials* from one part of the nervous system to another, whereas the function of nuclei and ganglia is to perform local analyses of neural signals. Accordingly, nuclei and ganglia are composed of many neurons with very short axons or no axons at all, in addition to cell bodies whose axons are part of tracts and nerves.

In studying the anatomy of the nervous system, it is important to keep in mind that each major nucleus, ganglion, tract, and nerve is composed of hundreds of thousands of individual neurons. Note, too, that the word *nucleus* has two different neuroanatomical meanings: As well as being a cluster of cell bodies in the CNS, it is the large spherical structure of the neural cell body.

**Nuclei** (NEW klee eye)
Structures of the CNS that are composed largely of neural cell bodies; their function is the local analysis of neural signals (singular: *nucleus)*.

**Tracts**
Structures of the CNS that are composed largely of axons; their function is to conduct action potentials from one part of the CNS to another.

**Ganglia** (GANG glee a)
Structures of the PNS that are composed largely of neural cell bodies; their function is the local analysis of neural signals (singular: *ganglion)*.

**Nerves**
Structures of the PNS that are composed largely of axons; their function is to conduct action potentials from one part of the PNS to another.

*Coloring notes*

*First, color the cell bodies in the nucleus one color and the cell bodies in the ganglion another. Then, color the axons in the tract and the axons in the nerve—again different colors.*

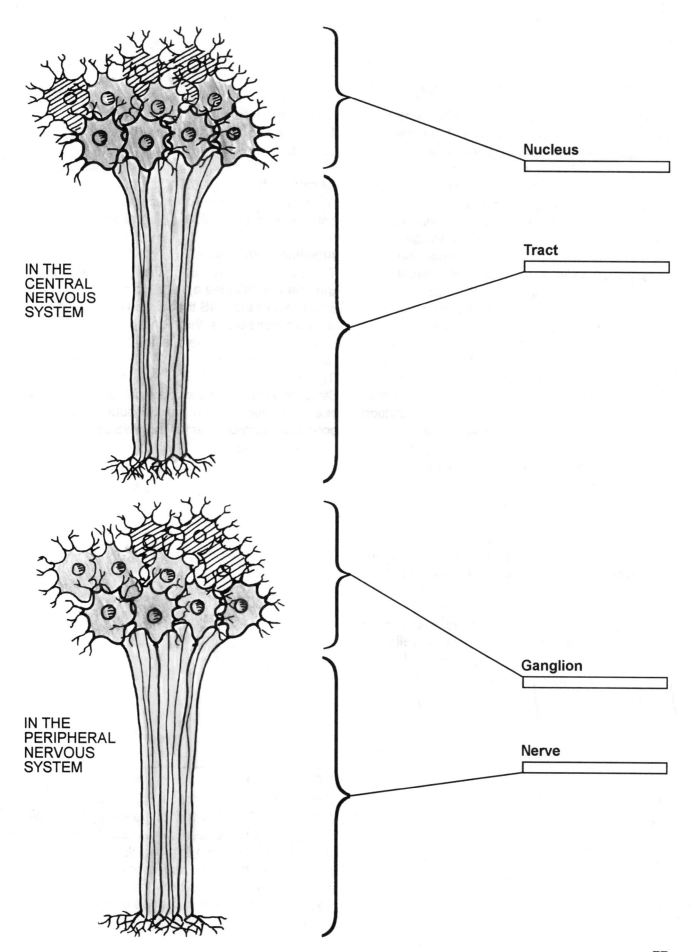

IN THE
CENTRAL
NERVOUS
SYSTEM

IN THE
PERIPHERAL
NERVOUS
SYSTEM

**Nucleus**

**Tract**

**Ganglion**

**Nerve**

## 5.6 The Cerebral Commissures

The two cerebral hemispheres are separated from each other by the **longitudinal fissure**—the longitudinal fissure is the long deep chasm between them. However, the cerebral hemispheres are connected to one another by a few large tracts that span the longitudinal fissure. These tracts are called the *cerebral commissures*. Because they are the only direct connections between the two largest, most complex, and most plastic parts of the brain; the cerebral commissures are, from a psychological perspective, very important structures indeed.

The best way of visualizing the cerebral commissures is by sectioning the brain along its midsagittal plane. A midsagittal section reveals the location and cross-sectional profile of each cerebral commissure.

By far the largest cerebral commissure is the **corpus callosum;** it is composed of about 200 million axons. Two other noteworthy commissures are the **anterior commissure** and the **massa intermedia**. The anterior commissure is located just inferior to the anterior tip of the corpus callosum, and it is the major route of communication between the parts of the brain near the left and right temples (i.e., the left and right *temporal lobes*). The massa intermedia is located in the middle of the *third ventricle*, and it connects the left and right lobes of the *diencephalon*. Although the massa intermedia is usually classified as a commissure because of its midline location, it is not a true commissure because it is primarily a nucleus rather than a tract.

**Longitudinal fissure**
The deep midline chasm between the two cerebral hemispheres.

**Corpus callosum** (ka LOW sum)
By far the largest cerebral commissure; it is composed of about 200 million axons.

**Anterior commissure**
The commissure that is located just inferior to the anterior tip of the corpus callosum; a major route of communication between the left and right temporal lobes.

**Massa intermedia**
The commissure that is located in the middle of the third ventricle; it is a route of communication between the left and right diencephalon, which is largely separated by the third ventricle.

---

*Coloring notes*

*First, in the coronal section, color the longitudinal fissure, which largely separates the left and right cerebral hemispheres. Next, color the massa intermedia in the midsagittal section. Finally, color the corpus callosum and the anterior commissure in both the midsagittal section and the coronal section using the same two colors in each section.*

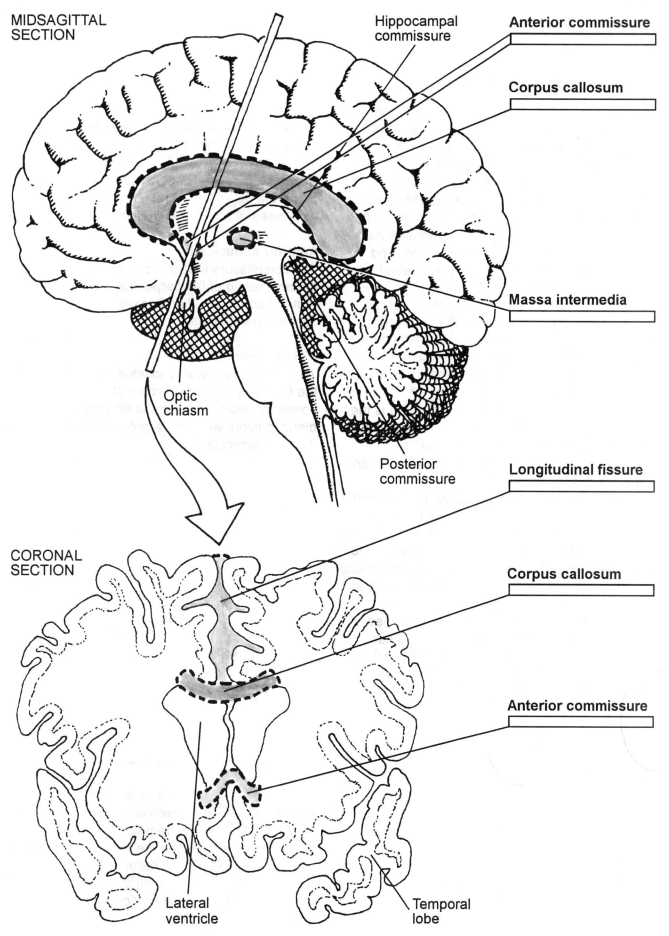

MIDSAGITTAL
SECTION

Hippocampal
commissure

**Anterior commissure**

**Corpus callosum**

**Massa intermedia**

Optic
chiasm

Posterior
commissure

**Longitudinal fissure**

CORONAL
SECTION

**Corpus callosum**

**Anterior commissure**

Lateral
ventricle

Temporal
lobe

## 5.7 The Cranial Nerves

Most *afferent* (i.e., sensory) nerves that enter the CNS do so at the level of the spinal cord; similarly, most *efferent* (i.e., motor) nerves that exit the CNS do so at the level of the spinal cord. There are 12 pairs of exceptions, the twelve pairs of *cranial nerves*. The cranial nerves are nerves that extend directly from the brain. Some of the cranial nerves are purely sensory, whereas others contain a mixture of sensory and motor fibers. The motor fibers of the cranial nerves compose the cranial division of the *parasympathetic nervous system*.

The 12 cranial nerves are numbered from anterior to posterior, from 1 to 12. The three purely sensory cranial nerves are the **olfactory** (the 1st), the **optic** (the 2nd), and the **vestibulocochlear** (the 8th) cranial nerves. The olfactory nerves conduct signals from the olfactory receptors of the nose, the optic nerves conduct signals from the visual receptors of the eyes, and the vestibulocochlear nerves conduct signals both from the auditory receptors and the organs of balance, both located in the inner ear.

Two of the mixed sensory and motor nerves are the **trigeminal** (the 5th) and the **vagus** (the 10th). The motor portions of the two trigeminal nerves control the muscles involved in chewing, and the sensory portions receive information back from the same muscles, as well as from other parts of the face—the prefix "tri" indicates that each trigeminal nerve has three major branches. The two vagus nerves are the longest cranial nerves; they conduct signals to and from many parts of the gut.

The aforementioned five cranial nerves are the ones that come up most frequently in the study of psychological phenomena. The other seven are labeled in the accompanying illustration.

**Olfactory nerves** (ole FAK tor ee)
The first pair of cranial nerves; they carry sensory signals from the olfactory receptors of the nose to the brain.

**Optic nerves**
The second pair of cranial nerves; they carry sensory signals from the visual receptors of the eyes to the brain.

**Vestibulocochlear nerves** (vess TIB yu loe COCK lee ar)
The eighth pair of cranial nerves, which carry sensory signals from the inner ear to brain; one branch carries sensory signals from the organs of balance (i.e., from the vestibular organs), and the other branch carries sensory signals from the organs of hearing (i.e., from the cochlea).

**Trigeminal nerves** (try JEM in al)
The fifth pair of cranial nerves, each of which has three major branches; they conduct motor signals from the brain to the muscles involved in chewing, and sensory signals from the same muscles and from other parts of the face to the brain.

**Vagus nerves** ((VAY gus)
The tenth and longest pair of cranial nerves; they conduct signals to and from the organs of the gut (e.g., to and from the heart, liver, and stomach).

*Coloring notes*

*Color each of the five pairs of cranial nerves that were emphasized in this learning unit. Be sure to color each of the five on both sides of the brain. Also, review the names of the other seven cranial nerves.*

INFERIOR VIEW

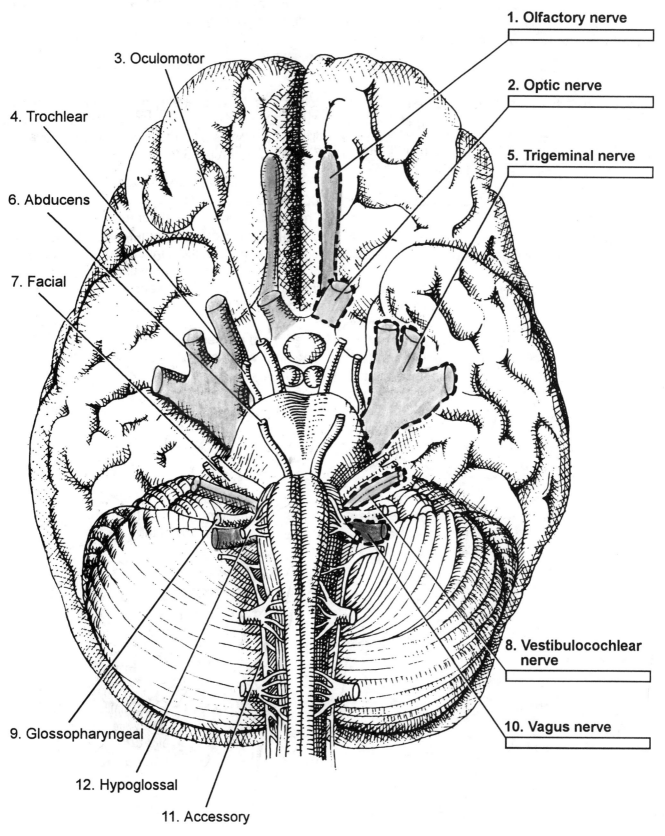

3. Oculomotor

4. Trochlear

6. Abducens

7. Facial

9. Glossopharyngeal

12. Hypoglossal

11. Accessory

1. Olfactory nerve

2. Optic nerve

5. Trigeminal nerve

8. Vestibulocochlear nerve

10. Vagus nerve

81

## Review Exercises: Gross Anatomy of the Human Brain

Now it is time for you to pause and consolidate the terms and ideas that you have learned in the seven learning units of Chapter 5. It is important that you overlearn them so that they do not quickly fade from your memory.

### Review Exercise 5.1

Turn to the illustrations in the seven learning units of Chapter 5, and use the cover flap at the back of the book to cover the terms that run down the right-hand edge of each illustration page. Study the seven illustrations in sequence until you can identify each of the labeled neuroanatomical structures. Once you have worked through all seven illustrations twice without making an error, advance to Review Exercise 5.2.

### Review Exercise 5.2

Fill in the missing terms in the following drawing of a midsagittal section of the human brain. The answers are provided at the back of the book. Carefully review the material related to your incorrect answers.

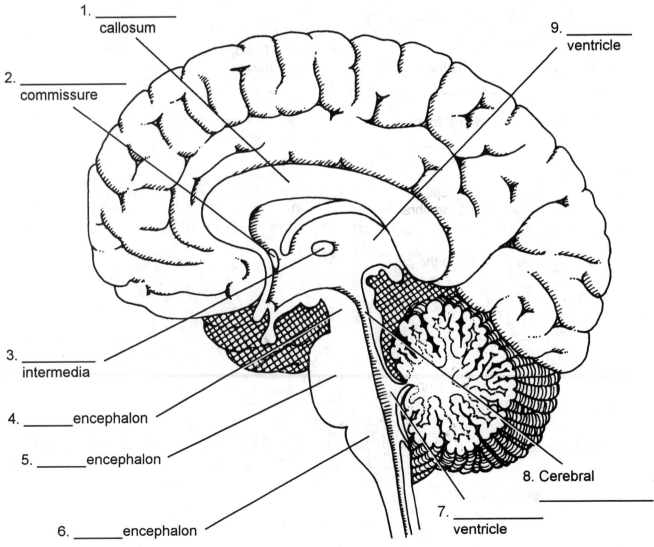

1. _____ callosum

2. _____ commissure

3. _____ intermedia

4. _____encephalon

5. _____encephalon

6. _____encephalon

7. _____ ventricle

8. Cerebral _____

9. _____ ventricle

## Review Exercise 5.3

Without referring to Chapter 5, fill in each of the following blanks with the correct term from the chapter. The correct answers are provided at the back of the book. Carefully review the material related to your incorrect answers.

1. The brain is composed of the two cerebral hemispheres and the _____.

2. The _____ nerve is the 10th cranial nerve; it is the longest cranial nerve, and it conducts signals to and from the organs of the gut.

3. Together, the diencephalon, mesencephalon, metencephlon, and myelencephalon compose the _____.

4. The toughest menynx is the _____.

5. Connecting the third and fourth ventricles is the cerebral _____.

6. Cerebrospinal fluid flows through the _____ space, the space between the arachnoid membrane and the pia mater.

7. The pia mater adheres to the surface of the _____ nervous system.

8. The spinal cord has no ventricles; instead, it has the _____.

9. The _____ is located in the third ventricle and connects the left and right diencephalon.

10. The _____ ventricles are the two ventricles of the cerebral hemispheres.

11. The inner menynx is the _____.

12. When babies are born with tumors near the cerebral aqueduct, _____ is often the result.

13. The most posterior area of the brain stem is the _____.

14. Tracts are to nuclei as nerves are to _____.

15. There are ____ pairs of cranial nerves.

16. The corpus callosum is the largest cerebral _____.

17. The _____ fissure divides the two cerebral hemispheres.

18. The olfactory, optic, and vestibulocochlear nerves are the three pairs of purely _____ cranial nerves.

19. The motor fibers of the cranial nerves are considered to be part of the _____ division of the autonomic nervous system.

20. Together, the two cerebral hemispheres compose the _____.

21. The _____ nerve is the 5th cranial nerve; it has three major branches, which carry signals to and from the face.

22. Tracts and nerves are composed mainly of _____.

23. The two cerebral ventricles that are located on the midline of the brain are the _____ and _____ ventricles.

24. The plural of *menynx* is _____.

## Review Exercise 5.4

Below in alphabetical order is a list of all the terms and definitions that you learned in Chapter 5. Cover the definitions with a sheet of paper, and work your way down the list of terms, defining them to yourself as you go. Repeat this process until you have gone through the list twice without an error. Then, cover the terms and work your way down the list of definitions, providing the correct terms as you go. Repeat this process until you have gone through the list twice without an error.

| | |
|---|---|
| Anterior commissure | The commissure that is located just inferior to the anterior tip of the corpus callosum; a major route of communication between the left and right temporal lobes. |
| Arachnoid membrane | The middle menynx; it has the texture of a gauze-like spider web. |
| Brain stem | The central neural stem on which the two cerebral hemispheres sit; many brain stem structures play key roles in the regulation of body's inner environment. |
| Central canal | The cerebrospinal-fluid-filled internal space that runs the length of the spinal cord. |
| Cerebral aqueduct | The narrow channel that connects the third and fourth ventricles; most of it is located in the mesencephalon. |
| Cerebral hemispheres | The two large neural structures that sit atop the vertebrate brain stem, one on the left and one on the right; they mediate complex psychological processes. |
| Cerebrospinal fluid | The fluid that fills both the subarachnoid space and the hollow core of the brain and spinal cord; it supports, nourishes, and cushions the central nervous system. |
| Corpus callosum | By far the largest cerebral commissure; it is composed of about 200 million axons. |
| Diencephalon | The region of the brain between the telencephalon and the mesencephalon; one of the two divisions of the forebrain (the other is the telencephalon); the most anterior region of the brain stem. |
| Dura mater | The outermost and toughest of the three meninges. |
| Fourth ventricle | The cerebral ventricle of the metencephalon; it connects the cerebral aqueduct and the central canal. |
| Ganglia | Structures of the PNS that are composed largely of neural cell bodies; their function is the local analysis of neural signals (singular: ganglion). |
| Lateral ventricles | The ventricles of the left and right cerebral hemispheres; they are the largest of the four cerebral ventricles. |
| Longitudinal fissure | The deep midline chasm between the two cerebral hemispheres. |

| | |
|---|---|
| Massa intermedia | The commissure that is located in the middle of the third ventricle; it is a route of communication between the left and right diencephalon, which is largely separated by the third ventricle. |
| Mesencephalon | The midbrain; the region of the brain stem between the diencephalon and the metencephalon. |
| Metencephalon | The region of the brain stem between the mesencephalon and the myelencephalon; one of the two divisions of the hindbrain (the other is the myelencephalon). |
| Myelencephalon | The most posterior region of the brain; the area of the brain stem between the metencephlon and the spinal cord; one of the two divisions of the hindbrain (the other is the metencephalon). |
| Nerves | Structures of the PNS that are composed largely of axons; their function is to conduct action potentials from one part of the PNS to another. |
| Nuclei | Structures of the CNS that are composed largely of neural cell bodies; their function is the local analysis of neural signals (singular: nucleus). |
| Olfactory nerves | The first pair of cranial nerves; they carry sensory signals from the olfactory receptors of the nose to the brain. |
| Optic nerves | The second pair of cranial nerves; they carry sensory signals from the visual receptors of the eyes to the brain. |
| Pia mater | The innermost and most delicate of the three meninges; it adheres to the surface of the CNS. |
| Subarachnoid space | The space between the arachnoid membrane and the pia mater; it contains cerebrospinal fluid, the web-like processes of the arachnoid layer, and many blood vessels. |
| Telencephalon | The cerebral hemispheres; one of the two divisions of the forebrain (the other is the diencephalon). |
| Third ventricle | The cerebral ventricle of the diencephalon; it is a vertical sheet-shaped chamber that lies along the midline. |
| Tracts | Structures of the CNS that are composed largely of axons; their function is to conduct action potentials from one part of the CNS to another. |
| Trigeminal nerves | The fifth pair of cranial nerves, each of which has three major branches; they conduct motor signals from the brain to the muscles involved in chewing, and sensory signals from the same muscles and from other parts of the face to the brain. |

| | |
|---|---|
| Vagus nerves | The tenth and longest pair of cranial nerves; they conduct signals to and from the organs of the gut (e.g., to and from the heart, liver, and stomach). |
| Vestibulocochlear nerves | The eighth pair of cranial nerves, which carry sensory signals from the inner ear to brain; one branch carries sensory signals from the organs of balance (i.e., from the vestibular organs), and the other branch carries sensory signals from the organs of hearing (i.e., from the cochlea). |

## Chapter 6: Major Structures of the Brain Stem

As you learned in the last chapter, the human brain is composed of the two cerebral hemispheres and the brain stem. This chapter introduces the major structures of the brain stem, and the following chapter introduces the major structures of the cerebral hemispheres.

This chapter's survey of structures is both systematic and selective. It is systematic in the sense that it begins at the brain stem's border with the spinal cord and ascends to its border with the telencephalon. It is selective in the sense that it focuses on only one category of brain stem structures.

The brain stem contains many large tracts that carry signals between the spinal cord and the cerebral hemispheres; a multitude of small nuclei interconnected by a network of local tracts, and a few large nuclei. This chapter focuses on the brain stem's large nuclei.

The following are the six learning units of Chapter 6:

6.1   Major Structures of the Myelencephalon

6.2   Major Structures of the Metencephalon

6.3   Major Structures of the Mesencephalon

6.4   Diencephalon: The Thalamus

6.5   Diencephalon: The Hypothalamus

6.6   The Hypothalamus and Pituitary

## 6.1  Major Structures of the Myelencephalon

The myelencephalon is commonly referred to as the **medulla**—or, more formally, the *medulla oblongata*. The medulla consists mainly of *white matter*, that is, it consists mainly of myelinated tracts, most of which carry signals between the rest of the brain and the spinal cord.

Prominent on the ventral surface of the medulla are two large bulges, called the **pyramids.** The pyramids are created by the *pyramidal tracts* coursing near the ventral surface of the medulla. The pyramidal tracts carry signals for voluntary movement from the cerebral hemispheres to the spine. They decussate in the lower part of the medulla, and consequently, each cerebral hemisphere controls the *contralateral* (opposite side) of the body. Similarly, many sensory fibers decussate in the medulla so that feelings on one side of the body tend to be perceived by the contralateral hemisphere.

Prominent on the lateral surfaces of the medulla are two large olive-shaped clusters of nuclei called the **olives**. The olives are strongly connected to the *cerebellum*, a metencephalic structure that you will learn about in the next learning unit.

The most prominent internal nuclear structure of the medulla is the **reticular formation**. The reticular formation is a complex network of nuclei and interconnecting fibers that runs up the core of the brain stem between the medulla and the midbrain. The circuits of the reticular formation serve many different functions, including the promotion of alertness and attention on one hand and sleep on the other.

Throughout the medulla, both within the reticular formation and without, are nuclei that play a role in controlling vital body functions such as muscle tone, pulse, blood pressure, respiration, swallowing, coughing, sneezing, and vomiting. These nuclei receive signals from or transmit signals to the body either through tracts that ascend or descend in the spinal cord or through the four pairs of cranial nerves (9, 10, 11, and 12) that exit the medulla.

**Medulla** (meh DULL la)
The most posterior region of the brain stem; the myelencephalon; its major structures include the pyramids, olives, medullary reticular formation, and the nuclei that contribute axons to cranial nerves 9, 10, 11, and 12.

**Pyramids**
Two large bulges, one left and one right, on the ventral surface of the medulla; they contain the pyramidal tracts, which carry signals for voluntary movement from the cerebral hemispheres to the motor circuits of the spinal cord.

**Olives**
The pair of large olive-shaped clusters of nuclei that are visible as bulges on the lateral surfaces of the medulla, one on each side; they are connected to the cerebellum.

**Reticular formation** (re TIK yu lar)
A complex network of nuclei and short interconnecting tracts that is located in the core of the brain stem, from the medulla to the midbrain; its nuclei play a role in controlling many vital body functions and in the promotion of arousal, attention, and sleep.

*Coloring notes*

*First, color the medulla in the midsagittal section; it is the shaded portion of the illustration. Then, notice the external bulges created by the pyramids and olives on the enlarged external illustration of the medulla. Finally, color the reticular formation, olives, and pyramids in the cross section of the medulla.*

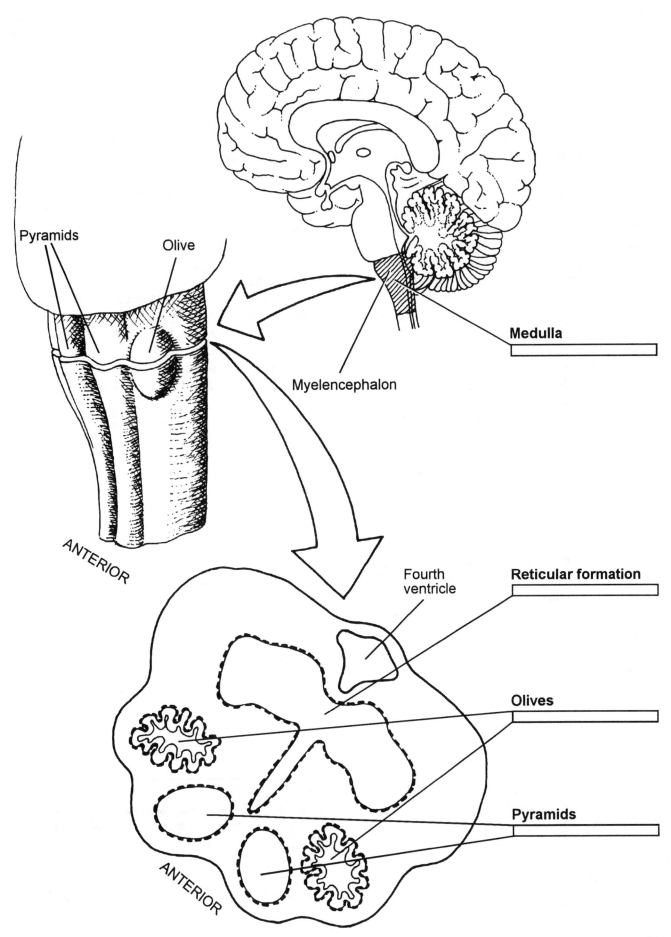

Pyramids

Olive

Myelencephalon

**Medulla**

ANTERIOR

Fourth
ventricle

**Reticular formation**

**Olives**

**Pyramids**

ANTERIOR

89

## 6.2 Major Structures of the Metencephalon

The metencephalon is composed of two distinct parts: the **cerebellum** and the **pons**. The cerebellum is the large striped structure that extends from the dorsal surface of the brain stem core—it is the third largest structure of the human brain—only the two cerebral hemispheres are larger. The cerebellum is connected to the rest of the brain stem by three large pairs of tracts called the **cerebellar peduncles** (inferior, middle, and superior)—the inferior peduncle is the major connection between the cerebellum and the olives of the medulla. The primary function of the cerebellum (which means *little brain*) is the coordination of movement. It does this by adjusting signals for movement descending from the cerebral hemispheres in the light of sensory information that it receives from muscles, joints, and tendons. Damage to the cerebellum results in *ataxia*, a condition characterized by jerky, uncoordinated, inaccurate movements.

The pons is the anterior extension of the medulla; it is the bulbous section of the brain stem to which the cerebellum is attached. The pons is like the medulla in three important respects: (1) It contains many ascending and descending tracts and many nuclei that are involved in the control of vital functions; (2) it contains the nuclei of four *cranial nerves* (in this case, 5, 6, 7, and 8); and (3) its major internal nuclear structure is the *reticular formation*. In addition, most of the *fourth ventricle* is located in the pons.

**Cerebellum** (serr uh BEL um)
The large striped metencephalic structure that is situated just dorsal to the pons; it plays a role in the coordination of movement.

**Cerebellar peduncles** (pe DUNK ulz)
Three large pairs of tracts (inferior, middle, and superior) that connect the cerebellum to the rest of the brain stem.

**Pons** (PONZ)
The ventral portion of the metencephalon; its major structures include the fourth ventricle, the metencephalic portion of the reticular formation, many ascending and descending tracts, and the nuclei of cranial nerves 5, 6, 7, and 8.

***Coloring notes***

*First, notice the location of the metencephalon on the midsagittal illustration; it is the portion that is shaded. Then, color the pons, cerebral peduncles, and cerebellum—in each case, by staying within the dashed lines. Notice that only two of the three cerebral peduncles are visible from this angle.*

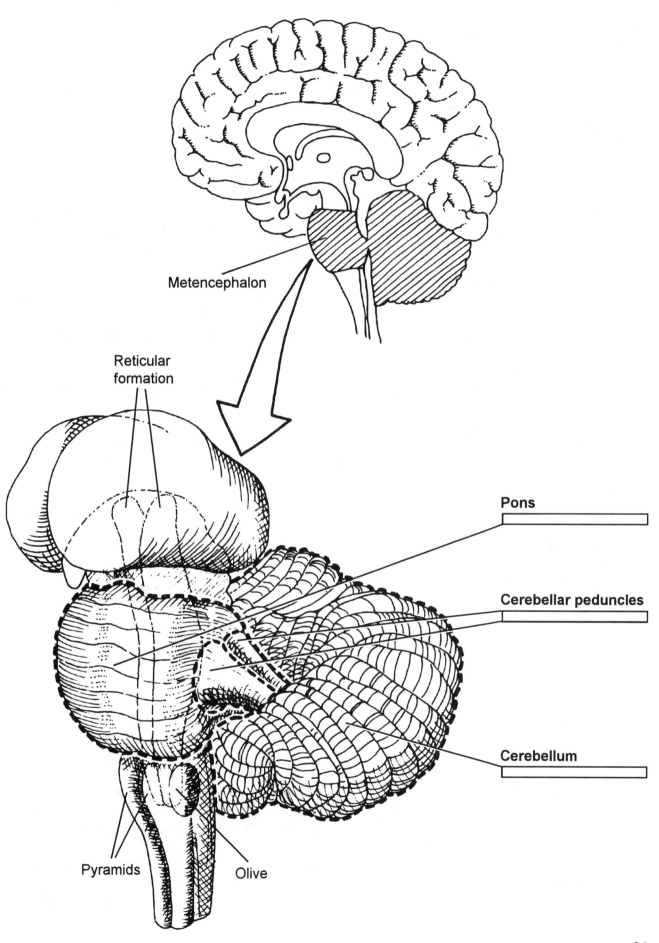

Metencephalon

Reticular formation

**Pons**

**Cerebellar peduncles**

**Cerebellum**

Pyramids

Olive

## 6.3  Major Structures of the Mesencephalon

The mesencephalon or midbrain is located just anterior to the pons. It has two regions: the *tectum* and *tegmentum*. The tectum (which means *roof*), forms the dorsal surface of the midbrain. In mammals it is composed of two pairs of nuclei. The more anterior pair, called the **superior colliculi,** play a role in the vision; the more posterior pair, called the **inferior colliculi,** play a role in audition (hearing).

The tegmentum is the portion of the midbrain ventral to the tectum. It contains the *cerebral aqueduct*, which connects the third and fourth ventricles; the midbrain portion of the *reticular formation*; and nuclei of cranial nerves 3 and 4.

I like to think of the tegmentum as the colorful area of the brain because it contains three important nuclear structures that are named after colors: the **red nucleus** (so named because it is faintly pink), the **periaqueductal gray** (so named because it is gray matter located around the cerebral aqueduct), and the **substantia nigra** (which means *black substance*; so named because many of its neurons contain a dark pigment). The red nucleus and substantia nigra are important structures in the sensorimotor system; the periaqueductal gray (PAG) is part of a circuit that suppresses pain and controls defensive behavior.

**Superior colliculi** (kuh LIK yu lee)
The more anterior of the two pairs of nuclei that constitute the mammalian tectum; they play a role in vision.

**Inferior colliculi**
The more posterior of the two pairs of nuclei that constitute the mammalian tectum; they play a role in audition.

**Red nuclei**
A pair of tegmental nuclei, one on the left and one on the right; they have a pinkish appearance and are important structures of the sensorimotor system.

**Periaqueductal gray** (PERR ee a kwuh DUK tal)
The tegmental gray matter that is located around the cerebral aqueduct; it plays a role in the suppression of pain and in defensive behavior.

**Substantia nigra** (sub STAN she a  NYE gra)
A pair of tegmental sensorimotor nuclei, one on the left and one on the right; they are so named because many of their neurons contain a dark pigment.

*Coloring notes*
*First, in the top midsagittal illustration, color the superior and inferior colliculi different colors by staying within the dashed lines. Then, using the same color that you used to color the midsagittal section of the superior colliculus, color the superior colliculi in the cross section. Finally, color the red nuclei and the substantia nigra in the cross section.*

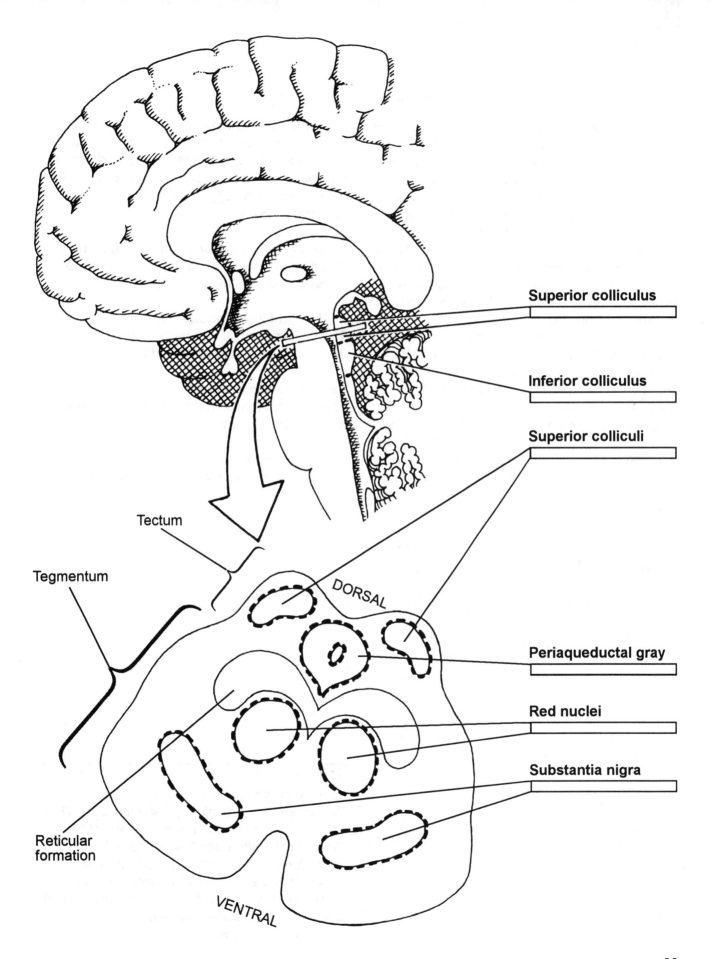

Superior colliculus

Inferior colliculus

Superior colliculi

Tectum

Tegmentum

DORSAL

Periaqueductal gray

Red nuclei

Substantia nigra

Reticular
formation

VENTRAL

## 6.4 Diencephalon: The Thalamus

The **thalamus** is one of the two major structures of the diencephalon; the *hypothalamus*, which will be discussed in the next learning unit, is the other. The thalamus is the large two-lobed structure that constitutes the top of the brain stem; one lobe sits on each side of the third ventricle. The two lobes of the thalamus are connected by the *massa intermedia*. The massa intermedia is a thalamic nucleus that is situated in the center of the third ventricle—it is often regarded as a cerebral commissure because of its midline position.

Several of the nuclei that compose the thalamus are relay nuclei in sensory systems; they receive sensory information from receptors and relay it to the appropriate areas of the *cerebral cortex*, the outer covering of the cerebral hemispheres. For example, the left and right **lateral geniculate nuclei, medial geniculate nuclei,** and **ventral posterior nuclei** relay visual, auditory, and tactual information, respectively.

Obvious neuroanatomical features of each lobe of the thalamus are the internal layers or lamina that are composed largely of myelinated axons. Because most of the thalamus is gray matter, the **internal lamina** of each lobe appear as white stripes against a gray background. Viewed from above, the dorsal lamina are apparent as a white Y-shape on the dorsal surface of each lobe.

**Thalamus** (THAL a mus)
The two-lobed diencephalic structure at the top of the brain stem, one lobe on each side of the third ventricle; several of its nuclei relay sensory information to the appropriate regions of the cerebral cortex.

**Lateral geniculate nuclei** (JEN ik yu luht)
The thalamic nuclei that relay visual information to the cerebral cortex.

**Medial geniculate nuclei**
The thalamic nuclei that relay auditory information to the cerebral cortex.

**Ventral posterior nuclei**
The thalamic nuclei that relay tactual information to the cerebral cortex.

**Internal lamina**
The layers of white matter in each lobe of the thalamus.

---

### Coloring notes

*First, color the shaded silhouette of the thalamus in the top midsagittal illustration. Then, color the internal lamina of both lobes of the thalamus. Finally, color the left medial geniculate, lateral geniculate, and ventral posterior nuclei. Notice the position of the massa intermedia, which connects the two lobes of the thalamus and is thus not visible in an external lateral view.*

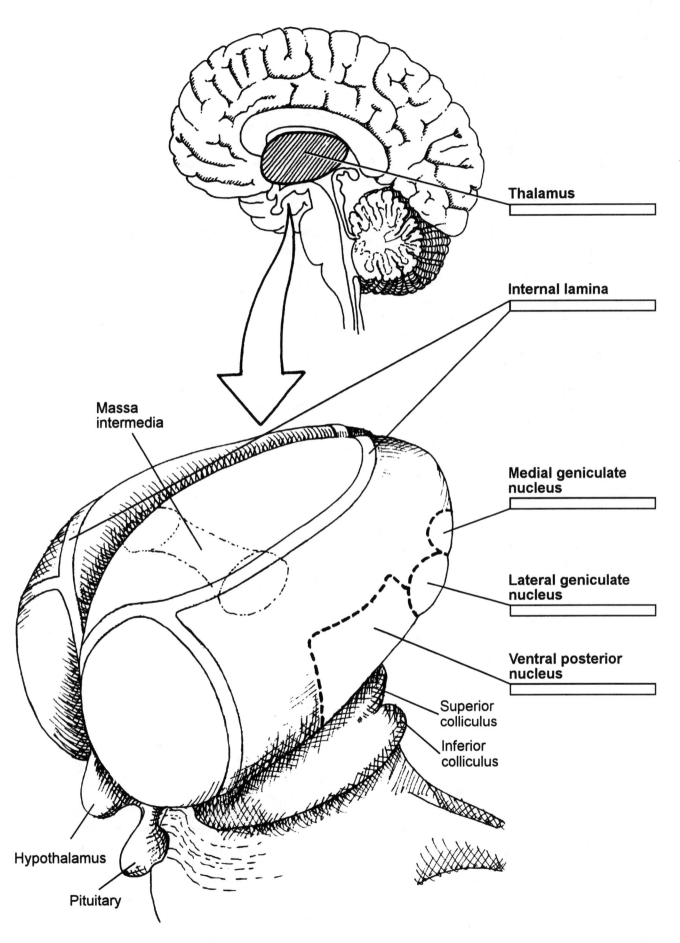

Thalamus

Internal lamina

Massa intermedia

Medial geniculate nucleus

Lateral geniculate nucleus

Ventral posterior nucleus

Superior colliculus

Inferior colliculus

Hypothalamus

Pituitary

## 6.5 Diencephalon: The Hypothalamus

The **hypothalamus** and thalamus together compose the diencephalon. The hypothalamus is located just inferior to the anterior end of the thalamus, and it is about one-tenth the size of the thalamus (*hypo* means *less than*). The *pituitary gland* is suspended from the hypothalamus.

Like the thalamus, the hypothalamus is composed of many pairs of nuclei, one member of each pair on the left and one on the right. The following are three of the pairs of hypothalamic nuclei: The **ventromedial nuclei** are located in the ventral part of the hypothalamus near the midline; they play a role in regulating the conversion of blood glucose to body fat. The **suprachiasmatic nuclei** are located just superior to the *optic chiasm* (the X-shaped decussation of the *optic nerves*); they play a role in timing 24-hour biological rhythms. And the **mammillary bodies** are located on the inferior surface of the hypothalamus, just posterior to the pituitary; they are part of a system that plays an important role in emotion.

Some parts of the hypothalamus are referred to as areas of the hypothalamus, rather than nuclei, because they include many small nuclei. One such area is the **preoptic area**, which is located on the anterior surface of the hypothalamus and plays a role in sexual behavior. The preoptic area on each side is composed of two parts: the *lateral preoptic area* and the *medial preoptic area*.

**Hypothalamus** (HYPE oh THAL a mus)
The diencephalic structure that is located just beneath the anterior end of the thalamus; the pituitary gland is suspended from it.

**Ventromedial nuclei**
The pair of hypothalamic nuclei, one on the left and one the right, that plays a role in regulating the conversion of blood glucose to body fat; they are located near the midline in the ventral part of the hypothalamus.

**Suprachiasmatic nuclei** (SUE pra KYE az ma tik)
The pair of hypothalamic nuclei, one on the left and one on the right, that play a role in the timing of 24-hour biological rhythms; they are located just dorsal to the optic chiasm.

**Mammillary bodies** (MAM i lair ee)
The pair of hypothalamic nuclei, one on the left and one on the right, that are part of a system that plays an important role in emotion; they are visible on the inferior surface of the hypothalamus as a pair of bumps just behind the pituitary.

**Preoptic area**
The most anterior area of the hypothalamus; it plays a role in sexual behavior.

*Coloring notes*
*First, color the hypothalamus in the top, midsagittal illustration; it is the shaded portion. Then, color the preoptic area, the ventromedial nucleus, the mammillary body, and the suprachiasmatic nucleus of the hypothalamus in the bottom illustration. Notice the position of the optic chiasm and pituitary.*

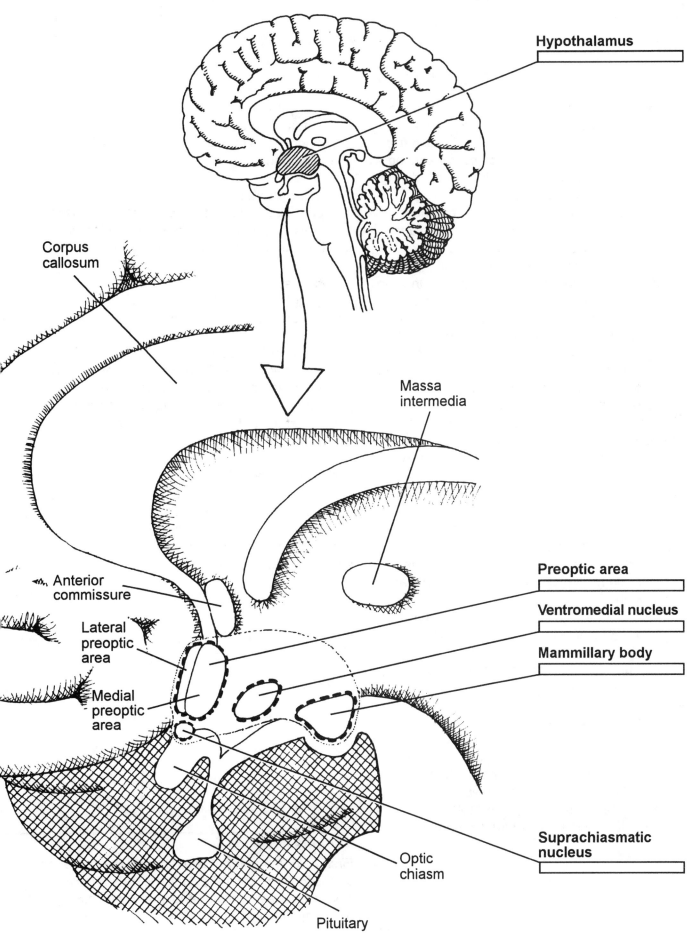

Hypothalamus

Corpus
callosum

Massa
intermedia

Preoptic area

Ventromedial nucleus

Mammillary body

Anterior
commissure

Lateral
preoptic
area

Medial
preoptic
area

Suprachiasmatic
nucleus

Optic
chiasm

Pituitary

## 6.6 The Hypothalamus and Pituitary

The pituitary is in fact two separate glands: the **anterior pituitary** and the **posterior pituitary**. The anterior and posterior pituitary develop from entirely different tissue and they become fused together on the end of the **pituitary stalk** during the course of development.

You learned in Learning Unit 1.6 that the pituitary gland is often called the *master gland* because it releases hormones, called *tropic hormones*, that stimulate the release of hormones from other endocrine glands. Only the anterior pituitary releases tropic hormones, and thus, strictly speaking, it is the anterior pituitary that is the master gland. One function of the hypothalamus is to regulate the release of pituitary hormones; thus, the hypothalamus is, in a sense, the master of the master gland.

The hypothalamus regulates the posterior pituitary via neurons whose axons project to the posterior pituitary from two hypothalamic nuclei: the **paraventricular nuclei** and the **supraoptic nuclei**. These neurons manufacture two pairs of hormones, *oxytocin* and *vasopressin*, which they release from their terminals in the posterior pituitary into the blood stream. Oxytocin stimulates contractions of the uterus during labor and the ejection of milk during suckling; vasopressin facilitates the reabsorption of water by the kidneys.

The hypothalamic regulation of the anterior pituitary is less direct; there are no neural connections between the hypothalamus and anterior pituitary. Neurons of the hypothalamus release chemicals called *releasing hormones* into a local network of fine blood vessels called the *hypothalamopituitary portal system*. The hypothalamopituitary portal system carries these releasing factors down the pituitary stalk to the anterior pituitary, where they trigger the release of particular anterior pituitary tropic hormones. There is a different hypothalamic releasing hormone for each anterior pituitary hormone.

### Anterior pituitary
The anterior portion of the pituitary; it releases tropic hormones in response to hypothalamic releasing hormones.

### Posterior pituitary
The posterior portion of the pituitary; it releases vasopressin and oxytocin from neuron terminals that have their cell bodies in the hypothalamus.

### Pituitary stalk
The stalk from which the anterior and posterior pituitary are suspended from the hypothalamus.

### Paraventricular nuclei
One of the two pairs of hypothalamic nuclei that contain neurons whose axons terminate in the posterior pituitary; this pair is located on the dorsal surface of the hypothalamus on each side of the third ventricle.

### Supraoptic nuclei
One of the two pairs of hypothalamic nuclei that contain neurons whose axons terminate in the posterior pituitary; this pair is located above the optic chiasm, just posterior to the suprachiasmatic nuclei.

### Coloring notes
*First, color the anterior pituitary and the posterior pituitary. Then, color the pituitary stalk. Finally, color the paraventricular and supraoptic nuclei of the hypothalamus.*

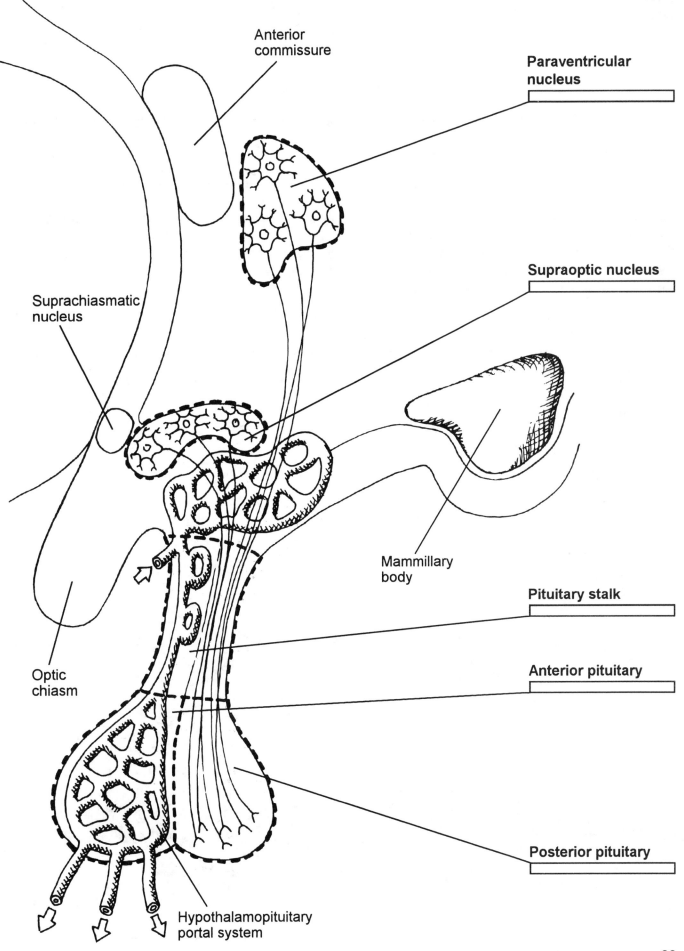

Anterior
commissure

Paraventricular
nucleus

Supraoptic nucleus

Suprachiasmatic
nucleus

Mammillary
body

Pituitary stalk

Anterior pituitary

Optic
chiasm

Posterior pituitary

Hypothalamopituitary
portal system

# Review Exercises: Major Structures of the Brain Stem

Now it is time for you to pause and consolidate the terms and ideas that you have learned in the six learning units of Chapter 6. It is important that you overlearn them so that they do not quickly fade from your memory.

## Review Exercise 6.1

Turn to the illustrations in the six learning units of Chapter 6, and use the cover flap at the back of the book to cover the terms that run down the right-hand edge of each illustration page. Study the six illustrations in chronological sequence until you can identify each labeled structure. Once you have worked through the six illustrations twice in a row without making an error, advance to Review Exercise 6.2.

## Review Exercise 6.2

Fill in the missing terms in the following illustration. The correct answers are provided at the back of the book. Carefully review the material related to your incorrect answers.

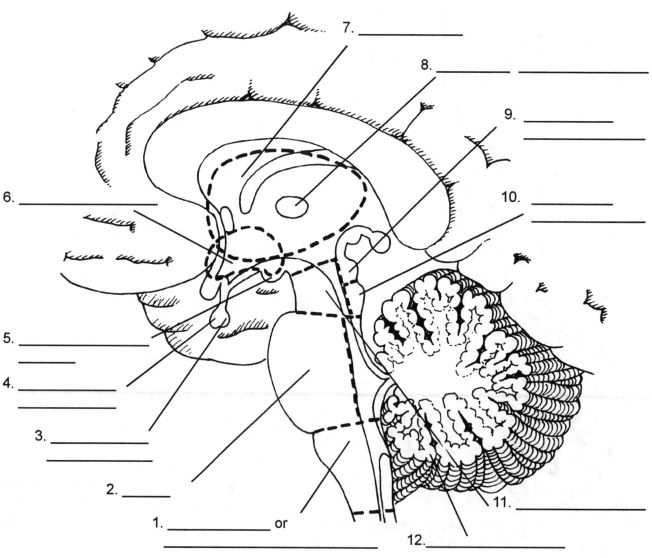

7. _____

8. _____ _____

9. _____ _____
   _____

6. _____

10. _____ _____
    _____ _____

5. _____
   _____

4. _____
   _____

3. _____
   _____

2. _____

1. _____ or
   _____

11. _____

12. _____

## Review Exercise 6.3

Without referring to Chapter 6, fill in each of the following blanks with the correct term from the chapter. The correct answers are provided at the back of the book. Carefully review the material related to your incorrect answers.

1. The myelencephalon is commonly called the _____.

2. Most of the fourth ventricle is located in the _____ of the metencephalon.

3. The tegmentum can be thought of as the most colorful region of the brain because it contains the _____ nucleus, the _____ gray, and the substantia _____.

4. In general, each cerebral hemisphere controls the _____ side of the body.

5. Running up the core of the brain stem from the medulla to the midbrain is the _____; it plays a role in alertness, attention, and sleep.

6. The tectum comprises two pairs of nuclei: the _____ colliculi, which play a role in vision, and the _____ colliculi, which play a role in audition.

7. The metencephalon minus the cerebellum equals the _____.

8. The _____ is located in the _____ ventricle between the two lobes of the thalamus.

9. Cranial nerves 5, 6, 7, and 8 extend from the _____ of the metencephalon.

10. The myelencephalon consists mainly of _____ matter.

11. The cerebellum is connected to the rest of the brain by the three pairs of cerebellar _____, the most inferior of which connects the cerebellum to the _____ of the medulla.

12. The _____ tracts, which are major descending movement pathways, decussate in the posterior part of the medulla.

13. Releasing factors are released by hypothalamic neurons into the hypothalamopituitary portal system, which carries them to the _____ pituitary.

14. The cerebellum is part of the _____.

15. Oxytocin and vasopressin are synthesized and released by neurons that have their cell bodies in the paraventricular and supraoptic nuclei of the _____ and their terminal buttons in the _____ pituitary.

16. The ventral posterior, lateral geniculate, and medial geniculate are sensory relay nuclei that are located in the _____.

17. Damage to the _____ results in ataxia.

18. The ventromedial nuclei, suprachiasmatic nuclei, and mammillary bodies are nuclei of the _____.

19. Strictly speaking, it is not the pituitary that releases tropic hormones; it is the _____ pituitary.

20. The cerebral aqueduct is located in the _____.

21. The mesencephalon minus the tegmentum equals the _____.

## Review Exercise 6.4

Below in alphabetical order is a list of the terms and definitions that you learned in Chapter 6. Cover the definitions with a sheet of paper, and work your way down the list of terms, defining them to yourself as you go. Repeat this process until you have gone through the list twice without an error. Then, cover the terms and work your way down the list of definitions, providing the correct terms as you go. Repeat this second process until you have gone through the list twice without an error.

| | |
|---|---|
| Anterior pituitary | The anterior portion of the pituitary; it releases tropic hormones in response to hypothalamic releasing hormones. |
| Cerebellar peduncles | Three large pairs of tracts (inferior, middle, and superior) that connect the cerebellum to the rest of the brain stem. |
| Cerebellum | The large striped metencephalic structure that is situated just dorsal to the pons; it plays a role in the coordination of movement. |
| Hypothalamus | The diencephalic structure that is located just beneath the anterior thalamus; the pituitary gland is suspended from it. |
| Inferior colliculi | The more posterior of the two pairs of nuclei that constitute the mammalian tectum; they play a role in audition. |
| Internal lamina | The layers of white matter in each lobe of the thalamus. |
| Lateral geniculate nuclei | The thalamic nuclei that relay visual information to the cerebral cortex. |
| Mammillary bodies | The pair of hypothalamic nuclei, one on the left and one on the right, that are part of a system that plays an important role in emotion; they are visible on the inferior surface of the hypothalamus as a pair of bumps just behind the pituitary. |
| Medial geniculate nuclei | The thalamic nuclei that relay auditory information to the cerebral cortex. |
| Medulla | The most posterior region of the brain stem; the myelencephalon; its major structures include the pyramids, olives, medullary reticular formation, and the nuclei that contribute axons to cranial nerves 9, 10, 11, and 12. |
| Olives | The pair of large olive-shaped clusters of nuclei that are visible as bulges on the lateral surfaces of the medulla, one on each side; they are connected to the cerebellum by the inferior peduncles. |
| Paraventricular nuclei | One of the two pairs of hypothalamic nuclei that contain neurons whose axons terminate in the posterior pituitary; this pair is located on the dorsal surface of the hypothalamus on each side of the third ventricle. |

| | |
|---|---|
| Periaqueductal gray | The tegmental gray matter that is located around the cerebral aqueduct; it plays a role in the suppression of pain and in defensive behavior. |
| Pituitary stalk | The stalk from which the anterior and posterior pituitary are suspended from the hypothalamus. |
| Pons | The ventral portion of the metencephalon; its major structures include the fourth ventricle, the metencephalic portion of the reticular formation, many ascending and descending tracts, and the nuclei that contribute axons to cranial nerves 5, 6, 7, and 8. |
| Posterior pituitary | The posterior portion of the pituitary; it releases vasopressin and oxytocin from neuron terminals that have their cell bodies in the hypothalamus. |
| Pyramids | Two large bulges, one left and one right, on the ventral surface of the medulla; they contain the pyramidal tracts, which carry signals for voluntary movement from the cerebral hemispheres to motor circuits of the spinal cord. |
| Red nuclei | A pair of tegmental nuclei, one on the left and one on their right; they have a pinkish appearance and are important structures of the sensorimotor system. |
| Preoptic area | The most anterior area of the hypothalamus, which is composed on each side of the brain of lateral and medial preoptic areas; it plays a role in sexual behavior. |
| Reticular formation | A complex network of nuclei and short interconnecting tracts that is located in the core of the brain stem, from the medulla to the midbrain; its various nuclei play a role in controlling numerous vital body functions and in the promotion of arousal, attention, and sleep. |
| Substantia nigra | A pair of tegmental sensorimotor nuclei, one on the left and one on the right; they are so named because many of their neurons contain a dark pigment. |
| Superior colliculi | The more anterior of the two pairs of nuclei that constitute the mammalian tectum; they play a role in vision. |
| Suprachiasmatic nuclei | The pair of hypothalamic nuclei, one on the left and one on the right, that play a role in the timing of 24-hour biological rhythms; they are located just dorsal to the optic chiasm. |
| Supraoptic nuclei | One of the two pairs of hypothalamic nuclei that contain neurons whose axons terminate in the posterior pituitary; this pair is located above the optic chiasm, just posterior to the suprachiasmatic nuclei. |

| | |
|---|---|
| Thalamus | The two-lobed diencephalic structure at the top of the brain stem, one lobe on each side of the third ventricle; several of its nuclei relay sensory information to the appropriate regions of the cerebral cortex. |
| Ventral posterior nuclei | The thalamic nuclei that relay tactual information to the cerebral cortex. |
| Ventromedial nuclei | The pair of hypothalamic nuclei, one on the left and one on the right, that plays a role in regulating the conversion of blood glucose to body fat; they are located near the midline in the ventral part of the hypothalamus. |

## Chapter 7: Major Structures of the Cerebral Hemispheres

In the preceding chapter, you were introduced to the major structures of the human brain stem. Your introduction began in the most inferior region of the brain stem, the medulla, and ascended to the most superior brain stem structure, the thalamus. This chapter completes your ascent of the human brain by introducing you to the major structures of the human cerebral hemispheres. Your cerebral hemispheres mediate your most complex psychological processes, and they constitute about 80% of your brain's total mass.

This chapter begins by examining some of the major external features of the human cerebral hemispheres. Then, it delves into their internal structure.

The following are the eight learning units of Chapter 7:

7.1   Major Fissures of the Cerebral Hemispheres

7.2   Lobes of the Cerebral Hemispheres

7.3   Major Gyri of the Cerebral Hemispheres

7.4   The Cerebral Cortex

7.5   Divisions of the Cerebral Cortex

7.6   Primary Sensory and Motor Areas

7.7   Subcortical Structures: The Limbic System

7.8   Subcortical Structures: The Basal Ganglia

## 7.1 Major Fissures of the Cerebral Hemispheres

The most obvious external features of the human cerebral hemispheres are its many grooves—the large ones are called **fissures,** and the small ones are called **sulci** (singular: *sulcus*). Not counting the *longitudinal fissure*, which separates the two cerebral hemispheres, the four largest cerebral fissures are the left and right **central fissures** and the left and right **lateral fissures**. The ridges between adjacent fissures are called **gyri** (singular: *gyrus)* or *convolutions.*

Not all vertebrates have deeply *convoluted* cerebral hemispheres. Indeed, most vertebrates, with the exception of large mammals, are relatively smooth-brained. The evolution of convoluted cerebral hemispheres is a product of the massive evolutionary increase in the area of the **cerebral cortex**, the outer layer of the cerebral hemispheres. In humans and other large mammals, the area of the cerebral cortex became so great that it became too large for the rest of the brain, and this caused the surfaces of the cerebral hemispheres to fold in on themselves. Accordingly, much of the human cerebral cortex is invisible to external view, hidden within the depths of the cerebral fissures and sulci.

The cerebral cortex is *gray matter*—it is gray in color because it is largely composed of cell bodies, dendrites, and short unmyelinated axons. Just beneath the cerebral cortex is a large layer of *white matter*, which is composed of large myelinated axons that connect various areas of the cerebral cortex with one another and with other parts of the brain. Any structure or area of the brain that is not cortical is generally referred to as *subcortical*.

**Fissures**
The large, deep grooves in the cerebral hemispheres.

**Sulci** (SUL kye)
The small grooves in the cerebral hemispheres (singular: sulcus).

**Central fissures**
The long, deep fissures on the lateral surfaces of the cerebral hemispheres, one on each side; they run from the longitudinal fissure down to the lateral fissure.

**Lateral fissures**
The long, deep fissures that run roughly horizontally on the lateral surface of the cerebral hemispheres, one on each side.

**Gyri** (GYE rye)
The large ridges, or convolutions, between adjacent fissures (singular: gyrus).

**Cerebral cortex**
The outer layer of the cerebral hemispheres (*cortex* means *bark*); it is largely composed of gray matter.

---

### Coloring notes

*First, color the general structures that are labeled on the upper illustration: fissure, gyrus, and sulcus. Then, color the central and lateral fissures on both illustrations—color both hemispheres of the lower illustration. Finally, color the cerebral cortex in the lower illustration, again coloring both hemispheres.*

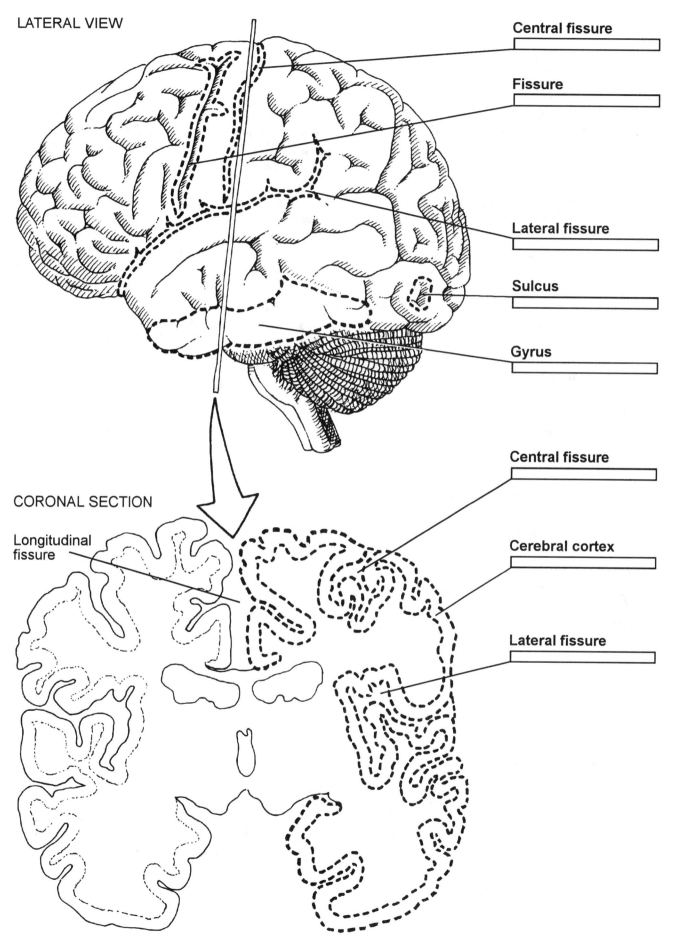

LATERAL VIEW

Central fissure

Fissure

Lateral fissure

Sulcus

Gyrus

CORONAL SECTION

Longitudinal
fissure

Central fissure

Cerebral cortex

Lateral fissure

107

## 7.2 Lobes of the Cerebral Hemispheres

Each human cerebral hemisphere is divided by the *central fissure* and *lateral fissure* into four *lobes:* (1) At the anterior end of each cerebral hemisphere, anterior to the central fissures and anterior and superior to the lateral fissures, are the **frontal lobes**. (2) At the top of each hemisphere, just posterior to the central fissures and superior to the lateral fissures, are the **parietal lobes**. (3) At the bottom of each hemisphere, inferior to the lateral fissures, are the **temporal lobes**. (4) And lastly, at the posterior pole of each hemisphere, posterior to the parietal and temporal lobes, are the **occipital lobes**.

It is important to understand that the lobes of the cerebral hemispheres are not functional units. The cerebral cortex is composed of many areas, each of which performs specific functions and has distinctive structural features; however, the boundaries of these functional units do not follow the boundaries between the lobes—the location of the major fissures is arbitrary with respect to cortical function. Each lobe is composed of many functional units, and many functional units lie across the boundaries of adjacent lobes. Accordingly, although knowing the general location of the four pairs of cerebral lobes is useful in describing the location of specific functional areas within the cerebral hemispheres, each hemisphere does not have a specific function.

**Frontal lobes**
The two regions of the cerebral hemispheres, one in each hemisphere, that are anterior to the central fissures.

**Parietal lobes** (pa RYE e tal)
The two regions of the cerebral hemispheres, one in each hemisphere, that are posterior to the central fissures and superior to the lateral fissures.

**Temporal lobes**
The two regions of the cerebral hemispheres, one in each hemisphere, that are inferior to the lateral fissures.

**Occipital lobes** (ok SIP i tal)
The two regions of the cerebral hemispheres that are at the posterior pole of each hemisphere.

*Coloring notes*

*First, color the temporal, frontal, parietal, and occipital lobes in the upper illustration. Then, using the same colors as you used in the upper view, color the frontal, parietal, and occipital lobes in the lower illustration.*

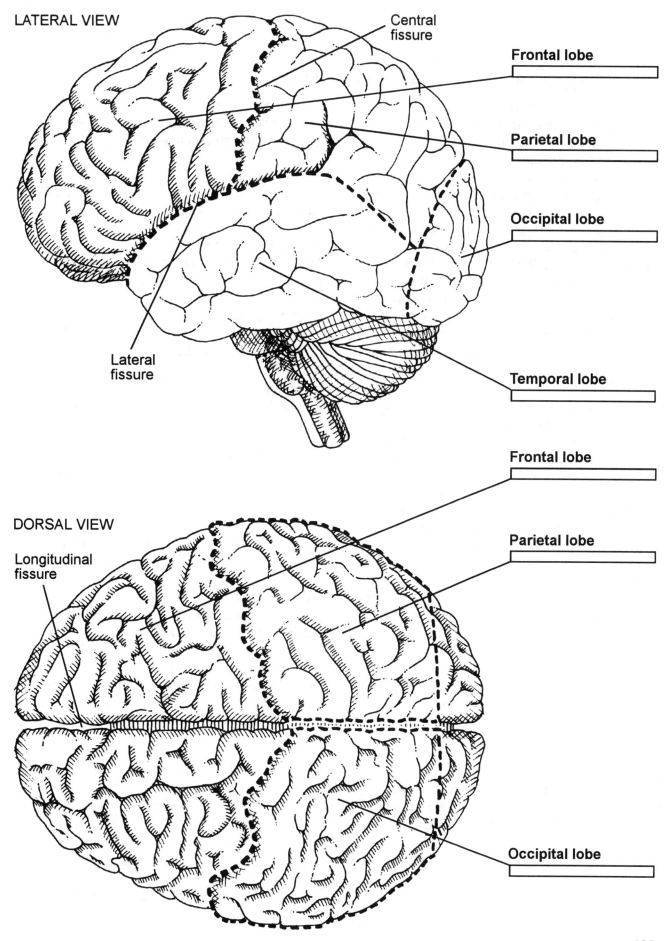

LATERAL VIEW

Central
fissure

**Frontal lobe**

**Parietal lobe**

**Occipital lobe**

Lateral
fissure

**Temporal lobe**

**Frontal lobe**

DORSAL VIEW

Longitudinal
fissure

**Parietal lobe**

**Occipital lobe**

## 7.3 Major Gyri of the Cerebral Hemispheres

Although the pattern of cerebral gyri, or convolutions, varies from person to person and even from one hemisphere to the other in the same person, the largest gyri are readily recognizable in virtually all humans. Not surprisingly, the largest gyri tend to be those adjacent to the largest fissures.

The following are some of the major gyri of the lateral surface of the human cerebral hemispheres. In each frontal lobe is the **precentral gyrus**, the **superior frontal gyrus**, the **middle frontal gyrus**, and the **inferior frontal gyrus**. In each temporal lobe is the **superior temporal gyrus**, the **middle temporal gyrus**, and the **inferior temporal gyrus**. And in each parietal lobe is the **postcentral gyrus** and the **angular gyrus**.

Notice that the names of most of the gyri provide an indication of their locations. For example, the precentral gyrus is just anterior to the central fissure, and the postcentral gyrus is just posterior to the central fissure.

Like the cerebral lobes, the gyri of the cerebral hemispheres should not be thought of as functional units. It is sometimes the convention to refer to a particular gyrus as having a single particular function, but it is never the case that the boundaries of the gyrus precisely define the boundaries of the functional area—the location of fissures is arbitrary with respect to cortical function.

**Precentral gyrus**
The frontal lobe gyrus that is located just anterior to the central fissure.

**Superior frontal gyrus**
The frontal lobe gyrus that runs horizontally along the top of the lobe.

**Middle frontal gyrus**
The frontal lobe gyrus that is located between the superior and inferior frontal gyri.

**Inferior frontal gyrus**
The frontal lobe gyrus that is located just inferior to the middle frontal gyrus.

**Superior temporal gyrus**
The temporal lobe gyrus that is located just inferior to the lateral fissure.

**Middle temporal gyrus**
The temporal lobe gyrus that is located between the superior and inferior temporal gyri.

**Inferior temporal gyrus**
The temporal lobe gyrus that is located just inferior to the middle temporal gyrus.

**Postcentral gyrus**
The parietal lobe gyrus that is located just posterior to the central fissure.

**Angular gyrus**
The parietal lobe gyrus that is located at the parietal lobe's border with the temporal and occipital lobes.

*Coloring notes*

*Color each of the nine labeled gyri of the brain's lateral surface of the right cerebral hemisphere.*

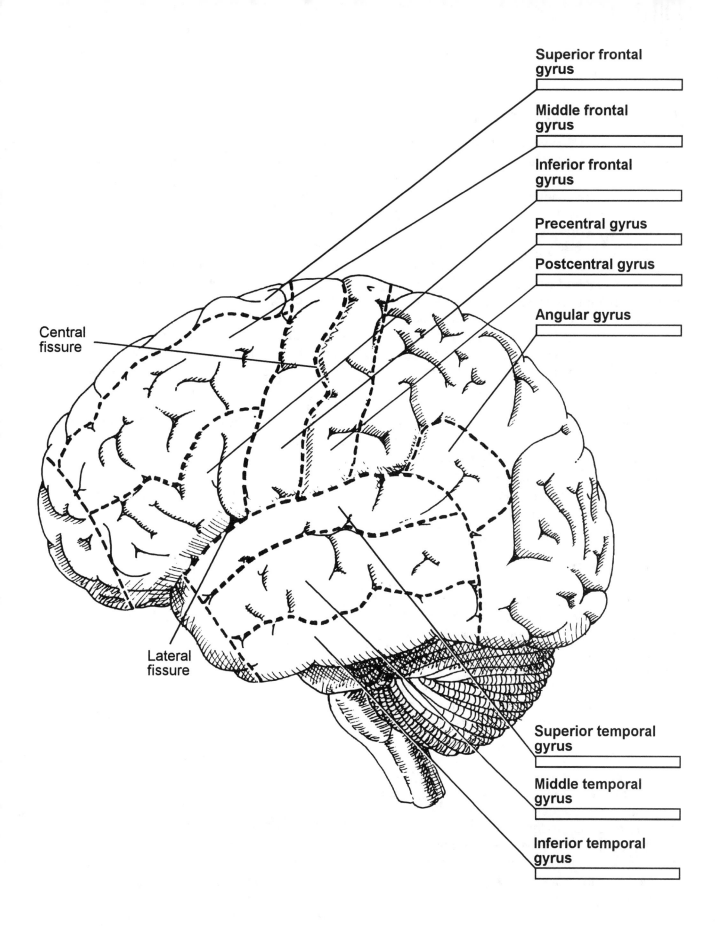

Superior frontal
gyrus

Middle frontal
gyrus

Inferior frontal
gyrus

Precentral gyrus

Postcentral gyrus

Angular gyrus

Central
fissure

Lateral
fissure

Superior temporal
gyrus

Middle temporal
gyrus

Inferior temporal
gyrus

## 7.4 The Cerebral Cortex

During the course of vertebrate evolution, the cerebral cortex underwent massive development. The cerebral cortex mediates the most complex psychological processes, processes that have achieved their highest level of complexity in the human species.

The first cerebral cortex to evolve was simple cortex composed of three layers, a layer of cell bodies sandwiched between two layers composed of cell processes—this is called **allocortex**. All the cerebral cortex of early vertebrates (e.g., fish, reptiles, and amphibians) is allocortex. In contrast, primates have little allocortex—the hippocampus and adjacent cortex comprises most of it. Most of the cortex of primates is of the more recently evolved six-layered variety, which is called **neocortex** (*neo* means *new*). The predominance of six-layered cortex in primates is why three-layered cortex is called *allocortex*—*allo* means *other*.

The layers of neocortex are numbered from 1 to 6; layer 1 is the most superficial layer, and layer 6 is the deepest layer. The layers can be differentiated from each other in stained sections because they differ in terms of the types of neurons that they contain, and whether they are composed primarily of neural processes or cell bodies. The structure of the neocortex differs somewhat from functional area to functional area, but its characteristic six layers are always present.

There are many different kinds of neurons in the cerebral cortex, but most fall into one of two distinct categories: **pyramidal cells** and **stellate cells** (*granule cells*). Pyramidal cells are neurons with large pyramid-shaped cell bodies, a large central dendrite that projects toward the surface of the cortex (an *apical dendrite*), and a long axon. Stellate cells are star-shaped cells (*stellate* means *star-shaped*) with many dendrites and a short axon. Pyramidal cells conduct signals to other parts of the cerebral cortex or to other CNS structures, whereas stellate cells participate in local cortical circuits.

**Allocortex** (AL oh KOR tex)
Three-layered cerebral cortex, which was the first type of cerebral cortex to evolve; humans have mostly neocortex (*allocortex* means *other cortex*).

**Neocortex**
Six-layered cerebral cortex of relatively recent evolutionary origin; most human cerebral cortex is neocortex.

**Pyramidal cells** (puh RAM i dal)
Cortical neurons with a pyramid-shaped cell body, an apical dendrite, and a long axon.

**Stellate cells**
Star-shaped cortical neurons with many short dendrites and a short axon.

---

*Coloring notes*

*First, color the allocortex and the neocortex in the top illustration, on both sides of the brain. Then, using the same two colors, color the borders around the bottom two illustrations. Finally, using different colors, color the one pyramidal cell and one stellate cell that are not shaded—be sure to color all their processes.*

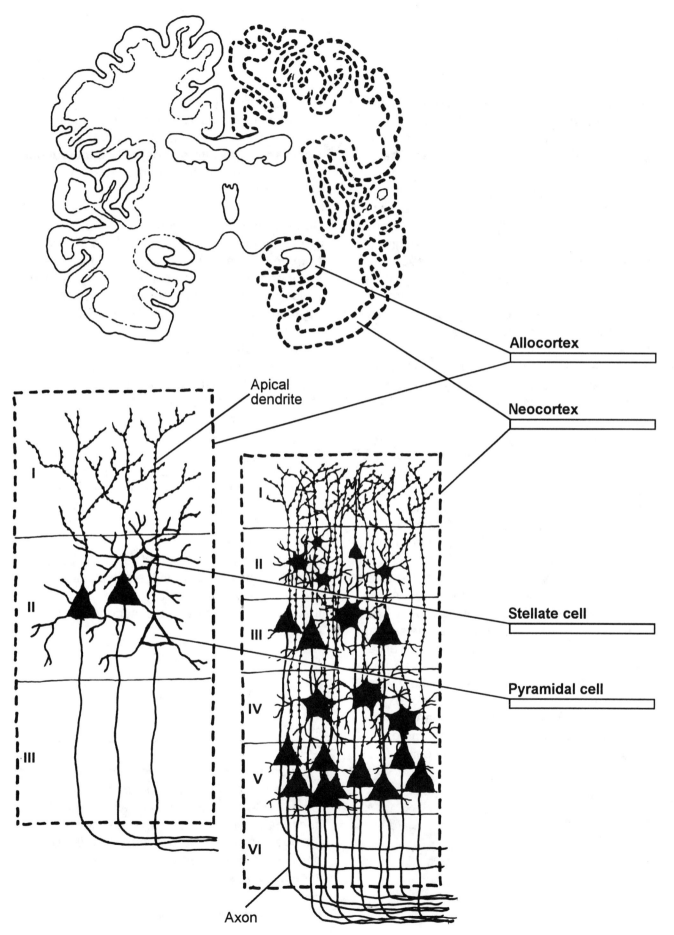

Apical
dendrite

Allocortex

Neocortex

Stellate cell

Pyramidal cell

I

II

III

I

II

III

IV

V

VI

Axon

113

# 7.5 Divisions of the Cerebral Cortex

Cerebral cortex is often divided into five kinds of areas: two kinds of sensory areas, two kinds of motor areas, and association areas. **Primary sensory areas** are those cortical areas that receive most of their input from the subcortical structures of a single sensory system, usually from the thalamic sensory relay nucleus for that system. **Secondary sensory areas** are areas of cortex that receive their input from a single primary cortical area and from other secondary areas of the same system—there are typically several areas of secondary sensory cortex adjacent to each area of primary sensory cortex.

**Primary motor areas** are the two cortical areas, left and right, from which most motor signals descend to motor circuits of the brain stem and spinal cord, and **secondary motor areas** are cortical areas that project directly to primary motor areas.

**Association areas** of cerebral cortex perform the most complex functions, and it is usually the case that we do not understand exactly what they do. By definition, they are areas that receive input from more than one sensory system, primarily from areas of secondary sensory cortex, and they often activate areas of secondary motor cortex.

Accordingly, input from each sensory system enters the cortex via the primary sensory area for that system, and it is conducted to the secondary sensory areas for the same system. Then, input from the secondary sensory areas of different sensory systems comes together in areas of association cortex. Association cortex activates areas of secondary motor cortex, which in turn activate areas of primary motor cortex. Finally, the output of primary motor cortex is conducted to the motor circuits of the brain stem and spinal cord.

## Primary sensory areas

Areas of cerebral cortex that receive most of their input from the thalamic relay nuclei of a single sensory system; most of their output goes to adjacent secondary sensory areas of the same system.

## Secondary sensory areas

Areas of sensory cortex that receive their input from one primary sensory area and from other secondary areas of the same system; there are typically several secondary sensory areas adjacent to each primary sensory area.

## Primary motor areas

Areas of motor cortex that send most of their output to subcortical and spinal motor circuits; much of their input comes from adjacent secondary motor areas.

## Secondary motor areas

Areas of motor cortex that send much of their output to areas of primary motor cortex; much of their input comes from association cortex.

## Association areas

Areas of cerebral cortex that receive input from more than one sensory system, typically via areas of secondary sensory cortex, much of their output goes to areas of secondary motor cortex.

---

### Coloring notes

*In coloring, work through the network of sensory, association, and motor cortex in sequence. Color the two primary sensory areas, the four secondary sensory areas, the association area, the two secondary motor areas, and finally the primary motor area. Note: This diagram is schematic; it is intended to show the general relations among the types of cortical areas, not their relative size or location.*

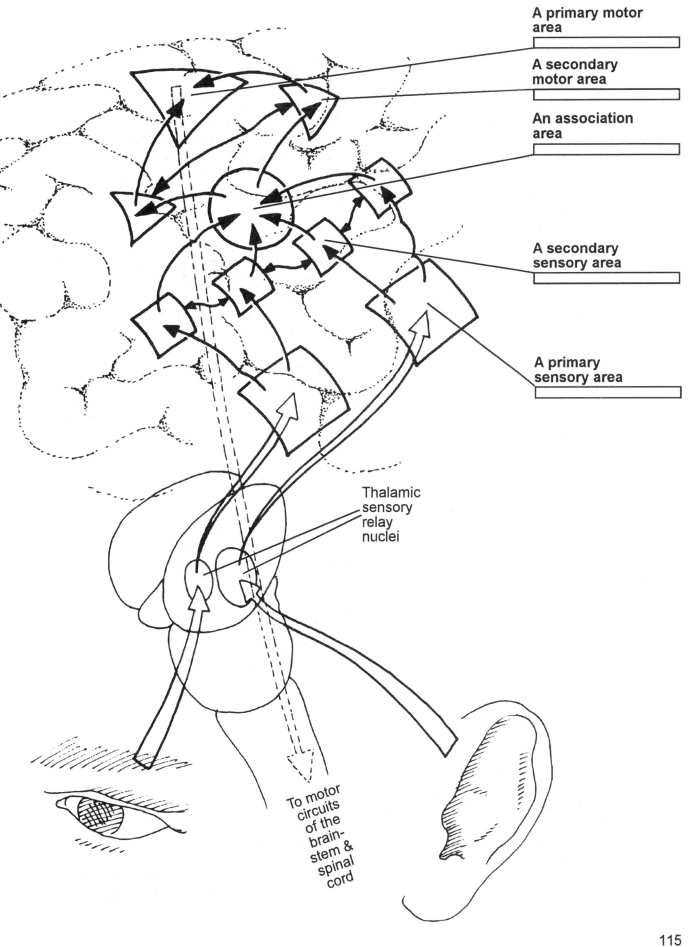

A primary motor area

A secondary motor area

An association area

A secondary sensory area

A primary sensory area

Thalamic sensory relay nuclei

To motor circuits of the brain-stem & spinal cord

## 7.6 Primary Sensory and Motor Areas

The primary sensory and motor areas are the best understood functional areas of the human cerebral neocortex. This learning unit describes the location of these areas. Each primary sensory or motor area comes in pairs, one area in each hemisphere at bilaterally symmetrical locations.

The areas of **primary visual cortex** are at the very back of the cerebral hemisphere; they take up much of the occipital lobes. Most primary visual cortex cannot be readily visualized because it is located in the depths of the longitudinal fissure. Similarly, the areas of **primary auditory cortex** and **primary gustatory cortex** (*gustatory* means *pertaining to taste*) are largely out of sight in the lateral fissures. Primary auditory cortex is in the temporal lobe side of the lateral fissures, and primary gustatory cortex is in the parietal lobe side.

The areas of **primary motor cortex** and **primary somatosensory cortex** lie on opposite sides of the central fissures, the primary motor cortex in the *precentral gyrus* of the frontal lobes, and the primary somatosensory cortex is in the *postcentral gyrus* of the parietal lobes. Finally, the neocortical areas of **primary olfactory cortex** are located on the inferior surface of the frontal lobes, near the two *olfactory nerves* (i.e., near the 1st cranial nerves). The olfactory system is unique; it is the only sensory system in which signals are conducted to an area of cortex (i.e., an area of allocortex in the medial temporal lobe) before being conducted to the thalamus and then to an area of neocortex.

### Primary visual cortex
The areas of cortex, one in each hemisphere, that receive most of their input from the visual relay nuclei of the thalamus (i.e., from the lateral geniculate nuclei); they are located in the occipital lobes, largely in the longitudinal fissure.

### Primary auditory cortex
The areas of cortex, one in each hemisphere, that receive most of their input from the auditory relay nuclei of the thalamus (i.e., from the medial geniculate nuclei); they are located in the superior temporal lobes, largely in the lateral fissures.

### Primary gustatory cortex (GUS ta tor ee)
The areas of cortex, one in each hemisphere, that receive most of their input from the gustatory relay nuclei of the thalamus; they are located on the inferior border of the parietal lobes, largely in the lateral fissures.

### Primary motor cortex
The areas of cortex, one in each hemisphere, that send most of their motor fibers to the motor circuits of the brain stem and spinal cord; they are located in the precentral gyri of the frontal lobes.

### Primary somatosensory cortex
The areas of cortex, one in each hemisphere, that receive most of their input from the somatosensory relay nuclei of the thalamus (e.g., from the ventral posterior nuclei); they are located in the postcentral gyri of the parietal lobes.

### Primary olfactory cortex (ole FAK tor ee)
The areas of cortex, one in each hemisphere, that receive most of their input from the olfactory relay nuclei of the thalamus; they are located on the inferior surface of the frontal lobes.

*Coloring notes*

*First, color the primary motor cortex. Then, color the five areas of primary sensory cortex. Note that much of the primary sensory cortex is not visible because it is located deep within fissures.*

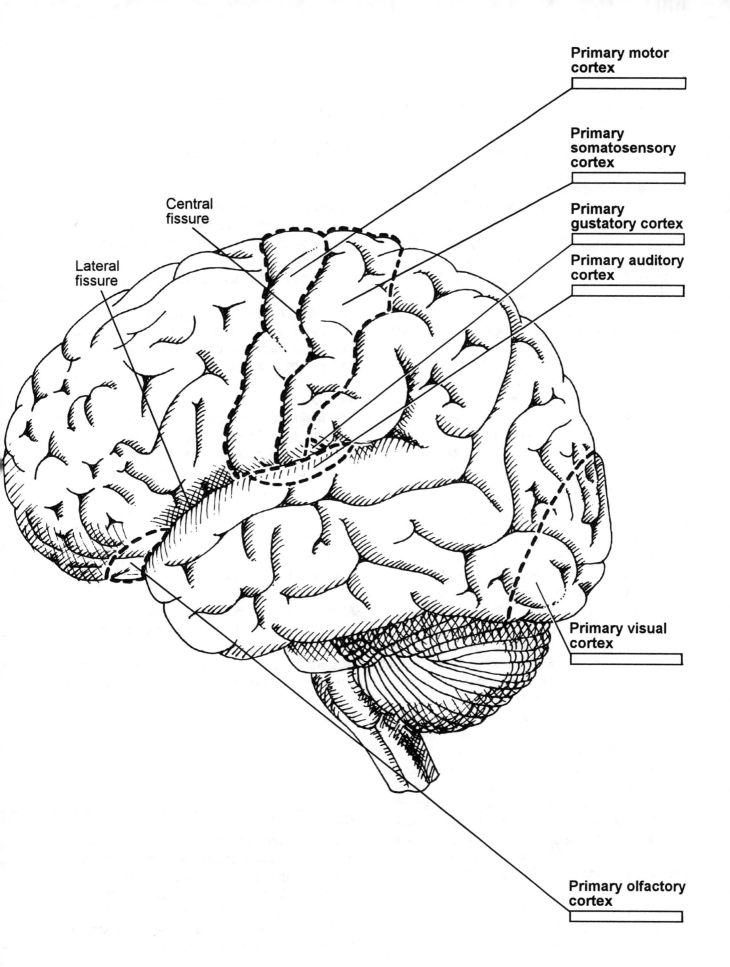

Primary motor
cortex

Primary
somatosensory
cortex

Primary
gustatory cortex

Primary auditory
cortex

Central
fissure

Lateral
fissure

Primary visual
cortex

Primary olfactory
cortex

## 7.7  Subcortical Structures: The Limbic System

The subcortical regions of the cerebral hemispheres are largely composed of white matter, but they also contain many nuclei. Several nuclei are part of a circuit called the **limbic system**. The limbic system is a circuit of midline structures that circles the thalamus (*limbus* means *ring*). The limbic system plays an important role in emotional behavior.

The following are major structures of the limbic system: the **amygdala**, the **hippocampus**, the **cingulate cortex**, the **fornix**, the **septum**, and the **mammillary bodies**. Let's begin tracing the limbic circuit at the amygdala, the almond-shaped nucleus in the anterior temporal lobe (*amygdala* means *almond*). Just posterior to the amygdala is the hippocampus, an area of *allocortex* that lies beneath the thalamus in the limbic ring, along the medial edge of the temporal cortex (*hippocampus* means *seahorse*; *cross sections* of the hippocampus look like a seahorse). Next in the ring are the cingulate cortex and fornix. The cingulate cortex is the large area of cortex in the cingulate gyrus on the medial surface of the cerebral hemispheres, just superior to the *corpus callosum*; it encircles the dorsal thalamus (*cingulate* means *encircling*). The fornix also encircles the dorsal thalamus; the major fiber tract of the limbic system, it leaves the dorsal end of the hippocampus and wraps around the thalamus, coursing along the superior surface of the third ventricle. It terminates in the septum and the mammillary bodies of the posterior hypothalamus (*fornix* means *arc*). The septum is a midline nucleus that is located at the anterior tip of the cingulate cortex. Several small tracts connect the septum and mammillary bodies with the amygdala thus completing the limbic ring.

The *olfactory nerves* (1st cranial nerves) are intimately connected to limbic system structures, and in vertebrate species of early evolutionary origin, the function of limbic structures is primarily olfactory rather than emotional.

**Amygdala** (a MIG duh luh)
The almond-shaped nucleus of the anterior temporal lobe.

**Hippocampus** (HIP oh CAMP us)
The allocortical limbic system structure of the medial temporal lobes; it extends from the amygdala at its anterior end to the cingulate cortex and fornix at its posterior end.

**Cingulate cortex** (SING gyu lut)
The large area of limbic cortex on the medial surface of each cerebral hemisphere, just dorsal to the corpus callosum.

**Fornix**
The major tract of the limbic system; it projects from the dorsal hippocampus of each hemisphere, circles the thalamus, and terminates in the septum and the mammillary bodies.

**Septum**
The limbic nucleus that is located on the midline at the anterior tip of the cingulate cortex; a major terminal of the fornix.

**Mammillary bodies** (MAM i lair ee)
A pair of hypothalamic nuclei that are visible as bumps on the inferior surface of the brain, just posterior to the pituitary; they are part of the limbic system and major terminals of the fornix.

---

### Coloring notes

*Color the major structures of the left limbic ring in a counter clockwise sequence beginning at the amygdala: In sequence color the left amygdala, hippocampus, cingulate cortex, fornix, septum, and mammillary body. Then, using the same colors, color the same structures on the right, where they are visible.*

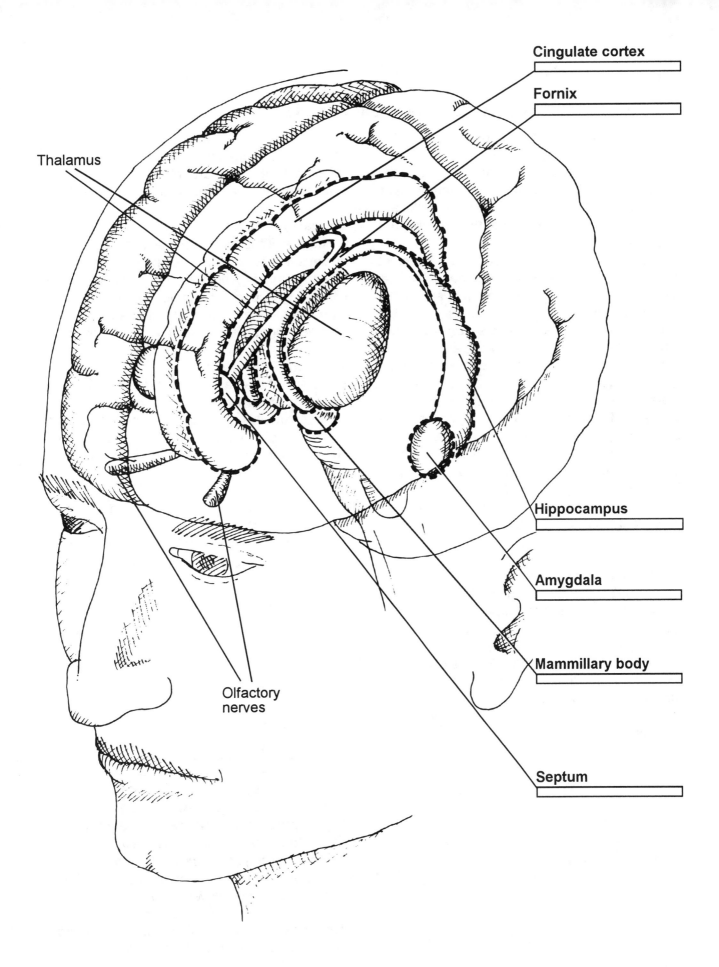

**Cingulate cortex**

**Fornix**

Thalamus

**Hippocampus**

**Amygdala**

Olfactory
nerves

**Mammillary body**

**Septum**

119

## 7.8 Subcortical Structures: The Basal Ganglia

The *basal ganglia* are two groups of cerebral nuclei, one in each hemisphere, which play a role in the control of movement. They include the **amygdala**, the **caudate**, the **putamen**, and the **globus pallidus**. In general, they are located just lateral and slightly anterior to the thalamus. The basal ganglia .

The amygdala is considered to be a structure of both the limbic system and the basal ganglia motor system. Sweeping out of each amygdala in the anterior temporal lobe is the caudate nucleus, which almost completely encircles the other nuclei of the basal ganglia (*caudate* means *tail-like*). The larger anterior end of the caudate nucleus, which is located anterior to the thalamus, is connected via a series of fiber bridges to the largest of the basal ganglia, the putamen, which is located lateral to the thalamus. However, between the putamen and the thalamus lies the globus pallidus (literally, the *pale globe*). Together, the caudate and putamen are known as the *striatum* because they have a striped appearance (*striatum* means *striped structure*).

The importance of the basal ganglia in the control of movement is apparent in people with *Parkinson's disease*. Parkinson's disease is characterized by the deterioration of *dopaminergic* (dopamine-releasing) neurons that project from the *substantia nigra* of the midbrain to the striatum. Parkinson's disease is characterized by muscular rigidity, slowness of movement, a shuffling wide-based gait, and tremor that is particularly pronounced during periods of inactivity.

**Amygdala**
The almond-shaped nucleus of the anterior temporal lobes; it is part of both the limbic system and the basal ganglia.

**Caudate** (KAW date)
A nucleus of the basal ganglia; it is a tail-like nucleus that extends in each hemisphere from the amygdala in a posterior direction and almost completely encircles the other basal gangliamus (*caudate* means *tail-like*); the caudate and putamen together are known as the striatum.

**Putamen** (PEW tay men)
A nucleus of the basal ganglia; it is located in each hemisphere just lateral to the globus pallidus, and it is connected to the anterior end of the caudate by a series of fiber bridges; the putamen and caudate together are known as the striatum.

**Globus pallidus** (GLOE bus   PAL i dus)
A nucleus of the basal ganglia; it is located in each hemisphere between the thalamus and the putamen (*globus pallidus* means *pale globe*).

---

***Coloring notes***

*First, color the small portion of the right globus pallidus that is visible behind the thalamus; the left globus pallidus is totally hidden by the putamen (do not color). Then, color the left caudate; it begins at the amygdala and almost completely circles the putamen, to which it is joined by fiber bridges. Then, color the left putamen and left amygdala. Finally—with the exception of the right globus pallidus, which you have already colored—color the basal ganglia of the right hemisphere.*

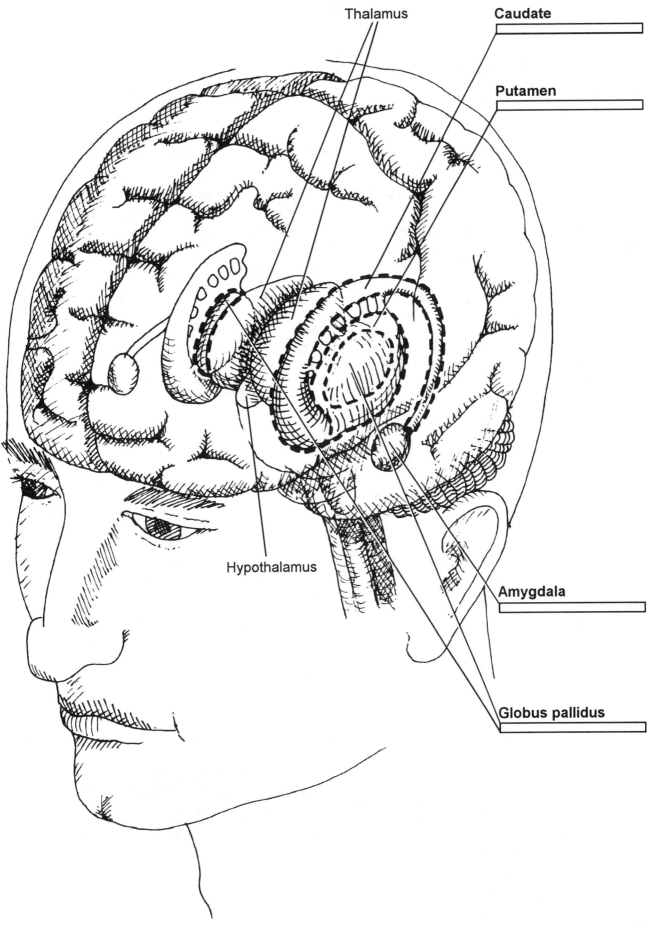

Thalamus

**Caudate**

**Putamen**

Hypothalamus

**Amygdala**

**Globus pallidus**

# Review Exercises: Major Structures of the Cerebral Hemispheres

Now it is time for you to pause and consolidate the terms and ideas that you have learned in the eight learning units of Chapter 7. It is important that you overlearn them so that they do not quickly fade from your memory.

## Review Exercise 7.1

Turn to the illustrations in the eight learning units of Chapter 7, and use the cover flap at the back of the book to cover the terms that run down the right-hand edge of each illustration page. Study the eight illustrations in sequence until you can iden- tify each of the labeled neuroanatomical structures. Once you have worked through the illustrations twice without making an error, advance to Review Exercise 7.2.

## Review Exercise 7.2

Fill in the missing terms in the following drawing of a midsagittal section of the human brain. The answers are provided at the back of the book. Carefully re- view the material related to your incorrect answers.

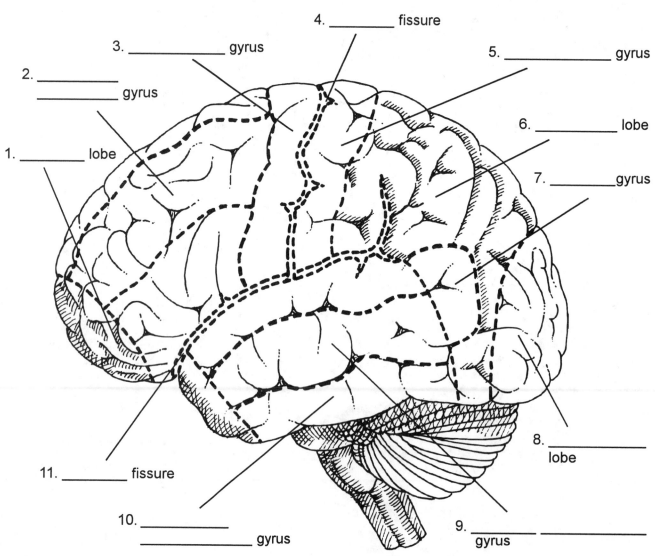

4. _____ fissure

3. _____ gyrus

2. _____ _____ gyrus

5. _____ gyrus

1. _____ lobe

6. _____ lobe

7. _____ gyrus

11. _____ fissure

10. _____ _____ gyrus

8. _____ lobe

9. _____ _____ gyrus

## Review Exercise 7.3

Without referring to Chapter 7, fill in each of the following blanks with the correct term from the chapter. The correct answers are provided at the back of the book. Carefully review the material related to your incorrect answers.

1. The left and right cerebral hemispheres are separated by the _____ fissure.

2. The _____ is an allocortical structure of the medial temporal lobes.

3. Just superior to the corpus callosum is the _____ cortex, which is a structure of the limbic system.

4. At the posterior pole of each hemisphere is the _____ lobe.

5. Most human cerebral cortex is neocortex; only about 10% is _____.

6. The caudate, putamen, globus pallidus, and amygdala are collectively referred to as the

    _____.

7. Association areas receive much of their input from _____ sensory areas.

8. The primary motor area receives substantial input from the _____ motor areas.

9. Caudate plus putamen equals

    _____.

10. The primary visual area is in the _____ lobe.

11. Parkinson's disease is characterized by a deterioration of dopaminergic neurons that project from the substantia nigra to the

    _____.

12. The _____ and _____ gyri are on opposite sides of the central fissure; their functions are motor and sensory, respectively.

13. Each area of secondary sensory cortex receives input from only one _____ sensory area.

14. The primary gustatory cortex is in the parietal lobe, largely out of site in the _____ fissure.

15. The hippocampus, cingulate cortex, septum, and fornix are all structures of the _____ system.

16. The central fissure separates the parietal lobe from the _____ lobe.

17. The lateral fissure separates the parietal lobe from the _____ lobe.

18. The fornix connects the _____ to the septum and mammillary bodies.

19. The _____ lies between the thalamus and putamen.

20. The primary motor cortex and primary somatosensory cortex are on opposite sides of the _____ fissure.

21. Neocortex is to allocortex as 6 is to ____.

22. Located between the lateral fissure and the middle temporal gyrus is the _____ temporal gyrus.

## Review Exercise 7.4

Below in alphabetical order is a list of all the terms and definitions that you learned in Chapter 7. Cover the definitions with a sheet of paper, and work your way down the list of terms, defining them to yourself as you go. Repeat this process until you have gone through the list twice without an error. Then, cover the terms and work your way down the list of definitions, providing the correct terms as you go. Repeat this second process until you have gone through the list twice without an error.

| | |
|---|---|
| Allocortex | Three-layered cerebral cortex, which was the first type of cerebral cortex to evolve; humans have mostly neocortex (*allocortex* means *other cortex*). |
| Amygdala | The almond-shaped nucleus of the anterior temporal lobe; it is part of both the limbic system and the basal ganglia. |
| Angular gyrus | The parietal lobe gyrus that is located at the parietal lobe's border with the temporal and occipital lobes. |
| Association areas | Areas of cerebral cortex that receive input from more than one sensory system, typically via areas of secondary sensory cortex; much of their output goes to areas of secondary motor cortex. |
| Caudate | A nucleus of the basal ganglia; it is a tail-like nucleus that extends from the amygdala in each hemisphere and almost completely encircles the other basal ganglia (*caudate* means tail-like); the caudate and putamen together are the striatum. |
| Central fissures | The long, deep fissures on the lateral surfaces of the cerebral hemispheres, one on each side; they run from the longitudinal fissure down to the lateral fissure. |
| Cerebral cortex | The outer layer of the cerebral hemispheres; it is largely composed of gray matter (*cortex* means *bark*). |
| Cingulate cortex | The large area of limbic cortex on the medial surface of each cerebral hemisphere, just dorsal to the corpus callosum. |
| Fissures | The large, deep grooves in the cerebral hemispheres. |
| Fornix | The major tract of the limbic system; it projects from the dorsal hippocampus of each hemisphere, circles the thalamus, and terminates in the septum and mammillary bodies. |
| Frontal lobes | The two regions of the cerebral hemispheres, one in each hemisphere, that are anterior to the central fissures. |
| Globus pallidus | A nucleus of the basal ganglia; it is located in each hemisphere between the thalamus and the putamen (*globus pallidus* means *pale globe*). |
| Gyri | The large ridges, or convolutions, between adjacent fissures (singular: gyrus). |

| | | | |
|---|---|---|---|
| Hippocampus | The allocortical limbic system structure of the medial temporal lobes; it extends from the amygdala at its anterior end to the cingulate cortex and fornix at its posterior end. | Parietal lobes | The two regions of the cerebral hemispheres, one in each hemisphere, that are posterior to the central fissures and superior to the lateral fissures. |
| Inferior frontal gyrus | The frontal lobe gyrus that is located just inferior to the middle frontal gyrus. | Postcentral gyrus | The parietal lobe gyrus that is located just posterior to the central fissure. |
| Inferior temporal gyrus | The temporal lobe gyrus that is located just inferior to the middle temporal gyrus. | Precentral gyrus | The frontal lobe gyrus that is located just anterior to the central fissure. |
| Lateral fissures | The long, deep fissures that run roughly horizontally on the lateral surface of the cerebral hemispheres, one on each side. | Primary auditory cortex | The areas of cortex, one in each hemisphere, that receive most of their input from the auditory relay nuclei of the thalamus (i.e., from the medial geniculate nuclei); they are located in the superior temporal lobes, largely in the lateral fissures. |
| Mammillary bodies | A pair of hypothalamic nuclei that are visible as bumps on the inferior surface of the brain, just posterior to the pituitary; they are part of the limbic system and major terminals of the fornix. | Primary gustatory cortex | The areas of cortex, one in each hemisphere, that receive taste input from the gustatory relay nuclei of the thalamus; they are located on the inferior border of the parietal lobes, largely in the lateral fissures. |
| Middle frontal gyrus | The frontal lobe gyrus that is located between the superior and inferior frontal gyri. | Primary motor areas | Areas of motor cortex that send most of their output to subcortical and spinal motor circuits; much of their input comes from adjacent secondary motor areas. |
| Middle temporal gyrus | The temporal lobe gyrus that is located between the superior and inferior temporal gyri. | | |
| Neocortex | Six-layered cerebral cortex of relatively recent evolutionary origin; most human cerebral cortex is neocortex. | Primary motor cortex | The areas of cortex, one in each hemisphere, that send most of their motor fibers to the motor circuits of the brain stem and spinal cord; they are located in the precentral gyri of the frontal lobes. |
| Occipital lobes | The two regions of the cerebral hemispheres that are located at the posterior pole of each hemisphere. | | |

| | | | |
|---|---|---|---|
| **Primary olfactory cortex** | The areas of cortex, one in each hemisphere, that receive most of their input from the olfactory relay nuclei of the thalamus; they are located on the inferior surface of the frontal lobes. | **Pyramidal cells** | Cortical neurons with a pyramid-shaped cell body, an apical dendrite, and a long axon. |
| **Primary sensory areas** | Areas of cerebral cortex that receive most of their input from the thalamic relay nuclei of a single sensory system; most of their output goes to adjacent secondary sensory areas of the same system. | **Secondary motor areas** | Areas of motor cortex that send much of their output to areas of primary motor cortex; much of their input comes from association cortex. |
| **Primary somatosensory cortex** | The areas of cortex, one in each hemisphere, that receive most of their input from the somatosensory relay nuclei of the thalamus (e.g., ventral posterior nuclei); they are located in the postcentral gyri of the parietal lobes. | **Secondary sensory areas** | Areas of sensory cortex that receive their input from one primary sensory area and from other secondary areas of the same system; there are typically several secondary sensory areas adjacent to each primary sensory area. |
| | | **Septum** | The limbic nucleus that is located on the midline near the anterior tip of the cingulate cortex; a major terminal of the fornix. |
| **Primary visual cortex** | The areas of cortex, one in each hemisphere, that receive most of their input from the visual relay nuclei of the thalamus (i.e., lateral geniculate nuclei); they are located in the occipital lobes, largely in the longitudinal fissure. | **Stellate cells** | Star-shaped cortical neurons with many short dendrites and a short axon. |
| | | **Sulci** | The small grooves in the cerebral hemispheres (singular: sulcus). |
| | | **Superior temporal gyrus** | The temporal lobe gyrus that is located just inferior to the lateral fissure. |
| **Putamen** | A nucleus of the basal ganglia; it is located in each hemisphere just lateral to the globus pallidus, and it is connected to the anterior end of the caudate by a series of fiber bridges; the putamen and caudate together are the striatum. | **Superior frontal gyrus** | The frontal lobe gyrus that runs horizontally along the top of the lobe. |
| | | **Temporal lobes** | The two regions of the cerebral hemispheres, one in each hemisphere, that are inferior to the lateral fissures. |

# Part 2: *Functional Neuroanatomy*

You are about to begin Part 2 of this book, *Functional Neuroanatomy*. In Part 2, you will be introduced to more of the brain's structures, but for the most part, you will revisit structures that you have already learned about in Part 1. However, in contrast to Part 1, which is organized primarily on the basis of where in the nervous system a particular structure is located, Part 2 is organized on the basis of function. Each learning unit of Part 2, rather than surveying the neural structures that are located in a particular region of the nervous system, surveys the neural structures associated with a particular psychological function. Accordingly, Part 2 reinforces what you have learned in Part 1 by providing you with a different perspective of the brain.

The following are the five chapters of Part 2—each is composed of several learning units:

8. **Sensory Systems of the Central Nervous System**
9. **Sensorimotor Pathways of the Central Nervous System**
10. **Brain Structures and Memory**
11. **Motivational Systems of the Brain**
12. **Cortical Localization of Language and Thinking**

## Chapter 8: Sensory Systems of the Central Nervous System

In order for you to function effectively, your brain requires two kinds of information: information about conditions inside your body and information about conditions in your external environment. The neural systems that are specialized for conducting and analyzing these two kinds of information are referred to as sensory systems. All sensory information is detected by specialized cells called *sensory receptors*, and then it is conducted to your central nervous system for analysis. In general, only those sensory signals that reach the level of your cerebral cortex enter your conscious awareness.

The learning units of this chapter focus on the sensory pathways of three systems: the visual system, the auditory system, and the somatosensory system. In each case, you will first follow the routes of sensory signals as they are conducted from sensory receptors to primary sensory cortex, and then you will follow their routes from primary sensory cortex to secondary and association areas.

The following are the seven learning units of Chapter 8:

8.1   Visual System: From Eye to Cortex

8.2   Cortical Visual Areas

8.3   Auditory System: From Ear to Cortex

8.4   Cortical Auditory Areas

8.5   Somatosensory System: From Receptors to Cortex

8.6   Cortical Somatosensory Areas

8.7   The Descending Analgesia Circuit

## 8.1 Visual System: From Eye to Cortex

Light enters the eye through the pupil and strikes the **retina**, the five-layered neural structure that lines the back of the eyeball. The last of these layers to be reached by the light contains the visual receptors. When the visual receptors are stimulated by the light, they produce signals that are conducted back through the retina to the first layer, which is composed of *retinal ganglion cells*. The retinal ganglion cells are the only retinal neurons with axons; their axons course across the inner surface of each eyeball and exit in a bundle, which is the **optic nerve** (i.e., the 2nd cranial nerve).

Most of the retinal ganglion cell axons pass through the **optic chiasm**, which is located on the inferior surface of the brain, just below the *hypothalamus*. At the optic chiasm, half the axons *decussate* (i.e., cross over to the other side of the brain), and half do not. Those with cell bodies in the medial *hemiretinas* (i.e., the medial half of each retina) decussate; those with cell bodies in the lateral hemiretinas do not. As a result, of this arrangement, information from your left visual field and right hemiretinas is conducted to your right hemisphere, and information from your right visual field and left hemiretinas is conducted to your left hemisphere, regardless of which eye it enters.

From the optic chiasm, the retinal ganglion cell axons enter the brain in two bundles, which are now referred to as the **optic tracts**. The neurons of the optic tracts terminate in the **lateral geniculate nuclei** of the thalamus. The axons of lateral geniculate nuclei neurons project via the **optic radiations** to the ipsilateral *primary visual cortex*.

The spatial relations among fibers leaving the surface of the retina are maintained all along the visual pathways to the primary visual cortex. As a result, the surface of the primary visual cortex is organized *retinotopically*, that is, its surface is laid out like a map of the surface of the retina, with the right visual cortex mapping the right hemiretinas and the left visual cortex mapping the left hemiretinas.

### Retina
The five-layered neural structure that lines the back of each eyeball; the furthest retinal layer from the pupil contains the visual receptors, and the closest contains the retinal ganglion cells.

### Optic nerves
The bundles of retinal ganglion cell axons that leave each eyeball; the second cranial nerves.

### Optic chiasm (KYE az im)
The X-shaped midline structure on the inferior surface of the hypothalamus; the retinal ganglion cell axons originating in the medial hemiretinas decussate via the optic chiasm.

### Optic tracts
The tracts, left and right, that project from the optic chiasm to the lateral geniculate nuclei; they are composed of the axons of retinal ganglion cells.

### Lateral geniculate nuclei
The thalamic nuclei that relay visual information from the optic tracts to the ipsilateral primary visual cortex via the optic radiations.

### Optic radiations
The diffuse neural pathways from each lateral geniculate nucleus to the primary visual cortex of the same hemisphere.

---

*Coloring notes*

*First, color the left retina—the one on the right side of the illustration, which has been drawn from the inferior perspective. Then, color each successive stage in the left visual pathway: optic nerve, optic chiasm, optic tract, lateral geniculate nucleus, and optic radiations. When you have finished coloring the visual system of the left hemisphere, color the visual system of the right hemisphere using the same colors.*

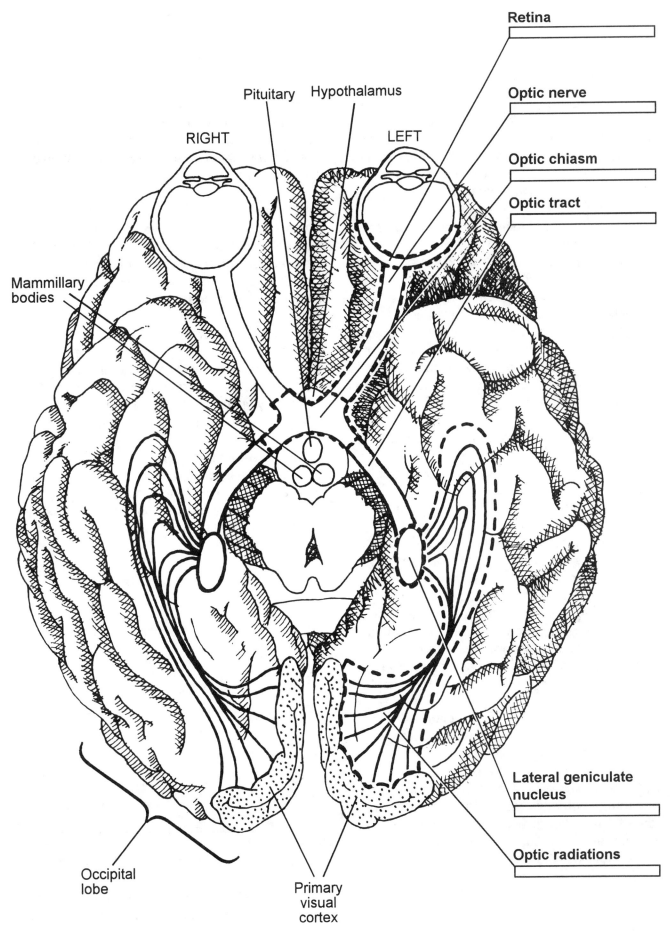

Retina

Optic nerve

Optic chiasm

Optic tract

Pituitary    Hypothalamus

RIGHT          LEFT

Mammillary
bodies

Lateral geniculate
nucleus

Optic radiations

Occipital
lobe

Primary
visual
cortex

## 8.2 Cortical Visual Areas

**Primary visual cortex** constitutes much of the cortex of the occipital lobes although it is largely hidden from view in the *longitudinal fissure*; it is the gateway of visual input from the thalamus to the cerebral cortex. Primary visual cortex is sometimes called *striate cortex* because it has a visible stripe in layer 4, where the optic radiations from the thalamus synapse (*striate* means *striped*).

From the primary visual cortex, visual signals are conducted through numerous areas of secondary visual cortex—close to 30 have been identified in the monkey. Each small area of secondary visual cortex is a complete *retinotopic* map of the contralateral visual field, and each area responds best to different features of the visual signal—for example, to color, form, location, or motion. The areas of secondary visual cortex are located in **prestriate cortex** and **inferotemporal cortex**. Prestriate cortex is a band of cortex surrounding primary visual cortex; inferotemporal cortex is the cortex of the *inferior temporal gyrus*.

Visual information flows through the various areas of secondary visual cortex along numerous paths, each dealing with a different aspect of the visual world. These paths follow two general routes: a *dorsal route* and a *ventral route*. The dorsal route projects from primary visual cortex, to dorsal areas of prestriate cortex, to **posterior parietal cortex**—posterior parietal cortex is an area of association cortex that receives substantial auditory and somatosensory input in addition to its visual input. This dorsal route of visual projections is primarily involved in the perception of location and motion. In contrast, the ventral route projects from the primary visual cortex, to ventral areas of prestriate cortex, to inferotemporal cortex; and it is primarily involved in the perception of color and form. In other words, in general, the dorsal route system tells us where things are and where they are going, and the ventral route system tells us what they are.

### Primary visual cortex
The areas of occipital cortex, one left and one right, that receive most of their input from the lateral geniculate nuclei of the thalamus; also referred to as *striate cortex*.

### Prestriate cortex
The areas of cerebral cortex, one in each hemisphere, that surround primary visual cortex; the prestriate cortex of each hemisphere contains several different functional areas of secondary visual cortex.

### Inferotemporal cortex
The cortex of the inferior temporal lobes; the inferotemporal cortex of each hemisphere contains several different functional areas of secondary visual cortex, each of which plays a role in the visual recognition of objects.

### Posterior parietal cortex
The area of association cortex in the posterior parietal lobe of each hemisphere; it receives input from visual, auditory, and somatosensory systems and plays a role in the perception of location and motion.

---

*Coloring notes*
*Use a different color for each of the four major cortical areas of the human visual system: primary visual cortex, prestriate cortex, posterior parietal cortex, and inferotemporal cortex.*

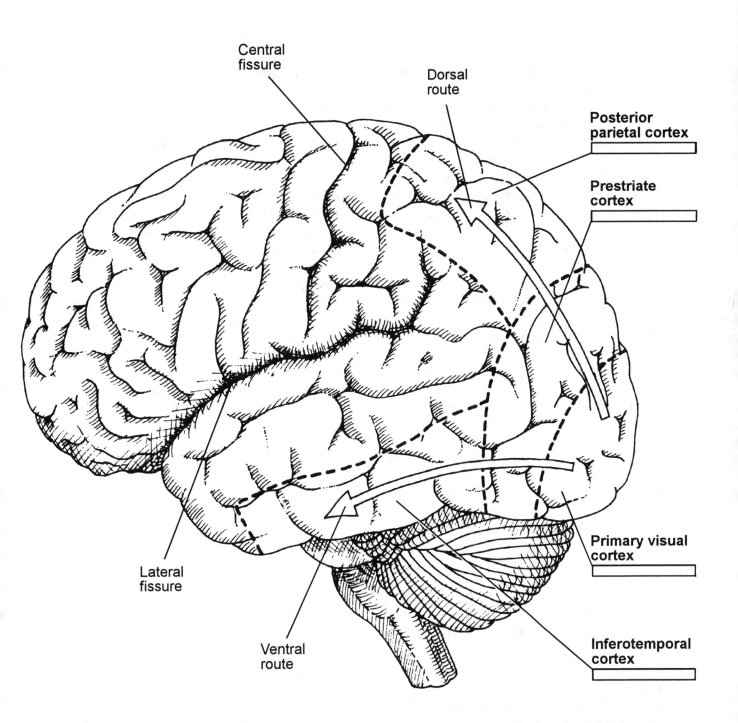

Central
fissure

Dorsal
route

**Posterior
parietal cortex**

**Prestriate
cortex**

Lateral
fissure

Ventral
route

**Primary visual
cortex**

**Inferotemporal
cortex**

## 8.3 Auditory System: From Ear to Cortex

The auditory receptors are in the **cochlea**, the long coiled structure of the inner ear—the cochlea looks like a snail (*cochlea* means *snail shell*). Sound waves produce vibrations in the fluid of the cochlea, and these excite the auditory receptors. The **auditory nerve** conducts auditory signals from the cochlea to the ipsilateral dorsal and ventral **cochlear nuclei** of the medulla. The auditory nerve is one branch of the *vestibulocochlear nerve* (i.e., of the 8th cranial nerve)—the other is the *vestibular nerve*, which carries signals from the organs of balance in the inner ear.

From each cochlear nucleus, axons project a short distance to the medial and lateral **superior olivary nuclei** on both sides of the medulla. Because each superior olivary nucleus receives *bilateral input* (i.e., input from both ears), they are able to play a role in localizing sound sources by comparing the relative volume and time of arrival of the same sounds at the two ears. From the superior olivary nuclei, fibers ascend in the **lateral lemnisci**, the major lower brain stem auditory pathways, to the **inferior colliculi** of the tectum.

The axons of inferior colliculi neurons ascend to the **medial geniculate nuclei** of the thalamus. From the medial geniculate nuclei, axons project via the **auditory radiations** to the *primary auditory cortex*. The primary auditory cortex is located in the superior temporal lobe, largely hidden within the lateral fissure.

### Cochlea (COCK lee a)
The coiled, snail-like inner-ear structure that contains the auditory receptors.

### Auditory nerve
The nerve that carries signals from each cochlea to the ipsilateral cochlear nuclei; one component of the vestibulocochlear nerve (i.e., of the eighth cranial nerve).

### Cochlear nuclei
The two pairs of medullary nuclei, two on the left and two on the right, that receive ipsilateral input from the nerves.

### Superior olivary nuclei (ol i VAIR ee)
The two pairs of medullary nuclei, two on the left and two on the right, that receive bilateral auditory signals from the cochlear nuclei.

### Inferior colliculi (kuh LIK yu lee)
The two nuclei of the tectum, one left and one right, that receive auditory input via the lateral lemnisci (singular: *colliculus*).

### Medial geniculate nuclei
The two auditory relay nuclei of the thalamus, one left and one right; their projections terminate in the ipsilateral primary auditory cortex.

### Auditory radiations
The ipsilateral projections from the medial geniculate nuclei to the primary auditory cortex.

---

*Coloring notes*

*First, color the left cochlea, the one on the right side of the illustration, which has been drawn from the anterior perspective. Then, color your way up through the structures on both sides of the brain through which signals from the left cochlea pass: the left auditory nerve, the left cochlear nuclei, the left and right superior olivary nuclei, the left and right inferior colliculus, the left and right medial geniculate nucleus, and the left and right auditory radiations.*

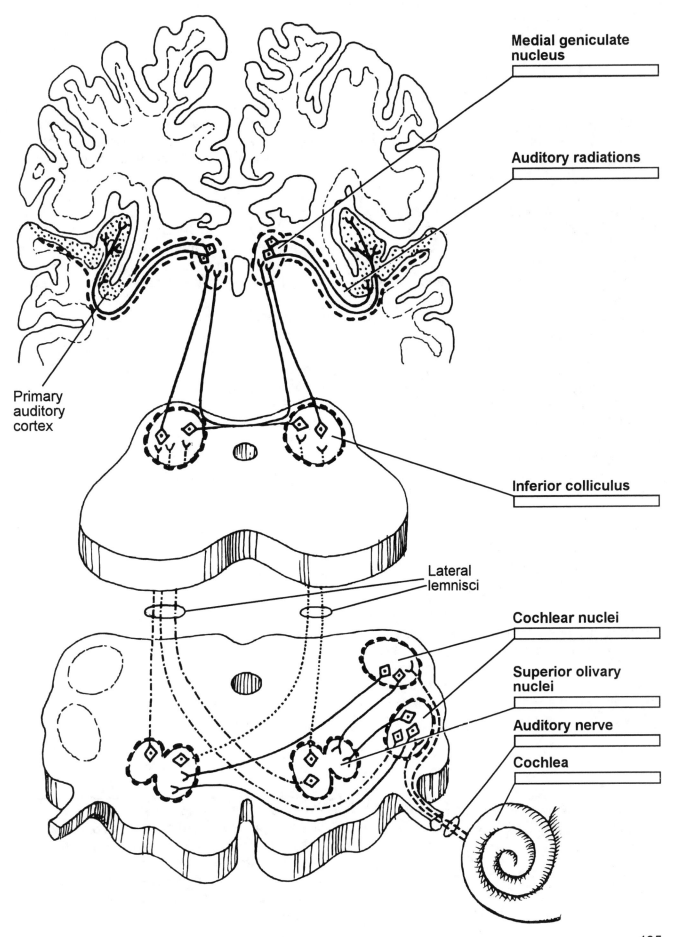

Medial geniculate nucleus

Auditory radiations

Primary auditory cortex

Inferior colliculus

Lateral lemnisci

Cochlear nuclei

Superior olivary nuclei

Auditory nerve

Cochlea

## 8.4 Cortical Auditory Areas

Most **primary auditory cortex** is located in **Heschl's gyrus**; Heschl's gyrus is located in the superior temporal lobe hidden from external view in the lateral fissure.

In contrast to primary visual cortex, which is organized *retinotopically*, primary auditory cortex is organized *tonotopically*. That is, it is organized on the basis of sound frequency or tone. Neurons in the more anterior regions of primary auditory cortex respond to higher frequencies, whereas neurons in the more posterior regions respond to lower frequencies. In most people, Heschl's gyrus is slightly larger on the side of the brain than the right.

Much of the output of primary auditory cortex is conducted to areas of **secondary auditory cortex**, which are located in adjacent areas of the temporal cortex. In turn, much of the output of secondary auditory cortex reaches the *posterior parietal association cortex*. Posterior parietal cortex plays a major role in the perception of spatial location on the basis of input that it receives from secondary areas of auditory, visual, and somatosensory cortex.

The human cortical auditory areas are not well understood, in part because of their location in the depths of the lateral fissure. When auditory cortex is damaged in humans, it is rarely destroyed entirely, and there is inevitably a great deal of damage to surrounding areas. However, monkeys with large bilateral surgical lesions of primary and secondary auditory cortex display profound hearing difficulties, particularly in discriminating complex sequences of sounds, and they have difficulty localizing sounds in space.

### Primary auditory cortex
The areas of cerebral cortex, one left and one right, that receive most of their input from the medial geniculate nuclei of the thalamus; most of primary auditory cortex is located in Heschl's gyrus.

### Heschl's gyrus (HESH uhls)
A superior temporal lobe gyrus that is located in the lateral fissure of each hemisphere; it is the location of most of the primary auditory cortex.

### Secondary auditory cortex
The areas of auditory cortex in each hemisphere that receive most of their input from primary auditory cortex; they are located in the superior temporal lobes.

*Coloring notes*

*First, color those portions of the left primary auditory cortex and left secondary auditory cortex that are visible in the top illustration. Then, color the same two areas on the left side of the bottom illustration. Finally, color Heschl's gyrus on the right side of the bottom illustration.*

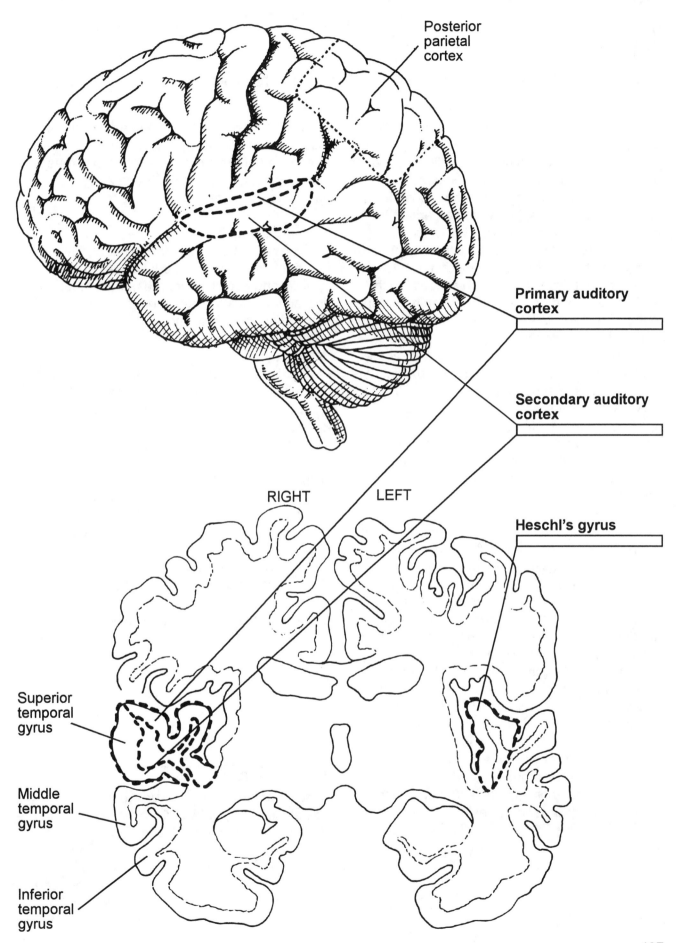

Posterior parietal cortex

Primary auditory cortex

Secondary auditory cortex

RIGHT    LEFT

Heschl's gyrus

Superior temporal gyrus

Middle temporal gyrus

Inferior temporal gyrus

137

## 8.5 Somatosensory System: From Receptors to Cortex

*Somatosensation* is a general term that refers to sensations of the body (*somato* means *of the body*). The somatosensory system is in fact three separate, but interacting, systems: (1) a *proprioceptive system*, which monitors information about the position of the body from receptors in muscles, joints, and organs of balance; (2) an *interoceptive system*, which monitors information about conditions within the body (e.g., blood pressure, temperature); (3) and an *exteroceptive system*, which senses touch, temperature, and pain stimuli through receptors in the skin. Information from touch receptors in skin and proprioception receptors in muscles and joints is conducted to the neocortex by the *dorsal-column medial-lemniscus system.* It is this system that is described here.

Sensory nerves carry proprioceptive and touch information into the spinal cord via the *dorsal roots*, and then without synapsing they ascend *ipsilaterally* in the dorsal part of the spinal cord as part of either the left or right **dorsal columns**. Many of the axons of the sensory neurons eventually synapse ipsilaterally in the medulla in the two pairs of **dorsal column nuclei**: one *nucleus gracilis* (from legs and lower trunk) and one *nucleus cuneatus* (from arms and upper trunk) on each side. The axons of dorsal column nuclei neurons decussate and ascend to the thalamus as part of either the left or right **medial lemnisci**. They are joined in their ascent in the medial lemnisci by neurons from the contralateral **trigeminal nucleus**, which receives tactual and proprioceptive information from the face via the three branches of the *trigeminal nerve* (i.e., the 5th cranial nerve).

Most of the axons of the medial lemniscus synapse on neurons in the **ventral posterior nucleus** of the thalamus. Most of the neurons of the ventral posterior nucleus in turn project to *primary somatosensory cortex.*

### Dorsal columns
The somatosensory tracts, left and right, that ascend in the dorsal spinal cord; they are composed of the axons of sensory neurons carrying information about touch and proprioception from ipsilateral receptors.

### Dorsal column nuclei
Two pairs of nuclei, two on the left and two on the right, in the dorsal medulla (i.e., nucleus gracilis and nucleus cuneatus); they receive ipsilateral somatosensory input via the ascending dorsal columns.

### Medial lemnisci
Two somatosensory tracts that ascend from the medulla to the thalamus; each ascends from dorsal column nuclei and decussates to the contralateral ventral posterior nucleus (singular: *lemniscus*).

### Trigeminal nuclei
The two medullary nuclei, left and right, that receive somatosensory input from the ipsilateral half of the face via the trigeminal nerves.

### Ventral posterior nuclei
The thalamic nuclei, left and right, that relay somatosensory information from the medial lemnisci to the ipsilateral primary somatosensory cortex.

### Coloring notes
*First, color the major structures of the somatosensory pathway from the left hand to the thalamus: the left dorsal column, the left dorsal column nuclei, and the right medial lemniscus. Then, color the trigeminal nucleus, which relays information from the left face. Finally, color the right ventral posterior nucleus. Pathways from only the left side of the body are shown.*

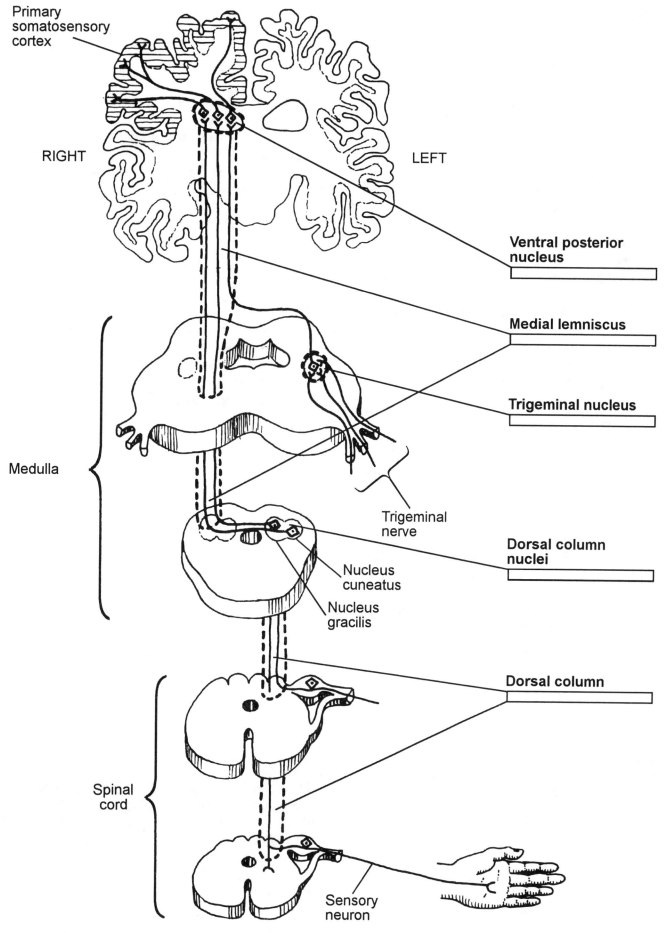

Primary somatosensory cortex

RIGHT

LEFT

**Ventral posterior nucleus**

**Medial lemniscus**

**Trigeminal nucleus**

Medulla

Trigeminal nerve

**Dorsal column nuclei**

Nucleus cuneatus

Nucleus gracilis

**Dorsal column**

Spinal cord

Sensory neuron

139

## 8.6 Cortical Somatosensory Areas

**Primary somatosensory cortex** receives input from the ventral posterior nucleus and from other thalamic nuclei carrying somatosensory information. It is located in the *postcentral gyrus* of the left and right parietal lobes.

The primary somatosensory cortex of each hemisphere is laid out *somatotopically;* that is, it is laid out according to a map of the body. Each primary somatosensory cortex is a map of the contralateral side of the body. Each somatotopic map is distorted; the largest areas of primary somatosensory cortex receive input from parts of the body, such as the mouth, face, and hands, that are capable of fine tactual discrimination. The somatotopic cortical map is often referred to as the **somatosensory homunculus** (*homunculus* means *little man*).

Much of the output of primary somatosensory cortex is conducted to **secondary somatosensory cortex**. Secondary somatosensory cortex is located just inferior to primary somatosensory cortex in the postcentral gyrus; much of it is hidden from view in the lateral fissure. Like primary somatosensory cortex, the two areas, left and right, of secondary somatosensory cortex are somatotopically organized. Because each receives input from both left and right primary somatosensory cortex, each responds to somatosensory signals from either side of the body. Much of the output of the secondary somatosensory cortex is conducted to the posterior parietal association cortex.

**Primary somatosensory cortex**
The areas of cerebral cortex, one left and one right, that receive somatosensory input from the thalamus, largely from the ventral posterior nuclei; primary somatosensory cortex is located in the postcentral gyrus of each hemisphere.

**Somatosensory homunculus** (HOE mung kyu lus)
The somatotopic maps that constitute primary somatosensory cortex.

**Secondary somatosensory cortex**
The areas of cortex in each hemisphere that receive most of their input from primary somatosensory cortex; they are located in the postcentral gyri just inferior to primary somatosensory cortex.

*Coloring notes*
*First, color the primary somatosensory cortex and secondary somatosensory cortex in the lateral view of the brain, that is, in the top illustration. Then, in the coronal section, color the primary somatosensory cortex and the somatosensory homunculus (the map of somatosensory input to the primary somatosensory cortex).*

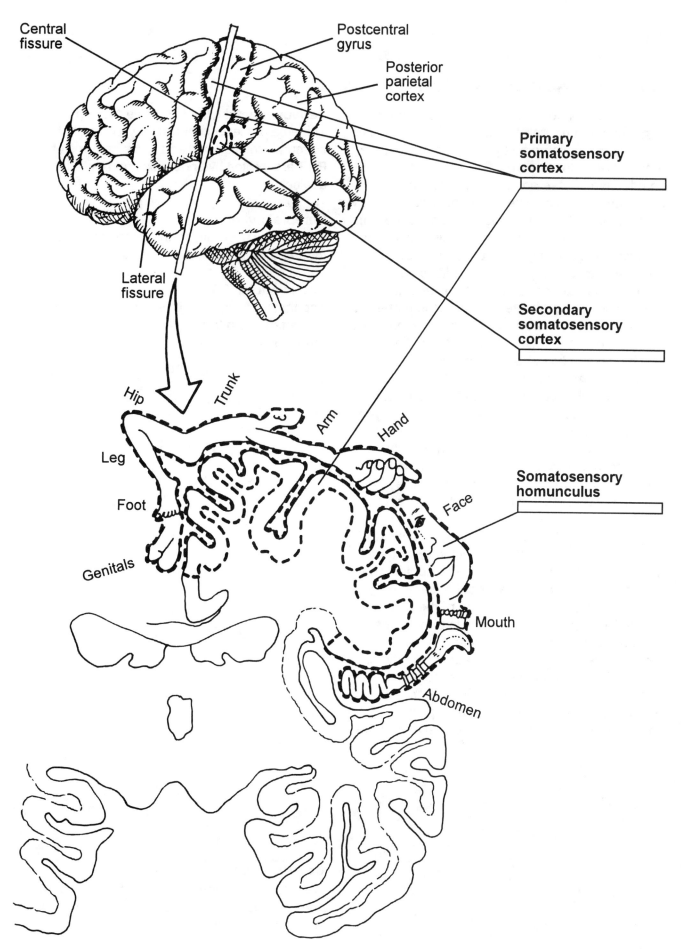

Central fissure

Postcentral gyrus

Posterior parietal cortex

**Primary somatosensory cortex**

Lateral fissure

**Secondary somatosensory cortex**

Hip

Trunk

Arm

Hand

Leg

Foot

Face

**Somatosensory homunculus**

Genitals

Mouth

Abdomen

141

## 8.7  The Descending Analgesia Circuit

The flow of sensory information into the brain is regulated to a degree by the brain itself. This is accomplished via pathways that run against the general receptor-to-cortex flow of sensory information. These are called *centrifugal pathways*. One example of a centrifugal pathway is the descending *analgesia* (i.e., pain-blocking) circuit. It is through the action of this circuit that people who suffer injuries during times of intense emotion (e.g., when their lives are in danger) feel little or no pain. This is adaptive; during times of intense emotion, it is important to be free from the disruptive effects of severe pain in order to deal effectively with the situation.

The descending analgesia circuit descends from the **periaqueductal gray** (PAG) of the midbrain to the gray matter of the dorsal spinal cord. The periaqueductal gray is an area of gray matter that surrounds the **cerebral aqueduct**. It contains neurons that are activated by both *opiate analgesics* (i.e., morphine-like pain-killing drugs) and *endorphins* (i.e., morphine-like chemicals that are synthesized by the brain itself).

When the PAG is activated by endorphins or analgesic drugs, axons descending from the PAG activate neurons in the **raphé nuclei**. The raphé nuclei are a vertical sheet of *serotonergic* nuclei that run down the midline of the *reticular formation*--*raphé* means *seam*. In turn, axons of the raphé nuclei neurons descend in the *dorsolateral spinal cord* with descending motor fibers. They synapse in the dorsal portion of the spinal gray matter i.e., in the *dorsal horn* on small inhibitory interneurons that suppress incoming pain signals before they ascend to the brain.

**Periaqueductal gray** (PEHR ee AK weh DUK tahl)
The area of mesencephalic gray matter that surrounds the cerebral aqueduct; neurons of the PAG are excited by endorphins and by opiate analgesics.

**Cerebral aqueduct**
The narrow midbrain channel that connects the third and fourth ventricles.

**Raphé nuclei** (RA fay)
The thin vertical sheet of serotonergic nuclei that is located along the midline of the reticular formation.

*Coloring notes*
*First, color the cerebral aqueduct; then color the periaqueductal gray, which surrounds it. Finally, color the raphé nuclei.*

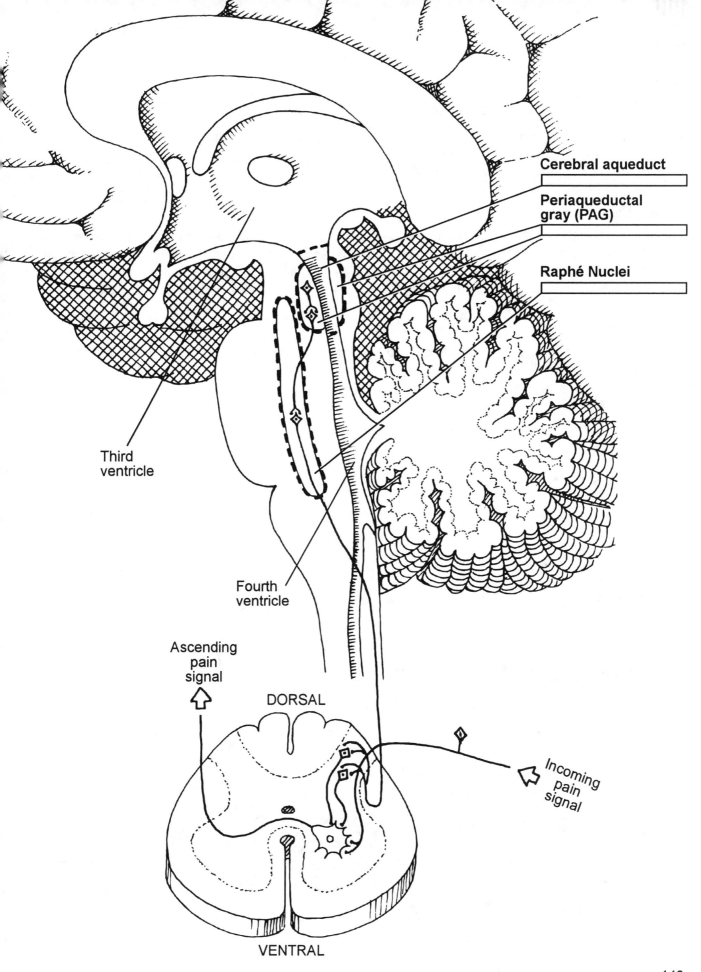

**Cerebral aqueduct**

**Periaqueductal gray (PAG)**

**Raphé Nuclei**

Third
ventricle

Fourth
ventricle

Ascending
pain
signal

DORSAL

Incoming
pain
signal

VENTRAL

143

## Review Exercises: Sensory Systems of the Central Nervous System

Now it is time for you to pause and consolidate the terms and ideas that you have learned in the seven learning units of Chapter 8. It is important that you overlearn them so that they do not quickly fade from your memory.

### Review Exercise 8.1

Turn to the illustrations in the seven learning units of Chapter 8, and use the cover flap at the back of the book to cover the terms that run down the right-hand edge of the illustration page. Study the seven illustrations in chronological sequence until you can identify each labeled structure. Once you have worked through all seven illustrations twice without making an error, advance to Review Exercise 8.2.

### Review Exercise 8.2

Fill in the missing terms in the following illustration. The answers are provided at the back of the book. Carefully review the material related to your incorrect answers.

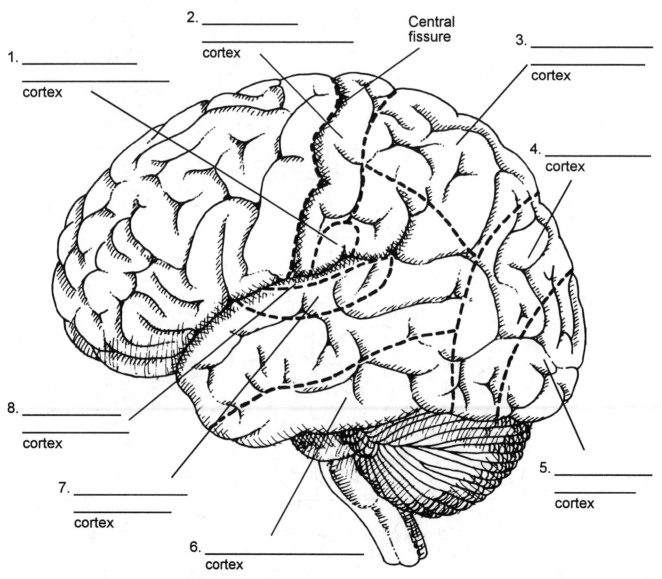

1. _____ cortex

2. _____ _____ cortex

Central fissure

3. _____ cortex

4. _____ cortex

5. _____ _____ cortex

6. _____ cortex

7. _____ cortex

8. _____ _____ cortex

144

## Review Exercise 8.3

Without referring to Chapter 8, fill in each of the following blanks with the correct term from the chapter. The correct answers are provided at the back of the book. Carefully review the material related to your incorrect answers.

1.  Retinal _____ cells carry signals out of the eye to the lateral geniculate nuclei.

2.  The _____ nerve leaves the cochlea as part of the 8th cranial nerve and terminates in the ipsilateral cochlear nuclei.

3.  Axons from the medial hemiretinas _____ in the optic chiasm; axons from the lateral hemiretinas do not.

4.  Primary somatosensory cortex is located in the _____ gyrus of each _____ lobe.

5.  As the result of the pattern of decussation in the visual pathways, information about any object that we see to the left of our center of gaze is conducted from the left eye to the _____ hemisphere and from the right eye to the _____ hemisphere.

6.  Information about touch and proprioception ascends the spinal cord ipsilaterally in the _____ spinal cord.

7.  The two general regions of secondary visual cortex in each hemisphere are the prestriate cortex and the _____ cortex.

8.  The optic nerves become known as the _____ once they have passed the optic chiasm and entered the brain.

9.  The superior olivary nuclei receive signals from the cochlear nuclei and conduct them via the lateral lemnisci to the inferior _____.

10. The thalamic relay nuclei of the auditory system are the medial _____ nuclei.

11. Primary auditory cortex is located in the superior region of each _____ lobe.

12. Much of the primary auditory cortex is in _____ gyri, which are located in the _____ fissure.

13. The primary visual cortex constitutes much of the _____ lobe.

14. The dorsal column nuclei are located in the _____.

15. The PAG is located in the midbrain around the cerebral _____.

16. Tactual and proprioceptive information from the face reaches the brain via the three branches of the _____ nerve, the fifth cranial nerve.

17. Primary visual cortex is organized _____; primary auditory cortex is organized _____; and primary somatosensory cortex is organized _____.

18. The topographic map in primary somatosensory cortex is often referred to as the somatosensory _____.

19. Secondary visual, auditory, and somatosensory cortexes all project to posterior _____ association cortex.

20. Endorphins excite neurons in the _____ gray.

21. The _____ nuclei are serotonergic nuclei of the midbrain reticular formation.

## Review Exercise 8.4

Below in alphabetical order is a list of all the terms and definitions that you learned in Chapter 8. Cover the definitions with a sheet of paper, and work your way down the list of terms, defining them to yourself as you go. Repeat this process until you have gone through the list twice without an error. Then, cover the terms and work your way down the list of definitions, providing the correct terms as you go. Repeat this second process until you have gone through the list twice without an error.

| | |
|---|---|
| Auditory nerve | The nerve that carries signals from each cochlea to the ipsilateral cochlear nuclei; a component of the vestibulocochlear nerve (i.e., of the eighth cranial nerve). |
| Auditory radiations | The ipsilateral projections from the medial geniculate nuclei to the primary auditory cortex. |
| Cerebral aqueduct | The narrow midbrain channel that connects the third and fourth ventricles. |
| Cochlea | The coiled, snail-like inner-ear structure that contains the auditory receptors. |
| Cochlear nuclei | The two pairs of medullary nuclei, two on the left and two on the right, that receive ipsilateral input from the auditory nerves. |
| Dorsal column nuclei | Two pairs of nuclei, two on the left and two on the right, in the dorsal medulla (i.e., nucleus gracilis and nucleus cuneatus); they receive ipsilateral somatosensory input via the ascending dorsal columns. |
| Dorsal columns | The somatosensory tracts, left and right, that ascend in the dorsal spinal cord; they are composed of the axons of sensory neurons carrying information about touch and proprioception from ipsilateral receptors. |
| Heschl's gyrus | A superior temporal lobe gyrus that is located in the lateral fissure of each hemisphere; it is the location of most of the primary auditory cortex. |
| Inferior colliculi | The two nuclei of the tectum, one left and one right, that receive auditory input via the lateral lemnisci (singular: colliculus). |
| Inferotemporal cortex | The cortex of the inferior temporal lobes; the inferotemporal cortex of each hemisphere contains several different functional areas of secondary visual cortex, each of which plays a role in the visual recognition of objects. |
| Lateral geniculate nuclei | The thalamic nuclei that relay visual information from the optic tracts to the ipsilateral primary visual cortex via the optic radiations. |
| Medial geniculate nuclei | The two auditory relay nuclei of the thalamus, one left and one right; their projections terminate in the ipsilateral primary auditory cortex. |

| | | | |
|---|---|---|---|
| Medial lemnisci | Two somatosensory tracts that ascend from the medulla to the thalamus; each ascends from dorsal column nuclei and decussates to the contralateral ventral posterior nucleus of the thalamus (singular: lemniscus). | Posterior parietal cortex | The area of association cortex in the posterior parietal lobe of each hemisphere; it receives input from visual, auditory, and somatosensory systems and plays a role in the perception of location and motion. |
| Optic chiasm | The X-shaped midline structure on the inferior surface of the hypothalamus; the retinal ganglion cell axons originating in the medial hemiretinas decussate via the optic chiasm. | Prestriate cortex | The areas of cerebral cortex, one in each hemisphere, that surround primary visual cortex; the prestriate cortex of each hemisphere contains several different functional areas of secondary visual cortex. |
| Optic nerves | The bundles of retinal ganglion cell axons that leave each eyeball; the second cranial nerves. | Primary auditory cortex | The areas of cortex, one left and one right, that receive most of their input from the medial geniculate nuclei of the thalamus; most of the primary auditory cortex is located in Heschl's gyrus. |
| Optic radiations | The diffuse neural pathways from each lateral geniculate nucleus to the primary visual cortex of the same hemisphere. | | |
| Optic tracts | The tracts, left and right, that project from the optic chiasm to the lateral geniculate nuclei; they are composed of the axons of retinal ganglion cells. | Primary visual cortex | The areas of occipital cortex, one left and one right, that receive most of their input from the lateral geniculate nuclei of the thalamus; also referred to as *striate cortex*. |
| Periaqueductal gray | The area of mesencephalic gray matter that surrounds the cerebral aqueduct; neurons of the PAG are excited by endorphins and by opiate analgesics. | Primary somatosensory cortex | The areas of cerebral cortex that receive somatosensory input from the thalamus, largely from the ventral posterior nuclei; primary somatosensory cortex is located in the postcentral gyrus of each hemisphere. |

| | |
|---|---|
| Raphé nuclei | The thin vertical sheet of serotonergic nuclei that is located along the midline of the reticular formation. |
| Retina | The five-layered neural structure that lines the back of each eyeball; the furthest retinal layer from the pupil contains the visual receptors, and the closest contains the retinal ganglion cells. |
| Secondary auditory cortex | The areas of auditory cortex in each hemisphere that receive most of their input from primary auditory cortex; they are located in the superior temporal lobes. |
| Secondary somatosensory cortex | The areas of cortex in each hemisphere that receive most of their input from primary somatosensory cortex; they are located in the postcentral gyri just inferior to primary somatosensory cortex. |
| Somatosensory homunculus | The somatotopic maps that constitute primary somatosensory cortex. |
| Superior olivary nuclei | The two pairs of medullary nuclei, two on the left and two on the right, that receive bilateral auditory signals from the cochlear nuclei. |
| Trigeminal nuclei | The two medullary nuclei, left and right, that receive somatosensory input from the ipsilateral half of the face via the trigeminal nerves. |
| Ventral posterior nuclei | The thalamic nuclei, left and right, that relay somatosensory information from the medial lemnisci to the ipsilateral primary somatosensory cortex. |

## Chapter 9: Sensorimotor Pathways of the Central Nervous System

This chapter is about the sensorimotor circuits of the central nervous system, the CNS circuits that control movement. They are referred to as *sensorimotor circuits,* rather than *motor circuits*, in acknowledgment of the critical role played by sensory input and feedback in guiding effective movement.

In the preceding chapter, you followed the pathways of three sensory systems as they ascended through a hierarchy of structures, from receptors to the association areas of the cerebral cortex. In contrast to the preceding chapter, this chapter begins in association cortex and traces the pathways of motor command that descend into the sensorimotor circuits of the spinal cord.

The following are the six learning units of Chapter 9:

9.1   Sensorimotor Cortical Pathways

9.2   Primary Motor Cortex

9.3   The Descending Dorsolateral Motor Pathways

9.4   The Descending Ventromedial Motor Pathways

9.5   The Cerebellum and Basal Ganglia

9.6   Parkinson's Disease and the Nigrostriatal Pathway

## 9.1 Sensorimotor Cortical Pathways

Before an accurate movement can be initiated, the sensorimotor system must know the current position of the body parts that are to be moved and the positions of external objects with which the body is going to interact. This information is supplied to the *posterior parietal cortex* by the visual, auditory, and somatosensory systems. The posterior parietal cortex in turn supplies this information to the motor areas of the frontal lobe, including the **dorsolateral prefrontal cortex**. The dorsolateral prefrontal cortex is association cortex that provides a mental representation of objects to which the subject is going to respond and initiates voluntarily movements.

Signals from dorsolateral prefrontal cortex project to four areas of **secondary motor cortex**. These are the **supplementary motor area,** the **premotor cortex**, and two **cingulate motor areas**. The supplementary motor area of each hemisphere is located in dorsal frontal cortex just anterior to the precentral gyrus; much of it is located in the *longitudinal fissure*. The premotor cortex of each hemisphere is located in ventral frontal cortex just anterior to the precentral gyrus; much of it is located in the lateral fissure. And the two cingulate motor areas are located in the cingulate gyrus.

The supplementary motor area and premotor cortex seem to be involved in planning sequences of voluntary movements before they are initiated; one difference between them is that the supplementary motor area is richly innervated by axons from somatosensory cortex, whereas premotor cortex is richly innervated by axons from visual cortex. The functions of the cingulate motor areas are not well understood.

Most of the output of the areas of secondary motor cortex goes to primary motor cortex. Primary motor cortex of each hemisphere is located in the *precentral gyrus* of the frontal lobe, just posterior to the supplementary motor area and the premotor cortex.

**Dorsolateral prefrontal cortex**
An area of association cortex in the frontal lobe that seems to play a role in providing a mental image of objects to which a person is going to respond and in initiating voluntary responses.

**Secondary motor cortex**
The supplementary motor area, the premotor cortex, and the two cingulate motor areas; areas of cortex whose major output is to primary motor cortex.

**Supplementary motor area**
The area of secondary motor cortex that is located in the dorsal frontal lobe, just anterior to the precentral gyrus; in addition to its input from posterior parietal cortex, it receives substantial input from somatosensory cortex.

**Premotor cortex**
The area of secondary motor cortex that is located in the ventral frontal lobe, just anterior to the precentral gyrus; in addition to its input from posterior parietal cortex, it receives substantial input from visual cortex.

**Cingulate motor areas**
Two areas of secondary motor cortex in the cingulate gyrus of each hemisphere.

### Coloring notes

*First, color all areas of secondary motor cortex in the top illustration. Then, color the individual areas of secondary motor cortex in the bottom illustration: the cingulate motor areas, the supplementary motor area, and the premotor cortex. Finally, color the dorsolateral prefrontal association cortex.*

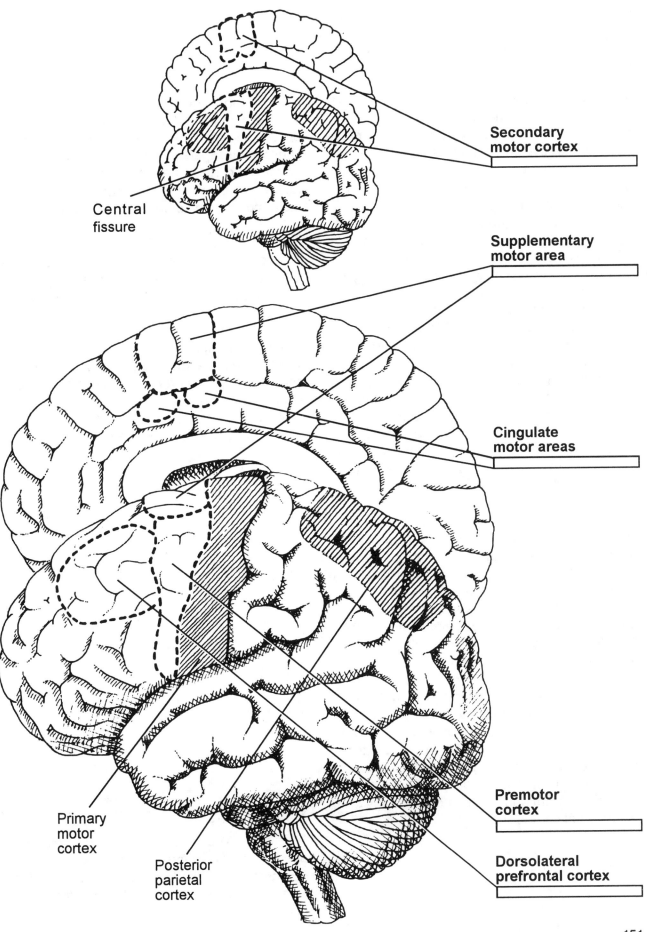

**Secondary motor cortex**

Central fissure

**Supplementary motor area**

**Cingulate motor areas**

**Premotor cortex**

**Dorsolateral prefrontal cortex**

Primary motor cortex

Posterior parietal cortex

151

## 9.2 Primary Motor Cortex

**Primary motor cortex** is the area of cortex that is the major point of departure for axons descending from the cortex to lower levels of the sensorimotor system. It is located in the precentral gyrus of the frontal lobe, and it receives its major input from the four areas of secondary motor cortex.

Electrical stimulation of each point on the surface of the primary motor cortex causes a muscle on the contralateral side of the body to contract. By stimulating each area of primary motor cortex and recording which muscle contracts in response to each stimulation, neuroscientists discovered that, like primary somatosensory cortex, primary motor cortex is organized *somatotopically*. The somatotopic map of the layout of primary motor cortex is called the **motor homunculus**. Areas of the motor homunculus that are capable of fine movements (e.g., areas that control the muscles of the fingers) are disproportionately larger than those that are not capable of fine movements (e.g., areas that control the muscles of the back).

All areas of the motor homunculus receive somatosensory input via the somatosensory cortex from receptors in the very muscles and joints that they control. Thus, when activity in an area of primary motor cortex initiates a movement, that area receives immediate *feedback* about the accuracy of the movement. This sensory feedback is critical for accurate movement.

Axons from each primary motor cortex gather together and descend as part of a large tract called the **internal capsule**. Each internal capsule passes through a channel bounded by the *putamen* and *globus pallidus* on one side and the *caudate* and *thalamus* on the other. Each internal capsule contains axons descending from and ascending to all parts of the cerebral cortex.

**Primary motor cortex**
The major point of departure for motor fibers descending from the cortex to lower levels of the sensorimotor system; it is located in the precentral gyrus of each hemisphere, and it receives major input from areas of secondary motor cortex and somatosensory cortex.

**Motor homunculus** (HOE mung kyu lus)
The somatotopic map of primary motor cortex; the primary motor cortex of each hemisphere exerts most of its control over the contralateral side of the body.

**Internal capsules**
The bundles of axons descending from, and ascending to, the cerebral cortex, that funnel through a channel bounded by the globus pallidus and putamen on one side and the caudate and thalamus on the other.

*Coloring notes*

*First, color the primary motor cortex in the top and bottom illustrations. Then, in the bottom illustration, color the internal capsule by staying within the dashed lines. Finally color the motor homunculus.*

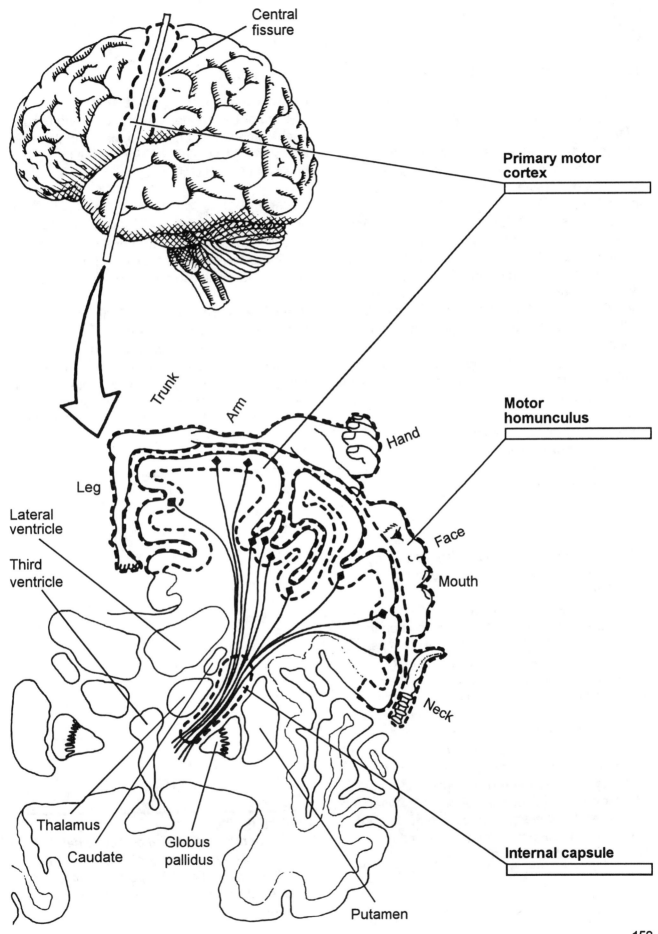

Central fissure

**Primary motor cortex**

Trunk

Arm

Hand

Leg

**Motor homunculus**

Lateral ventricle

Third ventricle

Face

Mouth

Neck

Thalamus

Caudate

Globus pallidus

**Internal capsule**

Putamen

## 9.3 The Descending Dorsolateral Motor Pathways

Four pairs of motor pathways descend from the primary motor cortex to the spinal cord via the *internal capsules*. Two pairs descend in the dorsolateral region of the spinal cord, and two pairs descend in the ventromedial region. The two pairs of dorsolateral pathways are described in this learning unit.

The axons of the **dorsolateral corticospinal tracts** descend ipsilaterally to the brain stem, where they can be seen on the ventral surface of the medulla as the **pyramids**. Then, without synapsing, each decussates and descends in the contralateral dorsolateral spinal cord. Most of the axons of the dorsolateral corticospinal tracts synapse on *interneurons* in the spinal gray matter, each of which synapses on a small number of *motor neurons* that project to muscles of the *distal* limbs (e.g., the muscles of the hands and fingers). However, a few neurons in the dorsolateral corticospinal tract synapse directly on motor neurons.

The other dorsolateral tracts, the **dorsolateral corticorubrospinal tracts**, are less direct. The axons of the primary motor cortex neurons that compose the first section of these tracts descend ipsilaterally to the **red nucleus** of the midbrain, where they synapse (*rubro* means *red)*. The axons of red nucleus neurons compose the second section of these tracts; they decussate and descend through the medulla, where some of them synapse on the nuclei of cranial nerves that control the muscles of the face. The remainder descend in the contralateral dorsolateral cord, where they synapse on interneurons of the spinal gray matter that in turn synapse on motor neurons that project to muscles of the distal limbs.

The major difference between the two pairs of tracts is that the output of each dorsolateral corticospinal tract neuron is focused on a much smaller number of muscle fibers. Thus, when the dorsolateral corticospinal tracts are destroyed, subjects can still move their fingers, but they cannot move them one at a time.

### Dorsolateral corticospinal tracts
The motor tracts whose axons descend from each primary motor cortex in the contralateral dorsolateral spinal cord; they control the muscles of the distal limbs.

### Pyramids
The two bulges on the ventral surface of the medulla, one on the left and one on the right, which are created by the axons of the dorsolateral corticospinal tracts.

### Dorsolateral corticorubrospinal tracts
The motor tracts that that are composed of axons that descend from each primary motor cortex to the ipsilateral red nucleus and of axons from each red nucleus that decussate and then descend in the contralateral dorsolateral spinal cord; they control the muscles of the distal limbs.

### Red nuclei
Important midbrain nuclei of the descending dorsolateral corticorubrospinal tracts.

*Coloring notes*

*First, color the dorsolateral corticospinal and the dorsolateral corticorubrospinal tracts. Then, color the pyramids and red nuclei. Notice that only the tracts descending from one hemisphere are shown.*

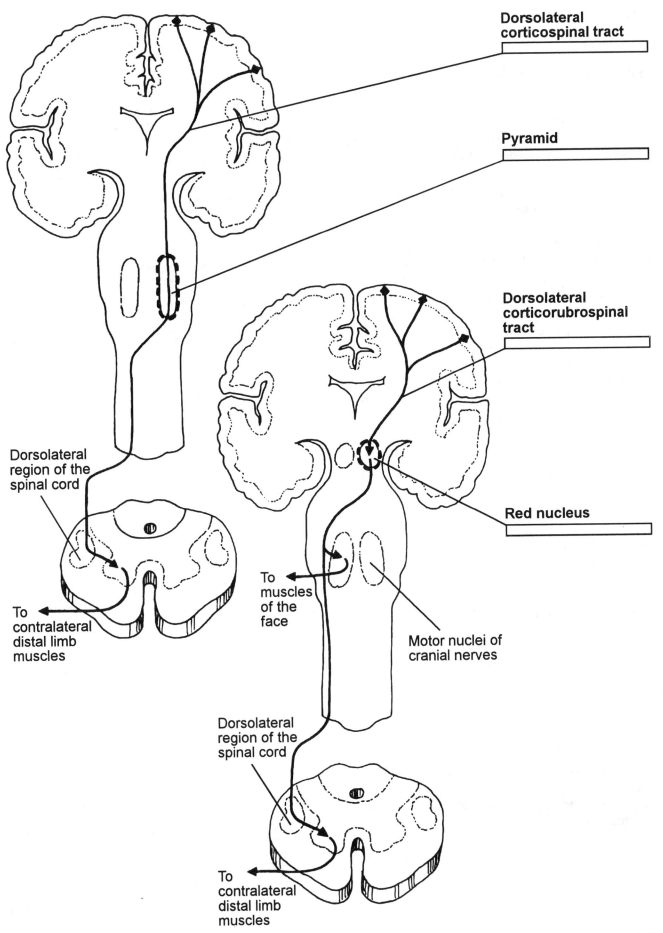

**Dorsolateral corticospinal tract**

**Pyramid**

**Dorsolateral corticorubrospinal tract**

**Red nucleus**

Dorsolateral region of the spinal cord

To contralateral distal limb muscles

To muscles of the face

Motor nuclei of cranial nerves

Dorsolateral region of the spinal cord

To contralateral distal limb muscles

## 9.4 The Descending Ventromedial Motor Pathways

Just as there are two pairs of dorsolateral motor tracts, descending from the primary motor cortex, one direct and one indirect; there are two pairs of ventromedial motor tracts, one direct and one indirect.

The direct ventromedial motor tracts are the **ventromedial corticospinal tracts**. The axons of these tracts descend from the primary motor cortex ipsilaterally in the ventromedial portion of the spinal cord. As they descend, each axon branches diffusely and innervates interneuron circuits at several levels of the spinal cord on both sides. The ventromedial corticospinal tracts control the muscles of the trunk, neck, and proximal limbs (e.g., shoulders).

The indirect ventromedial motor tracts are the **ventromedial cortico-brainstem-spinal tracts**. The axons of these tracts descend into a complex network of brain stem sensorimotor structures (which include the *tectum*, several nuclei of the *reticular formation*, and the nuclei of several cranial nerves including the *vestibular nucleus*, which receives information about balance from the inner ear via the 8th cranial nerve). Axons of each ventromedial cortico-brainstem-spinal tract descend from this complex brain stem circuit on both sides of the spinal cord in the ventromedial region. Each descending neuron synapses at several different levels of the spinal cord on interneuron circuits that synapse on motor neurons that project to the muscles of the trunk, neck, and *proximal* limbs (e.g., shoulders and hips).

The two pairs of ventromedial tracts are involved in the control of posture and in the coordination of activities that involve gross movements of the entire body—movements such as walking and crawling. Thus, in comparison to the neurons of the dorsolateral tracts, each neuron of the ventromedial tracts has consequences that are more proximal and less focused.

### Ventromedial corticospinal tracts
The motor tracts whose axons descend from each primary motor cortex in the ipsilateral ventromedial spinal cord; each axon descending from the motor cortex influences proximal muscles on both sides of the body.

### Ventromedial cortico-brainstem-spinal tracts
The motor tracts that are composed of axons that descend ipsilaterally from each primary motor cortex to sensorimotor circuits of the brain stem and of axons that descend bilaterally from the brain stem in the ventromedial spinal cord; each axon descending from the motor cortex influences proximal muscles on both sides of the body.

### Coloring notes
*First, color the ventromedial corticospinal tract. Then, color the ventromedial cortico-brainstem-spinal tract. Notice that only the tracts descending from one hemisphere are shown.*

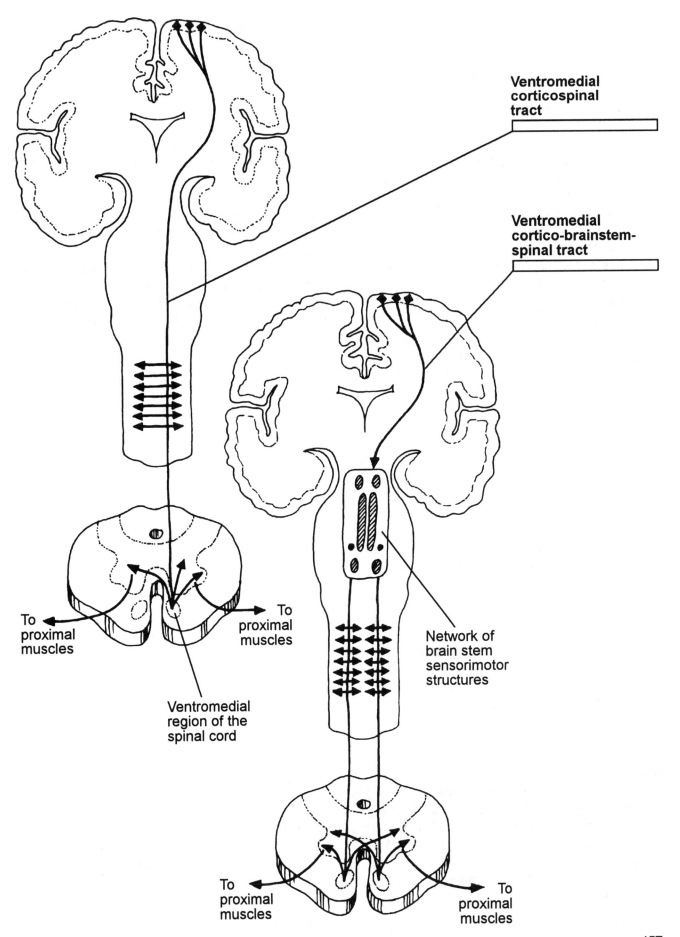

**Ventromedial corticospinal tract**

**Ventromedial cortico-brainstem-spinal tract**

Network of brain stem sensorimotor structures

Ventromedial region of the spinal cord

To proximal muscles

To proximal muscles

To proximal muscles

To proximal muscles

## 9.5 The Cerebellum and Basal Ganglia

The **cerebellum** and **basal ganglia** are important sensorimotor structures. However, unlike the structures of the descending motor pathways, they do not participate in the conduction of motor signals from the primary motor cortex to spinal motor circuits. Instead, their role seems to be to modulate and coordinate the activities of structures in the descending sensorimotor circuits—they both send fibers to, and receive fibers from, several sensorimotor structures.

Although the cerebellum constitutes only 10% of the brain's mass, it contains more than half its neurons. Its main input comes from sensory and motor areas of the cerebral cortex, the red nucleus, and the vestibular nucleus, and from receptors in muscles and joints via the *spinocerebellar tract*. Its main output goes to the red nucleus, vestibular nucleus, and reticular formation, and to the primary motor cortex via the thalamus.

The basal ganglia are a collection of independent cerebral nuclei: the *caudate* and *putamen* (together known as the *striatum)*, the *globus pallidus*, and the *amygdala*. The basal ganglia receive most of their input from the cerebral cortex, primarily from primary motor cortex. Their major output goes back to the primary motor cortex via the thalamus, but there is also output to the vestibular nucleus, pons, and reticular formation.

Given the complexity of the basal ganglia and the cerebellum and their respective connections, it is hardly surprising that it has proven difficult to precisely specify their functions. One hypothesis is that both are involved in modulating and coordinating movement through their interactions with descending motor pathways (e.g., with the primary motor cortex via the thalamus), in particular in the learning of new motor sequences and in adjusting responses to changing environmental conditions. The basal ganglia are thought to play the greater role in distal limb movements, and the cerebellum is thought to play the greater role in balance and postural adjustment.

**Cerebellum** (sair uh BEL um)
The large convoluted structure dorsal to the pons; it is thought to modulate and coordinate motor activity, particularly balance and postural adjustment.

**Basal ganglia** (BAZE ul)
The caudate, putamen, globus pallidus, and amygdala; a system of cerebral nuclei that modulates and coordinates motor activity, particularly distal limb activity, through its participation in a circuit that conducts signals from the primary motor cortex back to the primary motor cortex via the thalamus.

*Coloring notes*

*Color the visible portions of the basal ganglia staying within the dashed lines. Next color the visible portions of the cerebellum. Note that the globus pallidus is not visible behind the putamen.*

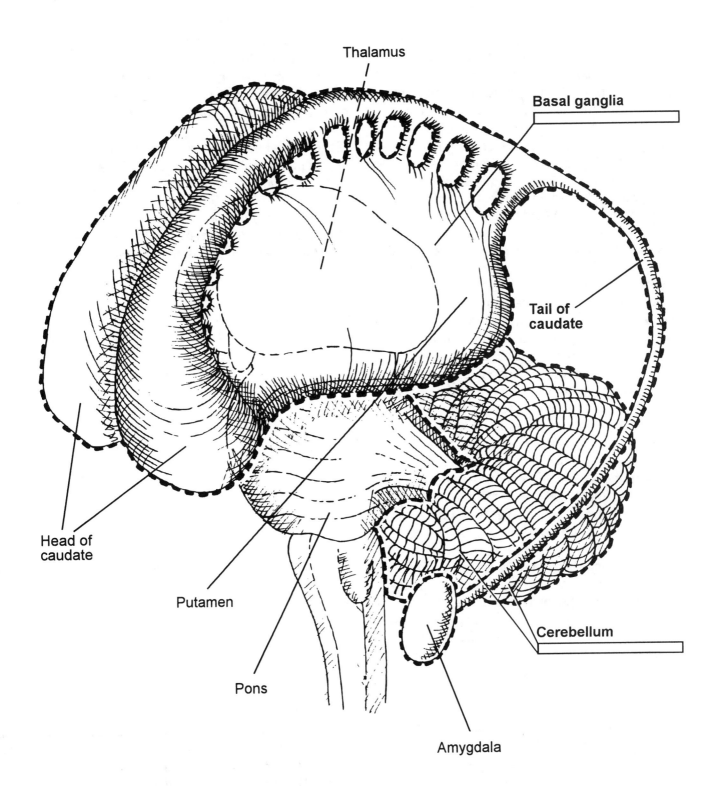

Thalamus

**Basal ganglia**

Tail of
caudate

Head of
caudate

Putamen

Cerebellum

Pons

Amygdala

159

## 9.6 Parkinson's Disease and the Nigrostriatal Pathway

Parkinson's disease is a movement disorder that strikes about 1% of the population, usually in adulthood. Its initial symptoms are mild—perhaps no more than a stiffness or tremor of the fingers—but they gradually increase in severity with advancing years. The following are the most common symptoms of the full-blown disorder: (1) *tremor at rest*, a tremor that is pronounced during inactivity but is suppressed during both voluntary movement and sleep; (2) muscular rigidity; (3) continual involuntary shifts in posture; (4) poverty and slowness of movement; and (5) a shuffling, wide-based gait with a forward-leaning posture. There is often little or no intellectual impairment.

Parkinson's disease seems to have no single cause. Brain infections, strokes, tumors, traumatic brain injury, and neurotoxins have all been implicated in specific cases; however, in the majority of cases no cause is obvious, and there is often no family history of the disorder.

Parkinson's disease is associated with degeneration of the **substantia nigra**, the dopaminergic midbrain nucleus whose neurons project via the **nigrostriatal pathway** to the **striatum** (the *caudate* plus *putamen*). As a result, there is an almost total lack of the neurotransmitter dopamine in the substantia nigras and striatums of long-term Parkinson's patients. Conversely, the symptoms of Parkinson's disease are sometimes alleviated by injections of *L-DOPA*, the chemical from which dopamine is synthesized—dopamine itself is ineffective because dopamine does not readily penetrate the CNS, whereas L-DOPA does. Unfortunately, even those patients who initially respond positively to the L-DOPA injections gain only temporary relief because they gradually become tolerant to the beneficial effects of the injections.

**Substantia nigra** (sub STAN she a   NYE gruh)
A midbrain nucleus whose dopaminergic neurons terminate in the striatum; in advanced cases of Parkinson's disease, substantia nigra neurons have largely degenerated.

**Nigrostriatal pathway** (NYE groe strye AY tal)
The dopaminergic tract from the substantia nigra to the striatum.

**Striatum** (strye AY tum)
The caudate and putamen; it is the terminal of the dopaminergic nigrostriatal pathway.

*Coloring notes*

*First, color the substantia nigra and the nigrostriatal pathway. Next color the visible portions of the striatum (the caudate plus the putamen). Color the striatum lightly so as not to obscure the structures hidden behind the putamen.*

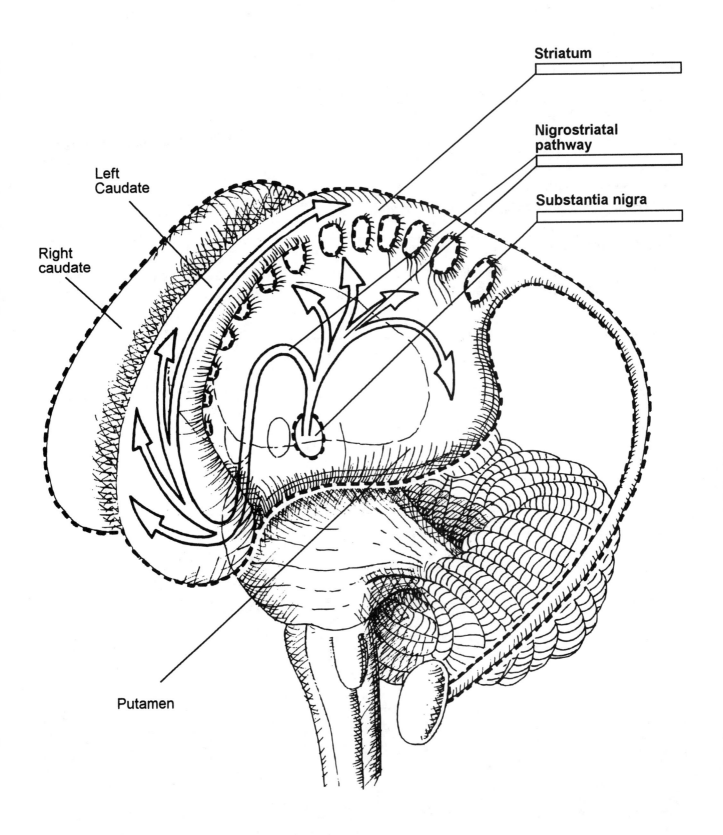

Striatum

Nigrostriatal
pathway

Substantia nigra

Left
Caudate

Right
caudate

Putamen

161

# Review Exercises: Sensorimotor Pathways of the Central Nervous System

Now it is time for you to pause and consolidate the terms and ideas that you have learned in the six learning units of Chapter 9. It is important that you overlearn them so that they do not quickly fade from your memory.

## Review Exercise 9.1

Turn to the illustrations in the six learning units of Chapter 9, and use the cover flap at the back of the book to cover the terms that run down the right-hand edge of each illustration page. Study the six illustrations in chronological sequence until you can identify each labeled structure. Once you have worked through all six illustrations twice without making any errors, advance to Review Exercise 9.2.

## Review Exercise 9.2

Fill in the missing terms in the following illustration. The answers are at provided at the back of the book. Carefully review the material related to your incorrect answers.

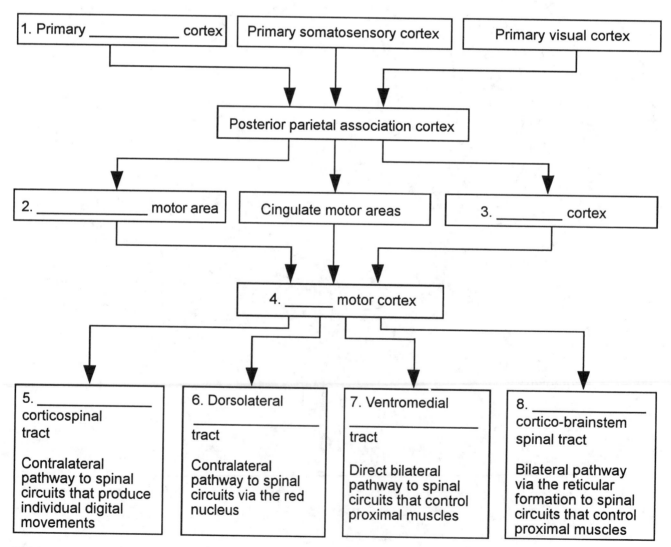

## Review Exercise 9.3

Without referring to Chapter 9, fill in each of the following blanks with the correct term from the chapter. The correct answers are provided at the back of the book. Carefully review the material related to your incorrect answers.

1. Signals from posterior parietal association cortex project to this area of association cortex in the frontal lobe: the

   _____ cortex.

2. The core of the body is said to be _____, whereas the hands and feet are said to be _____.

3. The axons of substantia nigra neurons compose the _____ pathway to the caudate and putamen.

4. Parkinson's disease is characterized by tremor _____.

5. They follow similar paths, but the dorsolateral corticorubrospinal tract takes a detour to the red nucleus while the dorsolateral _____ tract does not.

6. _____ is used in the treatment of Parkinson's disease.

7. The pyramids are bulges on the ventral surface of the medulla; they are created by the left and right dorsolateral _____ tracts.

8. The _____ and putamen compose the striatum.

9. Neurons projecting from the substantia nigra release dopamine in the _____.

10. The vestibular nucleus is a brain stem nucleus that receives sensory input from the organs of _____, which are located in the inner ear.

11. Axons from the cerebellum and basal ganglia project to the primary motor cortex via the _____.

12. The two _____ descending motor pathways control the voluntary muscles of the trunk, neck, and proximal limbs.

13. The amygdala, striatum, and _____ _____ compose the basal ganglia.

14. The _____ contains the cell bodies of many of the brain's dopaminergic neurons.

15. The motor homunculus is the _____ map of the primary motor cortex.

16. The dorsolateral _____ tract contains the axons of neurons that synapse directly on motor neurons.

17. Four major motor pathways descend into the spinal cord from the _____ motor cortex.

18. Most of the axons connecting the cortex with the brain stem and spinal cord funnel through the _____ capsule.

19. The two areas of secondary motor cortex located entirely within the longitudinal fissure are the two _____ motor areas.

20. Much of the output of secondary motor cortex goes to _____ motor cortex, which is located in the _____ gyrus.

21. Each internal capsule passes through a channel bounded by the globus pallidus and _____ on one side and the thalamus and _____ on the other.

## Review Exercise 9.4

Below in alphabetical order is a list of all the terms and definitions that you learned in Chapter 9. Cover the definitions with a sheet of paper, and work your way down the list of terms, defining them to yourself as you go. Repeat this process until you have gone through the list twice without an error. Then, cover the terms and work your way down the list of definitions, providing the correct terms as you go. Repeat this second process until you have gone through the list twice without an error.

| | |
|---|---|
| Basal ganglia | The caudate, putamen, globus pallidus, and amygdala; a system of cerebral nuclei that modulates and coordinates motor activity particularly distal limb activity, through its participation in a circuit that conducts signals from the primary motor cortex back to the primary motor cortex via the thalamus. |
| Cerebellum | The large convoluted structure dorsal to the pons; it is thought to modulate and coordinate motor activity, particularly balance and postural adjustment. |
| Cingulate motor areas | Two areas of secondary motor cortex in the cingulate gyrus of each hemisphere. |
| Dorsolateral corticorubrospinal tracts | The motor tracts that are composed of axons that descend from each primary motor cortex to the ipsilateral red nucleus and of axons from each red nucleus that decussate and then descend in the contralateral dorsolateral spinal cord; they control the muscles of the distal limbs. |
| Dorsolateral corticospinal tracts | The motor tracts whose axons descend from each primary motor cortex in the contralateral dorsolateral spinal cord; they control the muscles of the distal limbs. |
| Dorsolateral prefrontal cortex | An area of association cortex in the frontal lobe that seems to play a role in providing a mental image of objects to which a person is going to respond and in initiating voluntary responses. |
| Internal capsules | The bundles of axons descending from, and ascending to, the cerebral cortex that funnel through a channel bounded by the globus pallidus and putamen on one side and the caudate and thalamus on the other. |
| Motor homunculus | The somatotopic map of primary motor cortex; the primary motor cortex of each hemisphere exerts most of its control over the contralateral side of the body. |
| Nigrostriatal pathway | The dopaminergic tract from the substantia nigra to the striatum. |
| Premotor cortex | The area of secondary motor cortex that is located in the ventral frontal lobe just anterior to the precentral gyrus; in addition to its input from posterior parietal cortex, it receives substantial input from visual cortex. |

| | | | |
|---|---|---|---|
| Primary motor cortex | The major point of departure for motor fibers descending from the cortex to lower levels of the sensorimotor system; it is located in the precentral gyrus of each hemisphere, and it receives major input from secondary motor cortex and somatosensory cortex. | Supplementary motor area | The area of secondary motor cortex that is located in the dorsal frontal lobe, just anterior to the precentral gyrus; in addition to its input from posterior parietal cortex, it receives substantial input from somatosensory cortex. |
| Pyramids | The two bulges on the ventral surface of the medulla, one on the left and one on the right, which are created by the axons of the dorsolateral corticospinal tracts. | Ventromedial cortico-brainstem-spinal tracts | The motor tracts that are com-posed of axons that descend ipsilaterally from each primary motor cortex to sensorimotor circuits of the brain stem and of axons that descend bilaterally from the brain stem in the ventromedial spinal cord; each axon descending from the motor cortex influences proximal muscles on both sides of the body. |
| Red nuclei | Midbrain nuclei of the descending dorsolateral corticorubrospinal tract. | | |
| Secondary motor cortex | The supplementary motor area, the premotor cortex, and the two areas of cingulate motor cortex; areas of cortex whose major output is to primary motor cortex. | Ventromedial corticospinal tracts | The motor tracts whose axons descend from each primary motor cortex in the ipsilateral ventromedial spinal cord; each axon descending from the motor cortex influences proximal muscles on both sides of the body. |
| Striatum | The caudate and putamen; it is the destination of the dopaminergic nigrostriatal pathway. | | |
| Substantia nigra | A midbrain nucleus whose dopaminergic neurons terminate in the striatum; in advanced cases of Parkinson's disease, substantia nigra neurons have largely degenerated. | | |

# Chapter 10: Brain Structures and Memory

Memory is one of the brain's most important functions. Memory refers to the ability of an organism to store information about its experiences. The brain is changed in some way by its experiences, and these changes provide a record of them.

There are many important unresolved questions about the neural bases of memory. This chapter focuses on one of them: Which brain structures are involved in the memory process? You will learn in this chapter that memory functions are not evenly distributed throughout the brain. Specific structures of the brain play a role in memory, and in this chapter, you will learn about some of these important mnemonic (i.e., memory) structures. Each learning unit in this chapter deals with a particular area of the brain that has been implicated in memory by the study of memory loss in neuropsychological patients with damage to that area.

The following are the five learning units of Chapter 10:

10.1 Hippocampal Formation and Memory: The Case of H.M.

10.2 Rhinal Cortex and Memory

10.3 Hippocampus and Spatial Memory

10.4 Medial Diencephalon and Memory: Korsakoff's Amnesia

10.5 Basal Forebrain and Memory: Alzheimer's Amnesia

## 10.1 Hippocampal Formation and Memory: The Case of H.M.

In the early 1950s, H.M. had the medial portions of both his temporal lobes removed in an effort to control a life-threatening case of epilepsy. This *medial temporal lobectomy* greatly improved H.M.'s health, but it left him with a severe case of amnesia.

Since his surgery, H.M. has been incapable of forming new long-term *explicit memories*, long-term memories of which he has conscious awareness. In contrast, he has only mild amnesia for experiences that occurred before his surgery; he has a normal *short-term memory* (i.e., he can remember things for brief periods while he concentrates on them); and he has normal *implicit memory* (i.e., he can demonstrate retention of information by improved performance although he has no conscious awareness of the information). If you met H.M., he could chat with you quite normally until his attention was distracted, at which point he would have no recollection of you or your conversation.

H.M.'s case suggests that one or more of the structures of the medial temporal lobes plays a role in converting short-term memories into long-term memories—a process known as *memory consolidation*. Although several major structures are damaged by medial temporal lobectomy—which you may have surmised is no longer used as a treatment for epilepsy—it was initially assumed that H.M.'s memory deficit resulted from damage to his **hippocampal formation**. The **hippocampal formation** is composed of three cortical structures: the **hippocampus**, the **dentate gyrus**, and the **subicular cortex** (or subiculum). The hippocampus and dentate gyrus are *allocortex*; subicular cortex is part of a transitional area between the hippocampus and neocortex.

Many axons that project from the hippocampus run along its medial surface in a bundle called the **fimbria**. The axons of the fimbria project into the *fornix*.

### Hippocampal formation
The medial temporal lobe structure that is composed of the hippocampus, dentate gyrus, and subicular cortex; also referred to as the *hippocampal complex*.

### Hippocampus
The large fold of medial temporal lobe allocortex that is located between the edge of the cortical mantle and the subicular cortex; its structure in cross section reminded early neuroanatomists of a seahorse (*hippocampus* means *seahorse*).

### Dentate gyrus
The allocortical gyrus in the medial temporal lobe; in cross section, it is a C-shaped structure that curves around the edge of the hippocampus.

### Subicular cortex (sub IK yu lar)
An area of transitional cortex adjacent to the hippocampus; subicular cortex is folded like a supporting platform beneath the hippocampus and dentate gyrus (*subicular* means *supporting*).

### Fimbria
A bundle of axons that courses along the medial surface of the hippocampus; it carries signals from the hippocampus to the fornix.

---

*Coloring notes*

*First, color the position of the hippocampal formation in the upper illustration—note that the hippocampal formation would not be visible from this lateral view because it is a medial structure. Then, color the components of the hippocampal formation: the hippocampus, the dentate gyrus, and the subicular cortex. Finally, color the fimbria.*

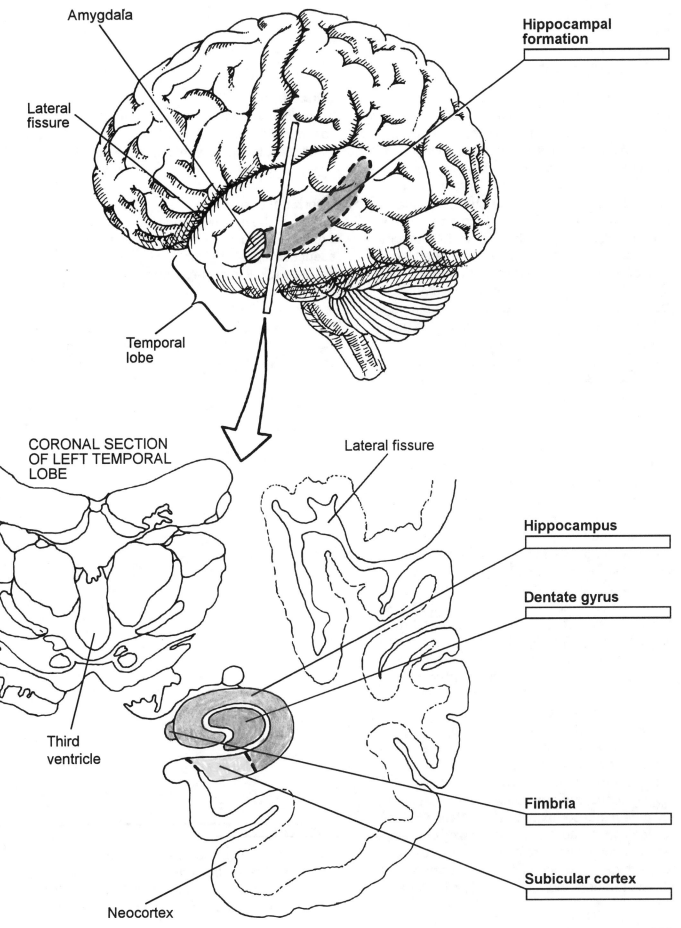

Amygdala

Lateral fissure

Temporal lobe

**Hippocampal formation**

CORONAL SECTION OF LEFT TEMPORAL LOBE

Lateral fissure

**Hippocampus**

**Dentate gyrus**

Third ventricle

**Fimbria**

**Subicular cortex**

Neocortex

169

## 10.2 Rhinal Cortex and Memory

Reports of H.M.'s case in the early 1950s triggered a major research effort to clarify the role of the medial temporal lobes in memory. Much of this research involved removing temporal lobe structures in laboratory species and assessing the effects of the removal on their memory. The first major success came in the 1970s from a line of research on monkeys. It was shown that large bilateral medial temporal lobe *lesions*, similar to H.M.'s, eliminated long-term *object-recognition memory* in monkeys—like H.M., the lesioned monkeys could not remember unfamiliar objects for more than a few seconds. Researchers then attempted to use this monkey model to identify the particular structures of the medial temporal lobes that are critical for the formation of long-term explicit memories of unfamiliar objects.

Some of the early research using the monkey model seemed to support the prevailing view that the hippocampal formation is the key memory structure of the medial temporal lobes; other early research also implicated the *amygdala*. However, in these early experiments, a large amount of *medial temporal cortex* was first removed to expose the hippocampus and amygdala above, and the contribution of its removal to the resulting memory deficits was never carefully assessed. Much of the medial temporal cortex damage in the experiments was to *rhinal cortex*. Rhinal cortex comprises two areas of cortex that lie around the **rhinal fissure**: **entorhinal cortex** and **perirhinal cortex**. Entorhinal cortex extends from subicular cortex to the upper lip of the rhinal fissure; perirhinal cortex is the cortex of the rhinal fissure. Much of the input to the hippocampus flows from the neocortex through the perirhinal and then entorhinal cortex.

Recent experiments have shown that hippocampus and amygdala lesions that do not damage rhinal cortex have little effect on object-recognition memory in either monkeys or rats. In contrast, monkeys or rats with lesions restricted to the rhinal cortex cannot remember unfamiliar objects for more than a few seconds.

### Rhinal fissure
A prominent fissure of the primate medial temporal lobe; *rhinal* means *of the nose* (in simple vertebrates, the function of the rhinal cortex is largely olfactory).

### Entorhinal cortex
An area of the medial temporal cortex that extends from subicular cortex to perirhinal cortex; recent evidence suggests that it plays an important role in object-recognition memory.

### Perirhinal cortex
The cortex of the rhinal fissure; recent evidence suggests that it plays an important role in object-recognition memory.

### Coloring notes
*First, color the rhinal fissure by coloring within the dashed lines. Then color the entorhinal and perirhinal cortices (singular: cortex). Notice the location of the hippocampal formation.*

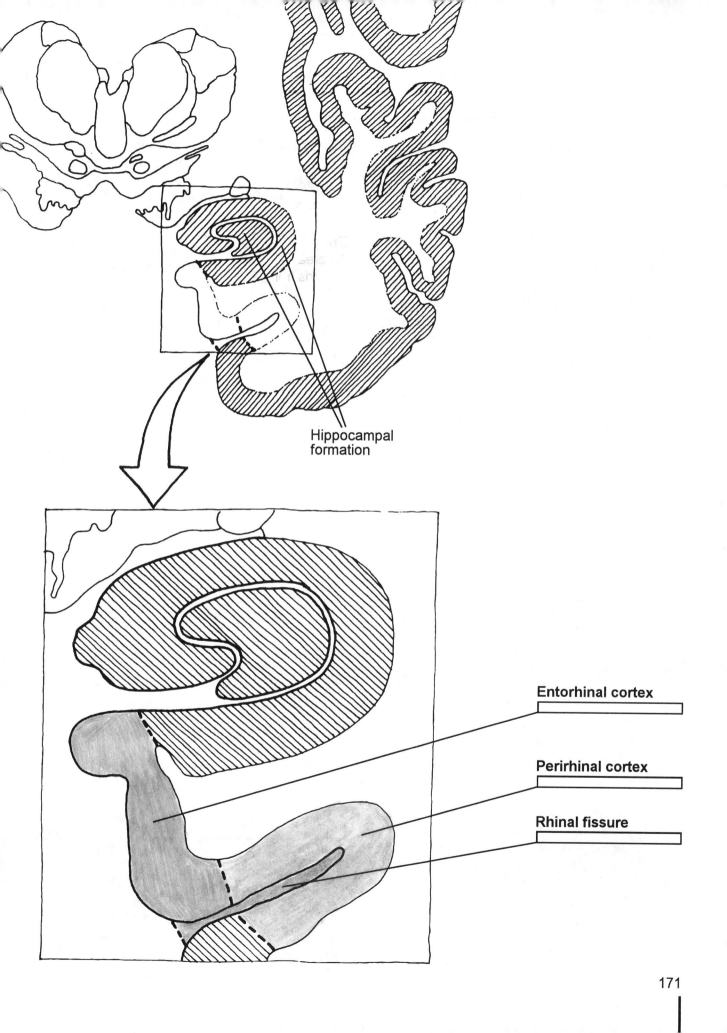

Hippocampal
formation

Entorhinal cortex

Perirhinal cortex

Rhinal fissure

## 10.3  Hippocampus and Spatial Memory

The recent discovery that the *rhinal cortex*, rather than the *hippocampal formation*, is the key object-recognition structure of the medial temporal lobes does not mean that the hippocampal formation is not involved in memory. Indeed, there is good evidence that the hippocampal formation plays a critical role in spatial memory, the ability to remember locations. For example, rats with lesions of the hippocampal formation have difficulty learning to run mazes, and food-caching birds with lesions of the hippocampal formation have difficulty finding seeds that they have cached.

Other evidence of the involvement of the hippocampal formation in spatial memory has come from neurophysiological studies of neurons in the **hippocampal pyramidal cell layer** of the hippocampus. The pyramidal cell layer is the middle of the three hippocampal layers; it is largely composed of the cell bodies of *pyramidal cells*—large cortical neurons with pyramid-shaped cell bodies, apical dendrites, and long axons. The key neurophysiological finding that has implicated the hippocampus in spatial memory is the finding that many pyramidal cells have *place fields*, that is, they fire at a high rate when the subject is in a particular location. For example, a particular hippocampal neuron may fire at a high rate only when the rat is in the start box of a familiar maze, but not when the rat is anywhere else in the maze. It seems, therefore, that the activity of hippocampal pyramidal cells is associated with the ability to recognize familiar places.

On the basis of differences in the architecture of the pyramidal cell layer, the hippocampus is often divided into four areas ($CA_1$, $CA_2$, $CA_3$, and $CA_4$) that are numbered in sequence from the subiculum to the tip of the hippocampus. *CA* stands for *cornu ammonis*, which is another term for *hippocampus*. The major **hippocampal circuit** runs from the entorhinal cortex, to the dentate gyrus, to $CA_3$, to $CA_1$.

### Hippocampal pyramidal cell layer
The middle layer of the hippocampus; it is largely composed of the cell bodies of pyramidal cells many of which have place fields.

### $CA_1$, $CA_2$, $CA_3$, and $CA_4$
The four regions of the hippocampus, numbered sequentially from the subiculum to the edge of the cortex.

### Hippocampal circuit
The major circuit of the hippocampal formation, which runs from the entorhinal cortex, to the dentate, to $CA_3$, to $CA_1$.

---

*Coloring notes*

*First, color the hippocampal pyramidal cell layer in the top illustration. Next, color all the arrows in the bottom illustration, which represent the major circuit of the hippocampus. Finally, color each of the four areas of the hippocampus a different color.*

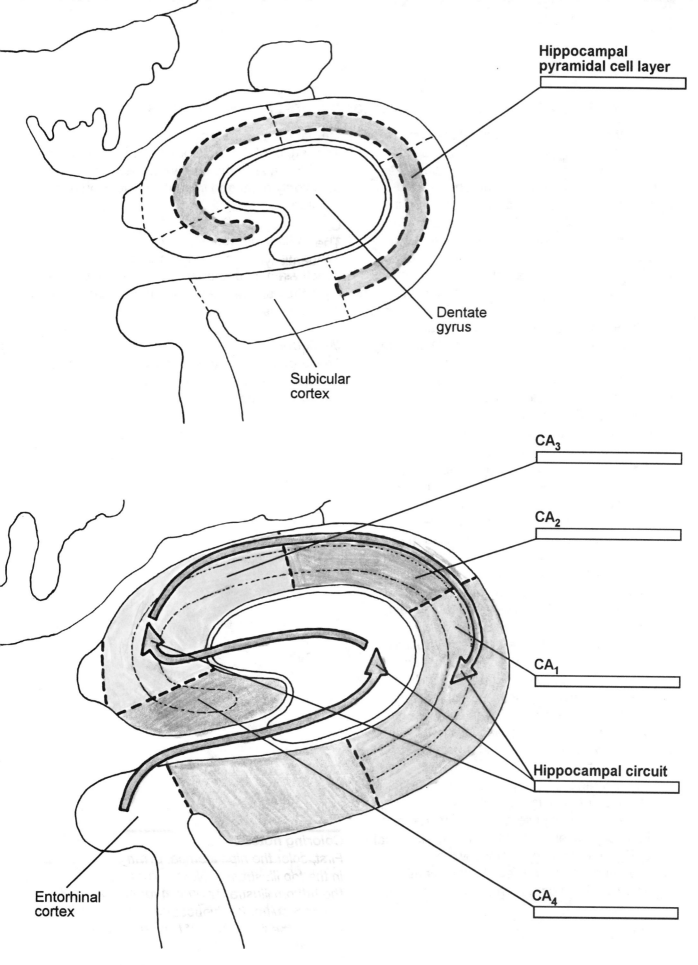

**Hippocampal
pyramidal cell layer**

Dentate
gyrus

Subicular
cortex

CA₃

CA₂

CA₁

Hippocampal circuit

Entorhinal
cortex

CA₄

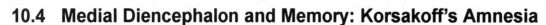

## 10.4 Medial Diencephalon and Memory: Korsakoff's Amnesia

Just as the case of H.M. provided the first indication of the important role played by the medial temporal lobes in memory, patients suffering from Korsakoff's syndrome were the first to implicate the **medial diencephalon** in memory.

Korsakoff's syndrome is a progressive disorder that is common in alcoholics; it results, to a large degree, from a deficiency in *thiamine* (vitamin B₁) consumption and a difficulty in metabolizing the little thiamine that is consumed.

Patients in the early stages of Korsakoff's syndrome often experience substantial memory impairment but are otherwise reasonably normal. Such patients typically have brain damage that is restricted to the medial diencephalon (i.e., to the areas of the *hypothalamus* and *thalamus* around the *third ventricle*). In its advanced stages, it is characterized by diffuse brain damage and a total breakdown of psychological functioning.

In order to identify the particular medial diencephalic structures that are involved in memory, neuroanatomists have studied the brains of deceased early Korsakoff's patients and have tried to identify those specific areas whose damage is associated with memory impairment. Early studies seemed to suggest that the **mammillary bodies** of the hypothalamus were the key memory structures, but then there were a few reports of patients with Korsakoff's amnesia but no mammillary body damage. More recent research has implicated the **mediodorsal nuclei** of the thalamus—virtually all Korsakoff patients with amnesia have damage to these nuclei.

Supporting the conclusion that mediosorsal nucleus damage is an important causal factor in Korsakoff's amnesia is the fact that neuropsychological patients with damage to the mediodorsal nuclei caused by strokes also suffer from memory impairment. Moreover, bilateral mediodorsal nucleus lesions cause memory deficits in both monkeys and rats.

**Medial diencephalon**
The region of the thalamus and hypothalamus on either side of the third ventricle; it is commonly damaged in patients with Korsakoff's disease.

**Mammillary bodies**
Two spherical nuclei of the medial hypothalamus, one on the left and one on the right; they are visible on the inferior surface of the brain just behind the pituitary.

**Mediodorsal nuclei**
The large nuclei of the medial dorsal thalamus; damage to these nuclei is associated with memory impairment.

**Coloring notes**

*Color the mammillary body and mediodorsal nucleus in the top illustration. Then, color the entire medial diencephalon in the bottom illustration.*

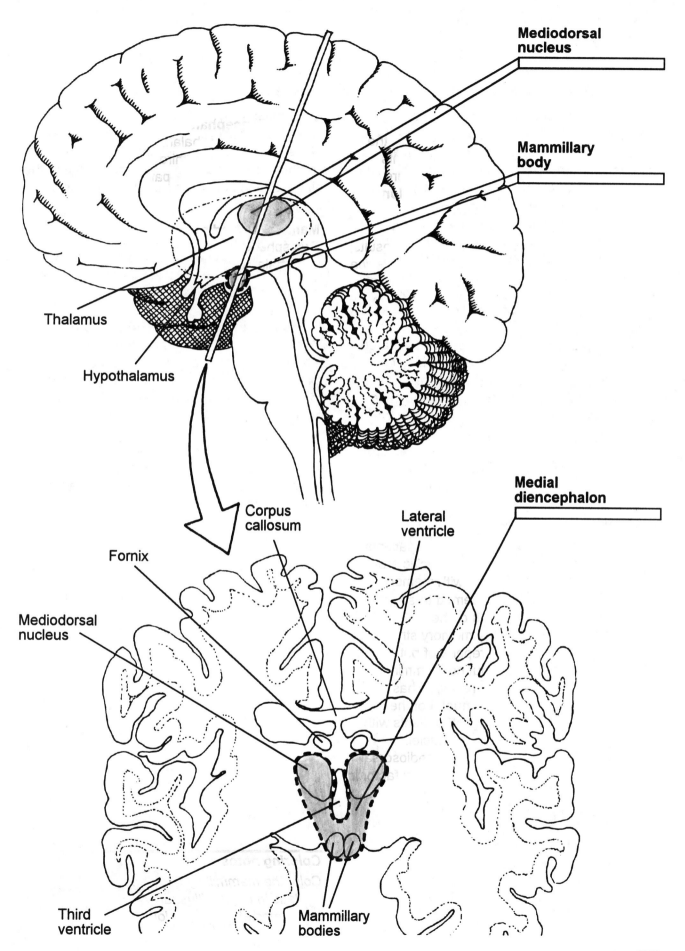

**Mediodorsal nucleus**

**Mammillary body**

Thalamus

Hypothalamus

**Medial diencephalon**

Corpus callosum

Lateral ventricle

Fornix

Mediodorsal nucleus

Third ventricle

Mammillary bodies

## 10.5 Basal Forebrain and Memory: Alzheimer's Amnesia

*Alzheimer's disease* is a cerebral degenerative disease of old age. Minor memory problems are among its early symptoms, but in its advanced stages, it is characterized by severe intellectual deterioration (e.g., by an inability to speak or even recognize one's own children). It culminates in death. Autopsy reveals widespread neural degeneration, *neurofibrils* (i.e., thread-like tangles in the cytoplasm of many neurons), and *amyloid plaques* (i.e., scar tissue composed of degenerating neurons interspersed with an abnormal protein called *amyloid*).

Although the neurodegeneration associated with Alzheimer's disease is widespread, it is particularly severe in the **basal forebrain**. The basal forebrain refers to the area at the base of the cerebral hemispheres just anterior to the *hypothalamus* in the vicinity of the *anterior commissure*. Three of its major structures are the **medial septum**, the **diagonal band of Broca**, and the **nucleus basilis of Meynert**.

The discovery of neurodegeneration in the basal forebrain of deceased Alzheimer's patients led to the hypothesis that the basal forebrain plays an important role in memory. The connections of the basal forebrain are consistent with this view; it is well connected to the medial temporal lobes, and it sends axons to all parts of the neocortex.

Many of the neurons of the basal forebrain are *cholinergic* (i.e., release the neurotransmitter *acetylcholine*). Indeed, the basal forebrain is the neocortex's only source of acetylcholine. Consequently, there is little acetylcholine in the cortexes of Alzheimer's patients. On the basis of this observation, it has been hypothesized that acetylcholine plays an important role in memory.

### Basal forebrain
The group of cholinergic structures at the base of the forebrain in the vicinity of the anterior commissure; it includes the medial septum, the diagonal band of Broca, and the nucleus basilis of Meynert.

### Medial septum
The medial region of the septal nucleus, which is located in the basal forebrain between the lateral ventricles.

### Diagonal bands of Broca (BROKE ah)
The major tracts, left and right, of the basal forebrain; they are largely composed of the axons of medial septal nuclei neurons coursing to the medial temporal lobes, but they also contain some cholinergic nuclei.

### Nuclei basilis of Meynert (MY nert)
A pair, left and right, of cholinergic basal forebrain nuclei located just below the anterior commissure.

---

*Coloring notes*

*In the top illustration, color the region of the basal forebrain by staying within the dashed lines. Then color the three pairs of basal forebrain structures in the bottom illustration.*

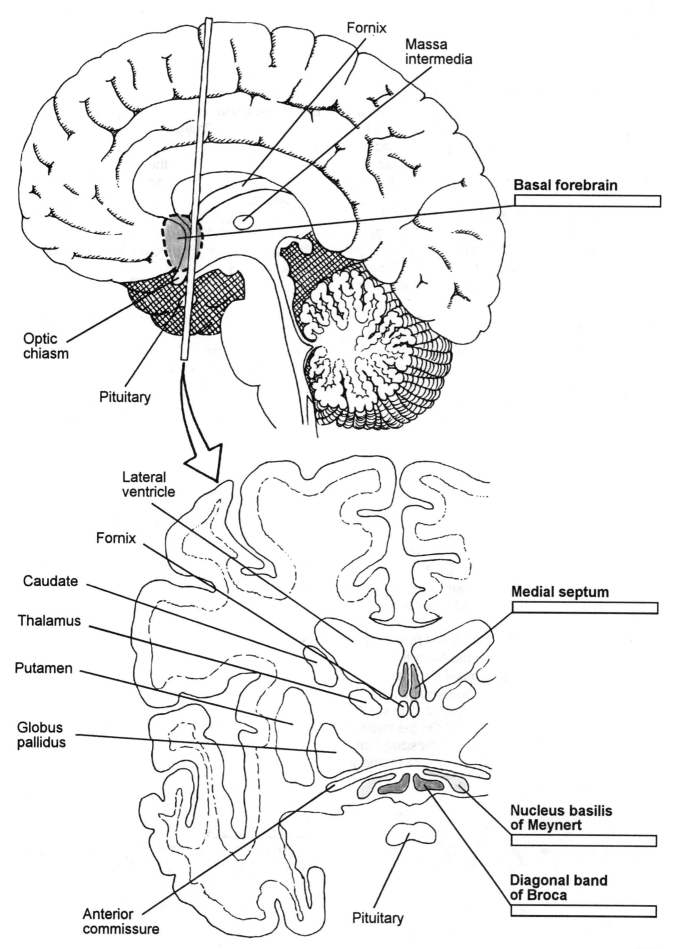

Fornix

Massa intermedia

**Basal forebrain**

Optic chiasm

Pituitary

Lateral ventricle

Fornix

Caudate

Thalamus

Putamen

Globus pallidus

Anterior commissure

Pituitary

**Medial septum**

**Nucleus basilis of Meynert**

**Diagonal band of Broca**

## Review Exercises: Brain Structures and Memory

Now it is time for you to pause and consolidate the terms and ideas that you have learned in the five learning units of Chapter 10. It is important that you overlearn them so that they do not quickly fade from your memory.

### Review Exercise 10.1

Turn to the illustrations in the five learning units of Chapter 10, and use the cover flap at the back of the book to cover the terms that run down the right-hand edge of each illustration page. Study the five illustrations in chronological sequence until you can identify each labeled structure. Once you have worked through the five illustrations twice without making an error, advance to Review Exercise 10.2.

### Review Exercise 10.2

Fill in the missing terms in the following illustrations. The correct answers are provided at the back of the book. Carefully review the material related to your incorrect answers.

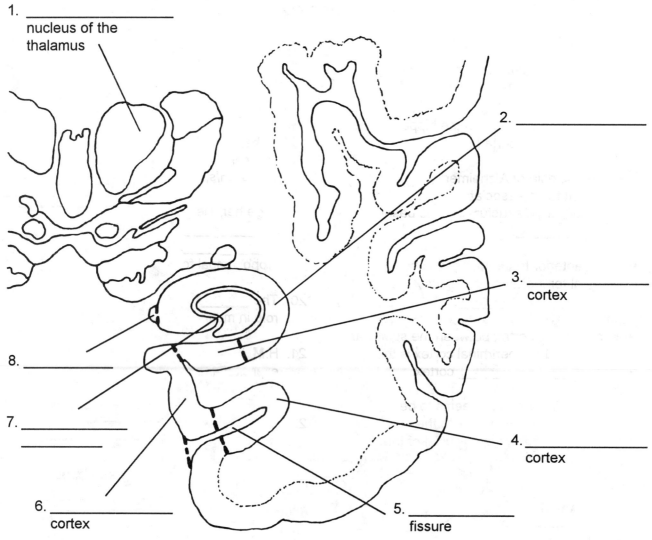

1. _____
   nucleus of the
   thalamus

2. _____

3. _____
   cortex

4. _____
   cortex

5. _____
   fissure

6. _____
   cortex

7. _____
   _____

8. _____

## Review Exercise 10.3

Without referring to Chapter 10, fill in each of the following blanks with the correct term from the chapter. The correct answers are provided at the back of the book. Carefully review the material related to your incorrect answers.

1. H.M.'s operation was a bilateral medial _____ lobectomy.

2. *CA* stands for *cornu ammonis*, which is another term for _____.

3. The neurons of the basal forebrain release _____ throughout the neocortex.

4. The process by which short-term memories are converted to long-term memories is called _____.

5. The hippocampus and adjacent _____ gyrus are allocortex.

6. The _____ cortex is a transition area of cortex between the hippocampus and entorhinal cortex.

7. The amnesia of Alzheimer's disease is thought to be associated with degeneration of cholinergic structures of the basal _____.

8. Just anterior to the hippocampus is another medial temporal lobe nucleus, the _____.

9. The area of cortex between the subicular cortex and the perirhinal cortex is the _____ cortex.

10. Korsakoff's amnesia seems to be associated with damage to the _____ nuclei of the thalamus.

11. At the very edge of the cortex is the hippocampal CA ____ region.

12. The diagonal band of Broca and the nucleus basilis of Meynert are located just inferior to the _____ commissure.

13. Many pyramidal cells of the hippocampus have _____ fields.

14. The middle layer of the hippocampus is the _____ cell layer.

15. H.M. cannot form new long-term _____ memories.

16. Korsakoff's patients almost always have extensive damage to the structures of the medial _____.

17. Bilateral lesions of _____ cortex disrupt object-recognition memory, even when they do not damage the hippocampal formation or amygdala.

18. Alzheimer's disease is associated with widespread neural degeneration, neurofibrils, and _____ plaques.

19. Together, the _____, the _____ gyrus, and the _____ cortex compose the hippocampal formation.

20. The _____ plays an important role in memory for spatial location.

21. H.M. can form normal _____ explicit memories and normal long-term _____ memories.

22. Marking the boundary between the entorhinal cortex and the perirhinal cortex is the superior lip of the _____ fissure.

## Review Exercise 10.4

Below in alphabetical order is a list of all the terms and definitions that you learned in Chapter 10. Cover the definitions with a sheet of paper, and work your way down the list of terms, defining them to yourself as you go. Repeat this process until you have gone through the list twice without an error. Then, cover the terms and work your way down the list of definitions, providing the correct terms as you go. Repeat this second process until you have gone through the list twice without an error.

| Basal forebrain | The group of cholinergic structures at the base of the forebrain in the vicinity of the anterior commissure; it includes the medial septum, the diagonal band of Broca, and the nucleus basilis of Meynert. |
| --- | --- |
| $CA_1$, $CA_2$, $CA_3$, and $CA_4$ | The four regions of the hippocampus, numbered sequentially from the subiculum to the edge of the cortex. |
| Dentate gyrus | The allocortical gyrus in the medial temporal lobe; in cross section, it is a C-shaped structure that curves around the edge of the hippocampus. |
| Diagonal bands of Broca | The major tracts, left and right, of the basal forebrain; they are largely composed of the axons of medial septal nuclei neurons coursing to the medial temporal lobes, but they also contain some cholinergic nuclei. |
| Entorhinal cortex | An area of the medial temporal cortex that extends from subicular cortex to perirhinal cortex; recent evidence suggests that it plays an important role in object-recognition memory. |
| Fimbria | A bundle of axons that courses along the medial surface of the hippocampus; it carries signals from the hippocampus to the fornix. |
| Hippocampal circuit | The major circuit of the hippocampal formation, which runs from the entorhinal cortex, to the dentate, to $CA_3$, to $CA_1$. |
| Hippocampal formation | The medial temporal lobe structure that is composed of the hippocampus, dentate gyrus, and subicular cortex; also referred to as the *hippocampal complex*. |
| Hippocampal pyramidal cell layer | The middle layer of the hippocampus; it is largely composed of the cell bodies of pyramidal cells, many of which have place fields. |
| Hippocampus | The large fold of medial temporal lobe allocortex that is located between the edge of the cortical mantle and the subicular cortex; its structure in cross section reminded early neuroanatomists of a seahorse (*hippocampus* means *seahorse*). |

| | |
|---|---|
| Mammillary bodies | Two spherical nuclei of the medial hypothalamus, one on the left and one on the right; they are visible on the inferior surface of the brain just behind the pituitary. |
| Medial diencephalon | The region of the thalamus and hypothalamus on either side of the third ventricle; it is commonly damaged in patients with Korsakoff's disease. |
| Medial septum | The medial region of the septal nucleus, which is located in the basal forebrain between the lateral ventricles. |
| Mediodorsal nuclei | The large nuclei of the medial dorsal thalamus; damage to these nuclei is associated with memory impairment. |
| Nuclei basilis of Meynert | A pair, left and right, of cholinergic basal forebrain nuclei located just below the anterior commissure. |
| Perirhinal cortex | The medial temporal cortex of the rhinal fissure; recent evidence suggests that it plays an important role in object-recognition memory. |
| Rhinal fissure | A prominent fissure of the primate medial temporal lobe; *rhinal* means *of the nose* (in simple vertebrates, the function of rhinal cortex is largely olfactory). |
| Subicular cortex | The area of transitional cortex between hippocampal allocortex and entorhinal cortex; subicular cortex is folded like a supporting platform beneath the hippocampus and dentate gyrus (*subicular* means *supporting*). |

# *Chapter 11:* Motivational Systems of the Brain

At any one time, we engage in only a small number of the behaviors that we have the capacity to perform. For example, right now, I am writing this introduction and sipping an espresso rather than sleeping, reading, beating my djembe, ironing my shirts, or any of the other innumerable acts of which I am capable. The processes that influence your choice of behaviors and the intensity with which you engage in them are called *motivational processes*.

The motivational processes that are critical for the survival of our species appear to have particular brain circuits dedicated to them. For example, there are structures in your brain that seem to be specifically involved in your motivation to eat, to drink, to sleep, to flee, to reproduce, and so on. It is these dedicated structures that are the focus of this chapter. The neural mechanisms of motivation have been studied almost exclusively in laboratory animals, but for the sake of consistency with the rest of the book, it is their human equivalents that are illustrated in this chapter.

The following are the six learning units of Chapter 11:

11.1 Hypothalamus and Eating

11.2 Subfornical Organ and Deprivation-Induced Thirst

11.3 Mesotelencephalic Dopamine System and Pleasure

11.4 Neural Mechanisms of Fear and Anxiety

11.5 Reticular Formation and Sleep

11.6 Suprachiasmatic Nucleus and Circadian Rhythms

11.7 Brain Stem Sex Circuits

## 11.1 Hypothalamus and Eating

In the 1950s, research suggested that the motivation to eat was controlled by two areas of the hypothalamus. Large bilateral lesions of the **ventromedial nucleus** (VMN), created rats that ate incessantly and gained massive amounts of weight. In contrast, large bilateral lesions of the **lateral hypothalamus** (LH) created rats that refused food and had to be force-fed in order to be kept alive. These findings led to the view that the VMN is a satiety center, which inhibits eating, and the LH is a hunger center, which stimulates eating.

Subsequent research has not been kind to the 1950s hypothalamic theory of hunger and satiety. It is now clear that LH lesions produce general motor impairment and a general insensitivity to sensory stimulation, not a specific disruption of eating. It is also clear that the idea that the VMN is a satiety center requires two important qualifications. The first of these qualifications is that the overeating and obesity produced by large VMN lesions result to a significant degree from damage to nuclei outside the VMN. In particular, VMN lesions damage fibers coursing through the area that ultimately terminate in the **paraventricular nuclei** of the hypothalamus, and some of the effects of VMN lesions result from damage to these fibers of passage. The second qualification is that the overeating produced by VMN lesions is a secondary, rather than a primary, effect of the lesions. VMN lesions promote the conversion of blood glucose to body fat and block the conversion of body fat back to glucose. Thus, rats and humans with VMN damage overeat, not because their satiety center has been destroyed, but because stores of utilizable energy (i.e., blood glucose) become dangerously low as soon as they stop eating. Thus, the VMN is more appropriately viewed as a metabolic center, not a satiety center.

### Ventromedial nucleus
The major nucleus of the ventral medial region of the hypothalamus; large bilateral lesions of this nucleus produce overeating and obesity by promoting the conversion of blood glucose to body fat.

### Lateral hypothalamus
The large lateral region of the hypothalamus; large bilateral lesions of this area produce various motor disturbances and a general insensitivity to stimulation.

### Paraventricular nucleus
A nucleus in the dorsal medial region of the hypothalamus, just above the dorsomedial nucleus; bilateral lesions to this nucleus or to the fibers that project to it through the ventromedial hypothalamus produce overeating and obesity.

### Coloring notes
*First, color the paraventricular nucleus, lateral hypothalamus, and ventromedial nucleus in the top illustration. Then, using the same three colors, color the same three structures in the bottom illustration. Note that in the top illustration the lateral hypothalamus is largely hidden by the other hypothalamic nuclei.*

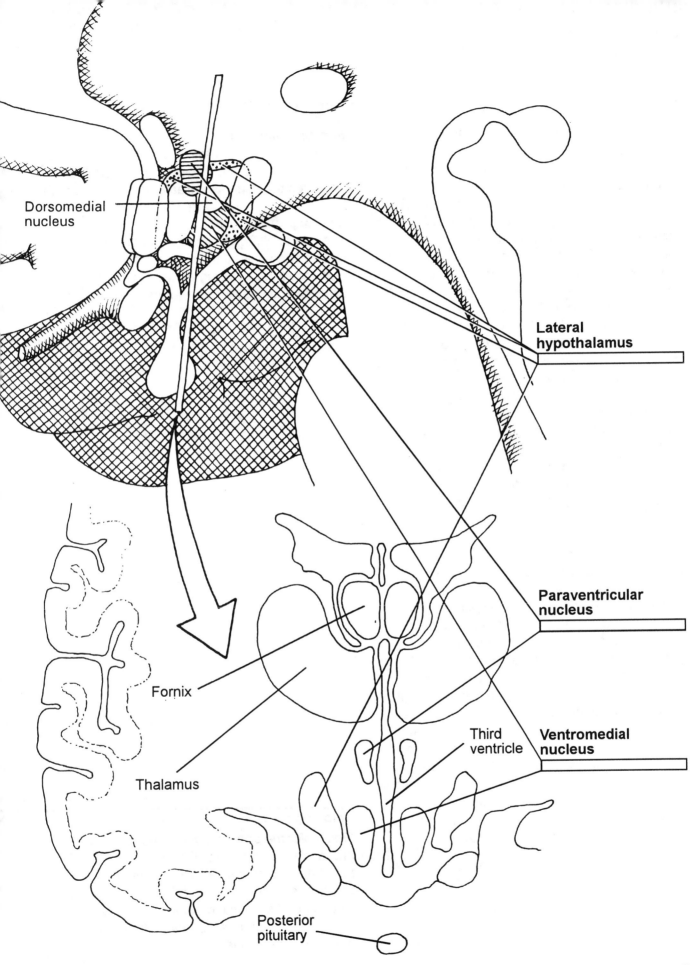

Dorsomedial
nucleus

**Lateral
hypothalamus**

**Paraventricular
nucleus**

Fornix

Third
ventricle

**Ventromedial
nucleus**

Thalamus

Posterior
pituitary

## 11.2  Subfornical Organ and Deprivation-Induced Thirst

Severe water deprivation disrupts the fluid balance of the body in two different ways. It produces *hypovolemia*, a reduction of blood volume, and it produces an increase in the concentration of salts in the extracellular fluid, which draws water out of cells by the resulting increase in *osmotic pressure* on cell membranes. Both disruptions of the body's fluid balance initiate physiological changes that reduce further water loss and its physiological consequences. In addition, both disruptions act on certain areas of the brain to induce thirst.

Hypovolemia causes the *kidneys* to release a hormone called *renin*, which causes *angiotensin II* to be synthesized in the blood, and then angiotensin II induces thirst by acting on the **subfornical organ**. The subfornical organ is a region of the brain that is located along the midline in the ceiling of the *third ventricle*, just below the *fornix,* as its name implies. It is a region of the brain that is rich in angiotensin II receptors. Microinjections of angiotensin II directly into the subfornical organ produce extreme thirst in experimental animals.

Increased osmotic pressure induces thirst by a mechanism different from the mechanism that mediates hypovolemic thirst. Increased osmotic pressure is detected by specialized cells in the brain that are called *osmoreceptors.* *Osmoreceptors* are located in the **lateral preoptic area** of the hypothalamus. Microinjections of concentrated salt solutions directly into this area produce extreme thirst in experimental animals.

### Subfornical organ
The structure in the ceiling of the third ventricle, just below the fornix, where angiotensin II acts to induce the thirst associated with hypovolemia.

### Lateral preoptic area
The lateral half of the preoptic region of the hypothalamus; it contains osmoreceptors that respond to increases in extracellular salt concentrations by inducing thirst.

### Coloring notes
*First, color the subfornical organ and lateral preoptic area in the top illustration. Then, using the same two colors, color the same two structures in the bottom illustration. Note the location of the medial preoptic area and the suprachiasmatic nucleus, optic chiasm, fornix, and anterior commissure.*

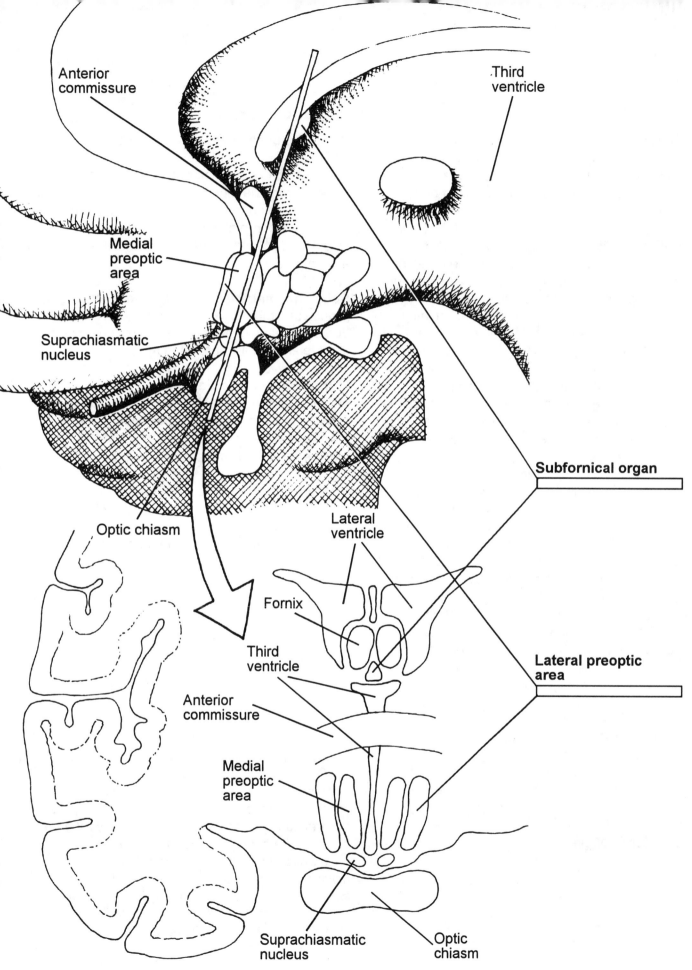

Anterior commissure

Third ventricle

Medial preoptic area

Suprachiasmatic nucleus

Optic chiasm

Subfornical organ

Lateral ventricle

Fornix

Third ventricle

Anterior commissure

Lateral preoptic area

Medial preoptic area

Suprachiasmatic nucleus

Optic chiasm

## 11.3  Mesotelencephalic Dopamine System and Pleasure

The members of many species, including humans, will press a lever or a button to deliver small electrical currents through implanted electrodes to certain sites in their own brains. This phenomenon is known as *intracranial self-stimulation* (ICSS). The discovery of intracranial self-stimulation was important because it provided a method of studying those areas of the brain involved in the experience of pleasure. The assumption has been that the sites in the brain that support intracranial self-stimulation are components of circuits that are normally active when subjects experience the pleasure associated with natural motivated behaviors (e.g., eating, drinking, and copulation).

Many of the sites in the brain that support intracranial self-stimulation are in a diffuse pathway known as the **mesotelencephalic dopamine system**--or they are directly connected to it. The neurons of the mesotelencephalic dopamine system have their cell bodies in one of two structures in the midbrain tegmentum: in the **substantia nigra** or the **ventral tegmental area**—the ventral tegmental area is just medial to the substantia nigra. The axons of these two structures project diffusely to a variety of telencephalic sites including *frontal cortex, striatum, septum, cingulate cortex, amygdala*, and **nucleus accumbens**, which is located between the striatum and the basal forebrain. The *nigrostriatal pathway*, which is damaged in cases of Parkinson's disease, is a component of the mesotelencephalic dopamine system.

Recent research has implicated the mesotelencephalic dopamine system in several motivated behaviors including self-administering addictive drugs, sexual behavior, and eating. The activity of the nucleus accumbens, in particular, appears to play a critical role in the experience of pleasure.

**Mesotelencephalic dopamine system**
(MEEZ oh TEL en se FAL ik)
The system of dopaminergic neurons that projects from the tegmentum of the mesencephalon to various telencephalic sites, including the frontal cortex, striatum, septum, cingulate cortex, amygdala, and nucleus accumbens.

**Substantia nigra** (sub STAN tchee a  NYE gra)
A nucleus of the tegmentum; it contains the cell bodies of many of the neurons that compose the mesotelencephalic dopamine system.

**Ventral tegmental area**
The area of the ventral tegmentum medial to the substantia nigra; it contains the cell bodies of many of the neurons that compose the mesotelencephalic dopamine system.

**Nucleus accumbens** (a KUM bens)
A nucleus that is located between the striatum and the basal forebrain; it is a major terminal of the mesotelencephalic dopamine system.

---

*Coloring notes*

*First, color the three dopaminergic structures in the top illustration: the nucleus accumbens, the substantia nigra, and the ventral tegmental area. Then, in the bottom illustration, color the substantia nigra and ventral tegmental area, using the same colors that you used for these structures in the top illustration. Finally, color all the projections (i.e., all the arrows) of mesotelencephalic dopamine system in the bottom illustration.*

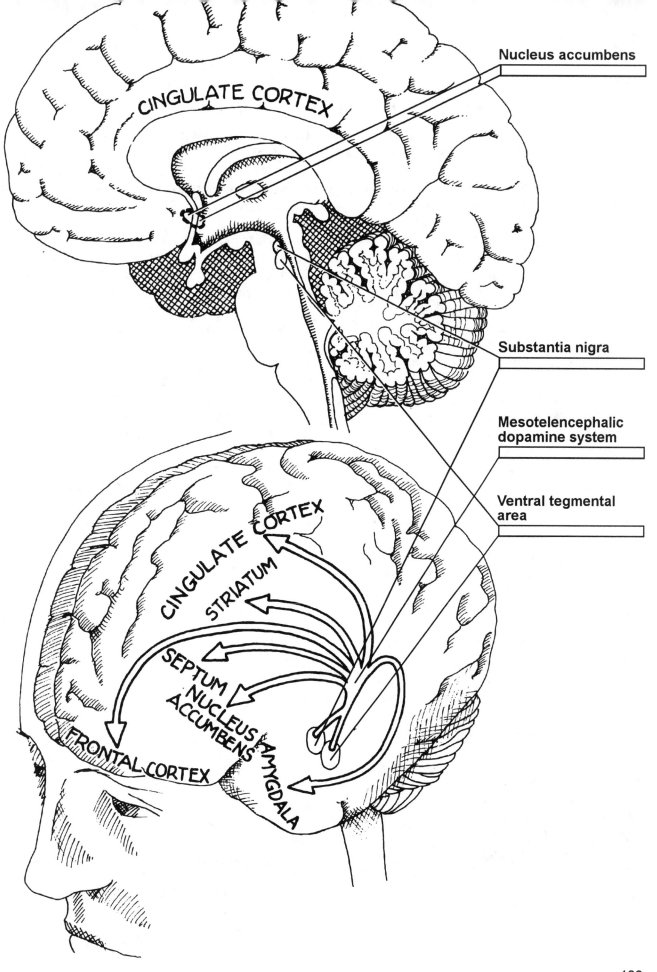

Nucleus accumbens

Substantia nigra

Mesotelencephalic
dopamine system

Ventral tegmental
area

CINGULATE CORTEX

CINGULATE CORTEX

STRIATUM

SEPTUM

NUCLEUS
ACCUMBENS

AMYGDALA

FRONTAL CORTEX

## 11.4   Neural Mechanisms of Fear and Anxiety

Much of the research on the neural bases of emotions has focused on fear and anxiety. *Fear* is an intense defensive reaction to the current or imminent presence of threat, whereas *anxiety* is a less intense, more long-term defensive reaction to the chronic anticipation of threat.

Two telencephalic structures have been implicated in the experience of fear and anxiety. One is **orbitofrontal cortex**, the area of cortex on the inferior surface of the frontal lobe. Both humans and monkeys with damage to this area experience little fear or anxiety. This is not always advantageous. Without the motivating force of fear and anxiety, orbitofrontal patients fail to complete tasks, to plan ahead, to consider the consequences of their misbehavior, or to be concerned about how they are viewed by others.

The other telencephalic structure that is important for the experience of fear and anxiety is the **amygdala**. Lesions of the amygdala reduce fear and anxiety, whereas electrical stimulation of the amygdala induces subjective feelings of fear and anxiety, elicits a variety of defensive behaviors, and activates the *sympathetic nervous system.*

The following is one view of the neural mechanisms of fear and anxiety. The orbitofrontal cortex is the site from which cognitive cortical processing influences the amygdala and other limbic structures, which mediate feelings of emotion. In particular, the amygdala, which receives input from all the sensory systems, is the limbic structure where feelings of fear and anxiety are linked to particular stimuli and to appropriate brain stem response circuits. These brain stem circuits activate and organize defensive responses—electrical stimulation of the **hypothalamus** or the **raphé nuclei** can activate various sequences of defensive behavior (e.g., flight, threat, defensive attack), depending on the location of the electrode and the situation.

### Orbitofrontal cortex
The cortex on the inferior surface of the frontal lobes (*orbito* means *near the eye sockets or orbits*); it is thought to be the area through which cortical processing influences the limbic system.

### Amygdala (a MIG duh la)
The almond-shaped limbic nucleus that is located in the medial temporal lobe, just anterior to the hippocampus; it is thought to link feelings of fear and anxiety to appropriate stimuli and defensive responses.

### Hypothalamus
The diencephalic structure that is located just inferior to the anterior thalamus; electrical stimulation of some areas of the hypothalamus can elicit defensive responses.

### Raphé nuclei (Ra fay)
The vertical sheet of serotonergic nuclei that runs along the midline of the reticular formation; electrical stimulation of some of the raphé nuclei can elicit defensive responses.

---

*Coloring notes*

*Color the major forebrain structures involved in fear and anxiety: the orbitofrontal cortex, the amygdala, and the hypothalamus. Then, color the raphé nuclei of the reticular formation.*

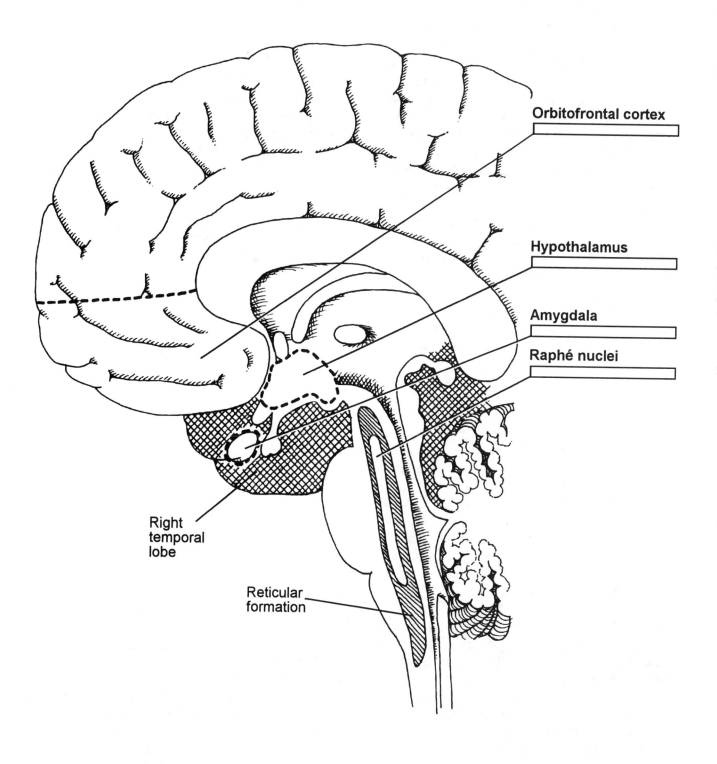

Orbitofrontal cortex

Hypothalamus

Amygdala

Raphé nuclei

Right
temporal
lobe

Reticular
formation

## 11.5 Reticular Formation and Sleep

Each night's sleep includes sleep of two fundamentally different sorts. *Slow-wave sleep* (SWS), the more prevalent of the two kinds of sleep, is associated with high-amplitude slow waves in the cortical EEG (electroencephalogram). In addition, each night there are four or five periods of *rapid-eye-movement sleep* (REM sleep), which typically last between 10 and 40 minutes each. REM sleep is associated with low-amplitude fast cortical EEG waves, rapid eye movements (REMs) behind closed lids, total relaxation of core body muscles, sympathetic nervous system activation, and dreaming.

Structures of the **pontine reticular formation** (i.e., the portion of the reticular formation within the pons) play a role in both REM sleep and SWS. Microinjections of *cholinergic agonists*, chemicals that increase the effects of the neurotransmitter *acetylcholine*, directly into the pontine reticular formation increase the proportion of REM sleep. Moreover, electrical stimulation of various nuclei within the pontine reticular formation elicits the various individual physiological responses that are associated with REM sleep (e.g., REMs, low-amplitude fast EEG, and core muscle relaxation). These findings indicate that REM sleep is controlled by a network of cholinergic nuclei within the pontine reticular formation.

Two other structures of the pontine reticular formation are involved in SWS: the **locus coeruleus** and the **raphé nuclei**. The locus coeruleus is a *noradrenergic* (norepinephrine-releasing) nucleus that is located in the pontine reticular formation near the boundary between the pons and the midbrain, and the raphé nuclei are a vertical sheet of *serotonergic* nuclei that run down the midline of the reticular formation. Both structures are active during SWS, but inactive during REM sleep.

Thus, it appears that the pontine reticular formation facilitates REM sleep through its cholinergic circuits and SWS through its noradrenergic and serotonergic circuits.

**Pontine reticular formation** (pon TEEN)
The portion of the reticular formation that is located in the pons; it contains cholinergic nuclei that play a role in REM sleep and noradrenergic and serotonergic nuclei that play a role in SWS.

**Locus coeruleus** (LOE kus  se RULE ee us)
A noradrenergic pontine nucleus near the boundary between the pons and midbrain; many of its neurons are active during SWS and inactive during REM sleep.

**Raphé nuclei** (RA fay)
The vertical sheet of serotonergic nuclei that runs along the midline of the reticular formation; many of its neurons are active during SWS and inactive during REM sleep.

---

### Coloring notes

*First, color the locus coeruleus. Then, color the raphé nuclei—cross the dashed lines to color those portions of the raphé nuclei that extend outside the pons. Finally, color the uncolored portions of the pontine reticular formation—stay within the dashed lines; color only the pintine prtion of the reticular formation.*

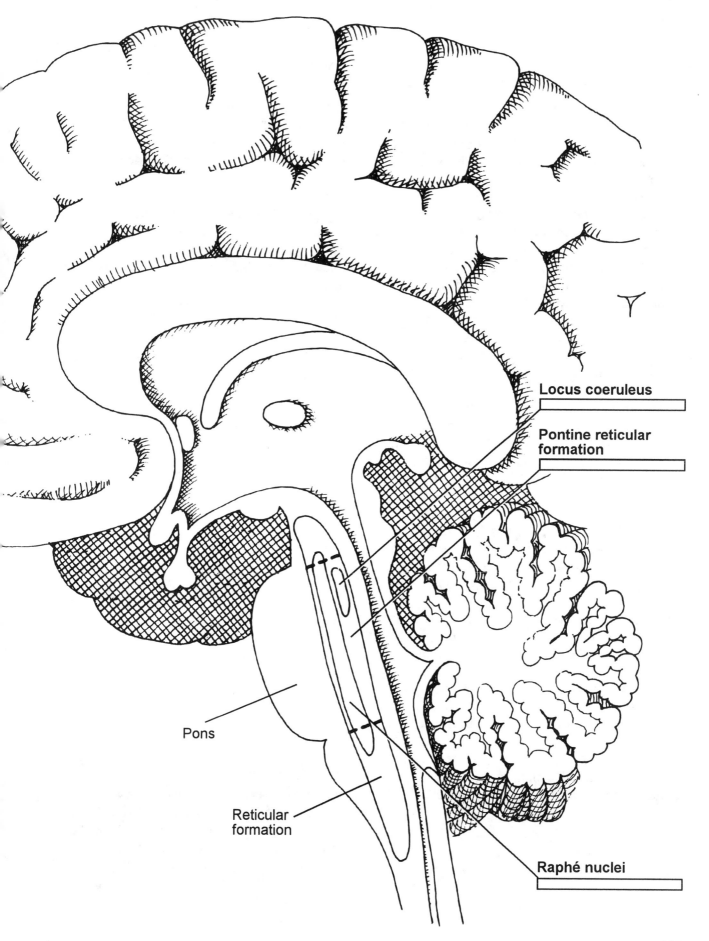

Locus coeruleus

Pontine reticular
formation

Pons

Reticular
formation

Raphé nuclei

193

## 11.6 Suprachiasmatic Nucleus and Circadian Rhythms

The behavioral and physiological responses of most surface-dwelling animals display *circadian rhythms* (rhythms lasting about 1 day). The most obvious circadian rhythm is the daily cycle of sleep and wakefulness that is displayed by virtually all surface-dwelling species.

Circadian rhythms do not require external cues such as changes in light; even animals maintained from birth in totally constant laboratory environments display circadian rhythms. The maintenance of circadian rhythms in the absence of external cues indicates that they are maintained by an internal timing mechanism referred to as a *circadian clock*. The circadian clock is located just above the *optic chiasm* in the **suprachiasmatic nuclei** of the hypothalamus. Lesions of the suprachiasmatic nuclei abolish all circadian rhythms, even in the presence of a circadian light-dark cycle.

Under constant laboratory conditions, each individual's circadian cycles are regular, but they are usually longer than 24 hours; for example, a subject maintained in a sound proof room with continuous lighting might display circadian cycles of 26.2 hours. In contrast, under natural conditions, circadian cycles average exactly 24 hours in length because they become synchronized to various precise temporal cues in the environment, the most important being the light-dark cycle. Cues that can set the duration of circadian cycles are called *zeitgebers* (pronounced ZITE gabe ers), which means *time givers*.

By which neural path does the light-dark zeitgeber influence circadian rhythms? The answer is by way of the **retinohypothalamic tracts**. A retinohypothalamic tract leaves each eye as part of the *optic nerve* and then branches off from it at the *optic chiasm* to project bilaterally to the suprachiasmatic nuclei.

### Suprachiasmatic nuclei

A pair of small hypothalamic nuclei that are located just superior to the optic chiasm; the location of the circadian timing mechanism.

### Retinohypothalamic tracts

Tracts that leave each eye as part of the optic nerve and project bilaterally to the suprachiasmatic nuclei; the neural paths by which the light-dark cycle influences circadian rhythms.

### Coloring notes

*First, color the tiny suprachiasmatic nucleus in the top illustration. Then, using the same color, color the suprachiasmatic nuclei in the bottom illustration. Finally, in the bottom illustration, color the retinohypothalamic tract by staying within the dashed lines. Note that for clarity the size of the retinohypothalamic tracts has been exaggerated.*

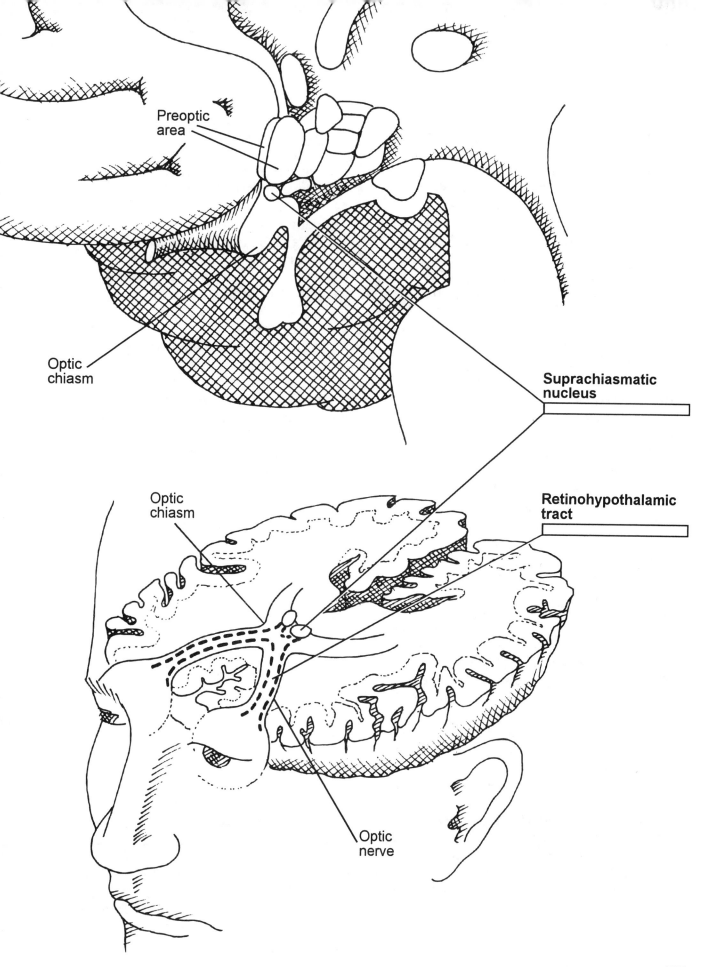

Preoptic
area

Optic
chiasm

**Suprachiasmatic
nucleus**

Optic
chiasm

**Retinohypothalamic
tract**

Optic
nerve

195

## 11.7 Brain Stem Sex Circuits

Research in laboratory rats suggests that the *hypothalamus* is an important structure for motivating both female and male copulatory behavior. In females, electrical stimulation of the **ventromedial nucleus** (VMN) of the hypothalamus facilitates copulation, and VMN lesions inhibit it. The influence of the VMN on female copulation seems to be mediated by a path that descends from the VMN to the **periaqueductal gray** (PAG); destruction of this tract or of the PAG itself eliminates copulation in females. Because the PAG also plays a role in *analgesia*, one of its functions may be to reduce in females any pain associated with copulation.

In contrast, in males it is the **medial preoptic area** of the hypothalamus that plays the major role in the motivation of copulatory behavior. Electrical stimulation of the medial preoptic area elicits copulatory behavior in males, and lesions of the area abolish it. Moreover, copulatory behavior can be reinstated in castrated males by medial preoptic area microimplants of *testosterone*. The influence of the medial preoptic area on male sexual behavior seems to be mediated by a pathway to the **lateral tegmental field** of the mesencephalic and pontine reticular formation; destruction of this pathway disrupts male copulatory behavior.

Given the differential involvement of various areas of the hypothalamus in male and female copulatory behaviors, it is not surprising that anatomical differences between male and female hypothalami have been identified in several species, including humans. The best documented of these gender differences is the rat **sexually dimorphic nucleus**. Located in the medial preoptic area, it is several times bigger in males than in females. The sexually dimorphic nuclei do not have an obvious direct equivalent in humans, but gender differences have been identified in several nearby hypothalamic nuclei.

In non primate mammals, estrogen and testosterone must be present for sexual motivation to occur in females and males, respectively. In humans, testosterone seems to be the critical hormone for both sexes.

**Ventromedial nucleus**
The major nucleus of the ventromedial hypothalamus; it plays a role in female copulatory behavior.

**Periaqueductal gray**
The area of the mesencephalon around the cerebral aqueduct; it plays a role in female copulatory behavior via a pathway from the ventromedial nucleus.

**Medial preoptic area**
The medial area of the preoptic hypothalamus; it plays a role in male copulatory behavior.

**Lateral tegmental field**
An area of the mesencephalic and pontine reticular formation just anterior to the fourth ventricle; it plays a role in male copulatory behavior via a pathway from the ventromedial nucleus.

**Sexually dimorphic nucleus**
A nucleus of the medial preoptic area that is several times bigger in male rats than in female rats.

---

*Coloring notes*
*First, color the sexually dimorphic nucleus. Then, color the medial preoptic area, which contains it, and the ventromedial nucleus. Finally, color the lateral tegmental field and the PAG.*

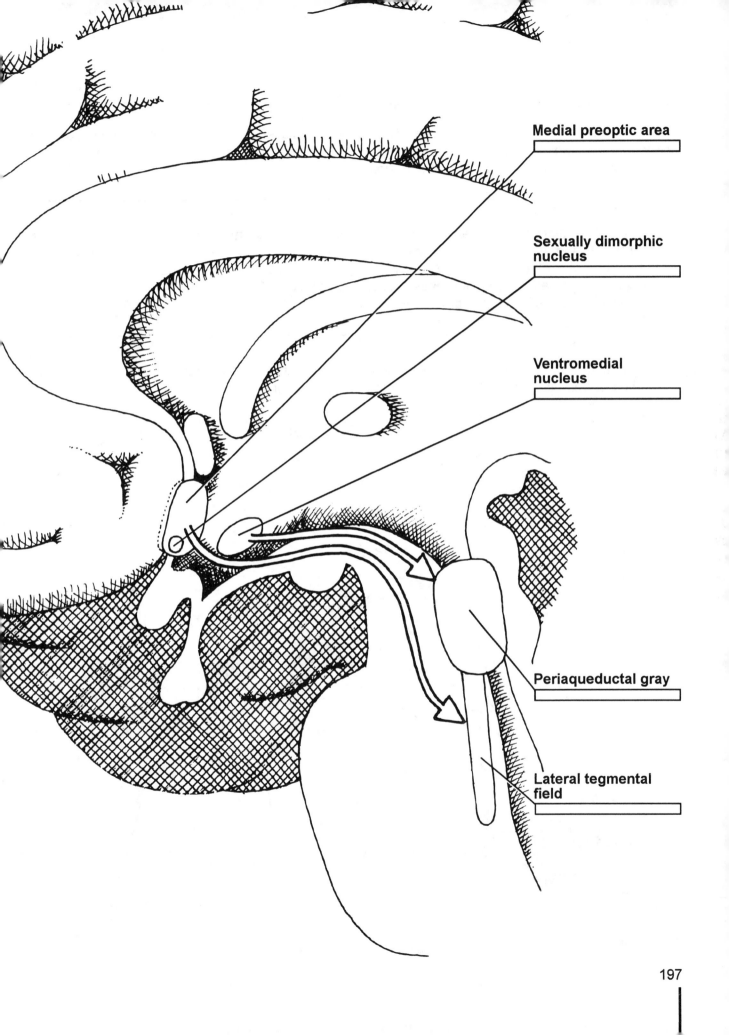

Medial preoptic area

Sexually dimorphic nucleus

Ventromedial nucleus

Periaqueductal gray

Lateral tegmental field

## Review Exercises: Motivational Systems of the Brain

Now it is time for you to pause and consolidate the terms and ideas that you have learned in the seven learning units of Chapter 11. It is important that you overlearn them so that they do not quickly fade from your memory.

### Review Exercise 11.1

Turn to the illustrations in the seven learning units of Chapter 11, and use the cover flap at the back of the book to cover the terms that run down the right-hand edge of each illustration page. Study the seven illustrations in chronological sequence until you can identify each labeled structure. Once you have worked through all seven illustrations twice without making an error, advance to Review Exercise 11.2.

### Review Exercise 11.2

Fill in the missing terms in the following illustration. The answers are provided at the back of the book. Carefully review the material related to your incorrect answers.

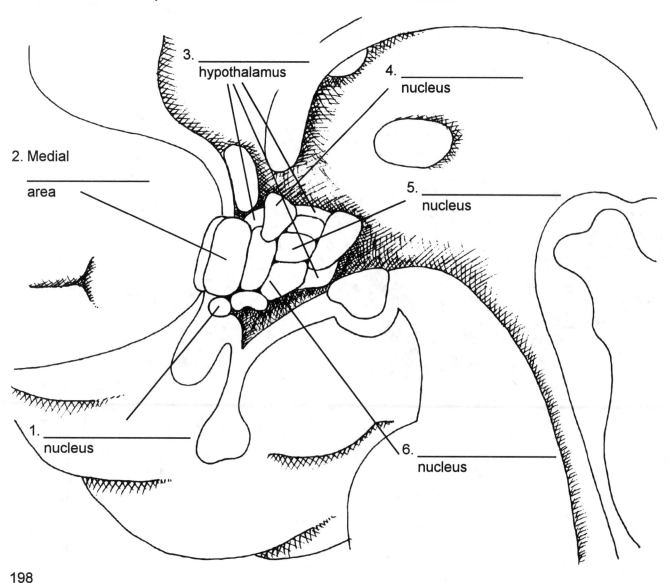

3. _____ hypothalamus

4. _____ nucleus

2. Medial _____ area

5. _____ nucleus

1. _____ nucleus

6. _____ nucleus

## Review Exercise 11.3

Without referring to Chapter 11, fill in each of the following blanks with the correct term from the chapter. The correct answers are provided at the back of the book. Carefully review the material related to your incorrect answers.

1. The _____ nucleus of the hypothalamus was once thought to be a satiety center; and the _____ hypothalamus was thought to be a hunger center.

2. Light influences the circadian clock via the _____ tracts.

3. Neurons of the serotonergic _____ nuclei and the noradrenergic locus _____ are active during SWS.

4. Angiotensin II induces thirst through its effect on the _____ organ.

5. The _____ nuclei are thought to be involved in defensive behavior and SWS.

6. Cell bodies of mesotelencephalic dopamine neurons are located in the _____ _____ and the ventral _____ area.

7. The circadian clock is located in the _____ nuclei.

8. Bilateral lesions of the _____ cortex reduce fear and anxiety.

9. REM sleep is controlled by cholinergic neurons in the _____ reticular formation.

10. The _____ is a limbic site at which fear is thought to be linked to particular sensory stimuli.

11. Increases in osmotic pressure are detected by osmoreceptors in the lateral _____ area.

12. Lesions of the _____ hypothalamus disrupt motor behavior and produce a general insensitivity to sensory stimulation.

13. Slow-wave sleep is punctuated by periods of _____ sleep.

14. Activation of the _____ nervous system is associated with feelings of fear and anxiety.

15. Some of the effects of large VMN lesions result from damage to fibers passing through the area from the _____ nuclei.

16. The nucleus accumbens is an important terminal of the _____ dopamine system.

17. Large bilateral lesions of the _____ nucleus of the hypothalamus increase eating by facilitating the conversion of blood glucose to body fat and blocking its conversion back to blood glucose.

18. Hypovolemia induces the release of renin from the kidneys, which increases the synthesis in the blood of _____.

19. The target sites of tracts from the hypothalamus that mediate female and male copulatory behavior, respectively, are the _____ and the _____ field.

20. The substantia nigra is located in the _____ of the midbrain.

21. Electrical stimulation of the raphé nuclei, amygdala, or some areas of the _____ can elicit defensive behaviors.

## Review Exercise 11.4

Below in alphabetical order is a list of all the terms and definitions that you learned in Chapter 11. Cover the definitions with a sheet of paper, and work your way down the list of terms, defining them to yourself as you go. Repeat this process until you have gone through the list twice without an error. Then, cover the terms and work your way down the list of definitions, providing the correct terms as you go. Repeat this second process until you have gone through the list twice without an error.

| Amygdala | The almond-shaped limbic nucleus that is located in the medial temporal lobe just anterior to the hippocampus; it is thought to link feelings of fear and anxiety to appropriate stimuli and defensive responses. |
| --- | --- |
| Hypothalamus | The diencephalic structure that is located just inferior to the anterior thalamus; electrical stimulation of some areas of the hypothalamus can elicit defensive responses. |
| Lateral hypothalamus | The large lateral region of the hypothalamus; large bilateral lesions of this area produce various motor disturbances and a general insensitivity to stimulation. |
| Lateral preoptic area | The lateral half of the preoptic region of the hypothalamus; it contains osmoreceptors that respond to increases in extracellular salt concentration. |

| Lateral tegmental field | An area of the mesencephalic and pontine reticular formation just anterior to the fourth ventricle; it plays a role in male copulatory behavior via a pathway from the ventromedial nucleus. |
| --- | --- |
| Locus coeruleus | A noradrenergic pontine nucleus near the boundary between the pons and midbrain; many of its neurons are active during SWS and inactive during REM sleep. |
| Medial preoptic area | The medial area of the preoptic hypothalamus; it plays a role in male copulatory behavior. |
| Mesotelencephalic dopamine system | The system of dopaminergic neurons that projects from the tegmentum of the mesencephalon to various telencephalic sites, including frontal cortex, striatum, septum, cingulate cortex, amygdala, and nucleus accumbens. |
| Nucleus accumbens | A nucleus that is located between the striatum and the basal forebrain; it is a major terminal of the mesotelencephalic dopamine system. |
| Orbitofrontal cortex | The cortex on the inferior surface of the frontal lobes (*orbito* means *near the eye sockets or orbits*); it is thought to be the area through which cortical processing influences the limbic system. |

| | | | |
|---|---|---|---|
| Paraventricular nucleus | A nucleus in the dorsal medial region of the hypothalamus, just above the dorsomedial nucleus; bilateral lesions to this nucleus or to the fibers that project to it through the ventromedial hypothalamus produce overeating and obesity. | Sexually dimorphic nucleus | A nucleus of the medial preoptic area that is several times bigger in male rats than in female rats. |
| | | Subfornical organ | The structure in the ceiling of to the third ventricle, just below to the fornix, where angiotensin II acts to induce the thirst associated with hypovolemia. |
| Periaqueductal gray | The area of the mesencephalon around the cerebral aqueduct; it plays a role in female copulatory behavior via a pathway from the ventromedial nucleus. | Substantia nigra | A nucleus of the tegmentum; it contains the cell bodies of many of the neurons that compose the mesotelen-cephalic dopamine system. |
| Pontine reticular formation | The portion of the reticular formation that is located in the pons; it contains cholinergic nuclei that play a role in REM sleep and noradrenergic and serotonergic nuclei that play a role in SWS. | Suprachiasmatic nuclei | A pair of small hypothalamic nuclei that are located just superior to the optic chiasm; the location of the circadian timing mechanism. |
| | | Ventral tegmental area | The area of the ventral tegmentum medial to the substantia nigra; it contains the cell bodies of many of the neurons that compose the mesotelencephalic dopamine system. |
| Raphé nuclei | The vertical sheet of serotonergic nuclei that runs along the midline of the reticular formation; electrical stimulation of some of the raphé nuclei can elicit defensive responses and many of its neurons are active during SWS. | Ventromedial nucleus | The major nucleus of the ventral medial region of the hypothalamus; large bilateral lesions of this nucleus produce overeating and obesity by promoting the conversion of blood glucose to body fat; it also plays a role in female copulatory behavior. |
| Retinohypo-thalamic tracts | Tracts that leave each eye as part of the optic nerve and project bilaterally to the suprachiasmatic nuclei; the neural paths by which the light-dark cycle influences circadian rhythms. | | |

## Chapter 12: Cortical Localization of Language and Thinking

It is appropriate that this book ends with a chapter on the neuroanatomy of language and thinking. They are two of the human species' most complex psychological processes.

Although humans are not the only species that possess the ability to think and use language, human capacities for language and thought far outstrip those of all other species, including those of our closest primate relatives. As a result, neuroscientists have not been able to directly explore the neural bases of language and thought in controlled laboratory experiments on other species; they have been largely limited to clinical research on human neurological patients. Nevertheless, substantial progress has recently been made in our understanding of the neural bases of language and thought thanks to the development of exciting new techniques for visualizing the structure and function of the living human brain.

The following are the five learning units of Chapter 12:

12.1   The Wernicke-Geschwind Model of Language

12.2   Cortical Areas Involved in Reading: Mapped by PET

12.3   Cortical Areas Involved in Naming Objects: Mapped by Stimulation

12.4   Cortical Areas Involved in Thinking: Mapped by Blood Flow Measurement

12.5   Cognitive, Social, and Emotional Effects of Prefrontal Cortex Lesions

## 12.1 The Wernicke-Geschwind Model of Language

The Wernicke-Geschwind model of language was proposed in 1965. The Wernicke-Geschwind model attributes the various processes involved in language to specific areas of the left cortex—right cortical lesions rarely disrupt language. The Wernicke-Geschwind model, although incorrect in several respects, has provided a framework for the study and treatment of *aphasia* (brain-damage-produced language dysfunction).

According to the Wernicke-Geschwind model, the following seven areas of the left hemisphere mediate language-related activities: (1) The *primary auditory cortex* mediates hearing the spoken word. (2) The *primary visual cortex* mediates seeing the written word. (3) The mouth and throat area of the *primary motor cortex* mediates the motor responses of speech. (4) **Wernicke's area**, an area in the left temporal lobe just posterior to primary auditory cortex, mediates comprehension of spoken language. (5) The left **angular gyrus**, the parietal lobe gyrus located on its border with the temporal lobe, translates the image of the written word into an auditory code, and passes it on to Wernicke's area for comprehension. (6) **Broca's area**, an area of the left frontal lobe just anterior to the mouth area of the primary motor cortex, stores programs of speech production and produces speech by activating the adjacent primary motor cortex. And, finally, (7) the **arcuate fasciculus**, a major tract that connects Wernicke's area with Broca's area, enables the Wernicke comprehension center to activate speech programs in Broca's area.

According to the Wernicke-Geschwind model, this is what happens when we read aloud. The visual signal is received by primary visual cortex and is conducted to the angular gyrus of the left hemisphere, where it is translated into an auditory code and conducted to Wernicke's area for comprehension. Wernicke's area then activates, via the left arcuate fasciculus, the appropriate programs of speech in Broca's area, and these produce speech by driving the mouth area of the primary motor cortex.

**Wernicke's area** (VER ni keys)
The area in the superior temporal cortex of the left hemisphere just posterior to primary auditory cortex; according to the Wernicke-Geschwind model, it is the center of language comprehension.

**Angular gyrus** (ANG gyu lar)
The parietal-lobe gyrus that is located on its boundary with the temporal lobe; according to the Wernicke-Geschwind model, the angular gyrus of the left hemisphere translates images of written words into an auditory code.

**Broca's area** (BROE kahz)
The area of the left frontal cortex, just anterior to the mouth region of the primary motor cortex; according to the Wernicke-Geschwind model, it contains the motor programs for speech.

**Arcuate fasciculus** (AR kyu ate   fa SIK yu lus)
The large tract that connects Wernicke's area with Broca's area.

---

*Coloring notes*

*Color each of the four labeled Wernicke-Geschwind areas that are enclosed within dashed lines. Note the position of the other three Wernicke-Geschwind areas: primary motor, primary auditory, and primary visual areas.*

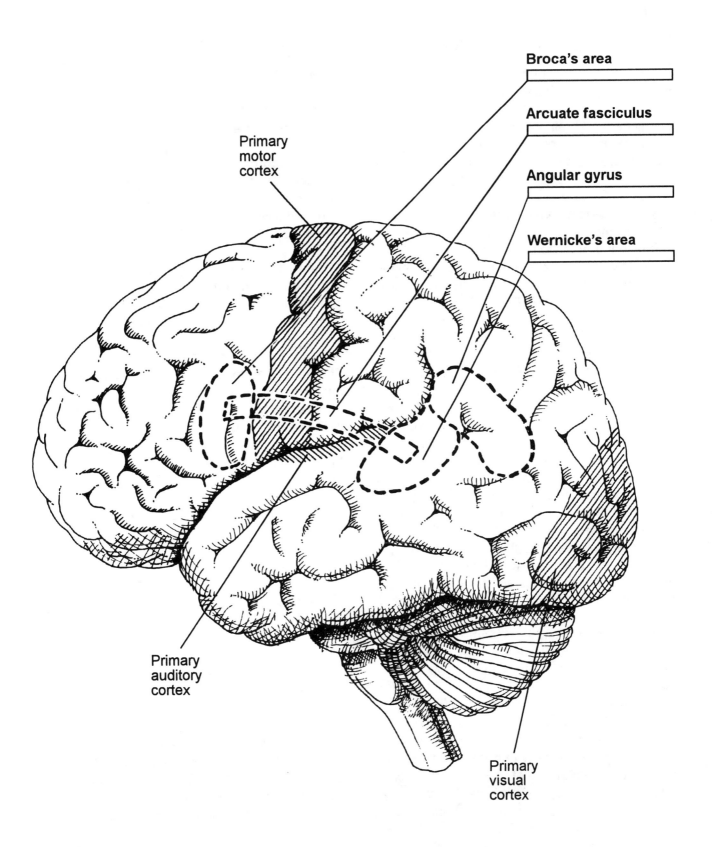

**Broca's area**

**Arcuate fasciculus**

**Angular gyrus**

**Wernicke's area**

Primary
motor
cortex

Primary
auditory
cortex

Primary
visual
cortex

## 12.2  Cortical Areas Involved in Reading:  Mapped by PET

The Wernicke-Geschwind model of the cortical localization of language was based on the analysis of neurological patients with diffuse and poorly defined brain damage. It is thus not surprising that the results of research using modern brain scanning techniques are inconsistent with some of the predictions of the Wernicke-Geschwind model.

Several studies have used *positron emission tomography* (PET) to map the areas of the cortex that are active in the brains of human subjects while they engage in language-related activities. In one such study, Petersen and his colleagues (*Nature, 1988, 331*:585-589) recorded PET scans in subjects who either stared at a blank display screen, stared at the screen while printed nouns were presented, stared at the screen while reading the printed nouns aloud, or stared at the screen while responding to the nouns with related verbs (e.g., cake: eat). Looking at the nouns produced bilateral activity in **primary visual cortex** that was not present when the subjects merely stared at a blank screen. Reading printed nouns aloud produced additional bilateral activity in **primary motor cortex**, **primary somatosensory cortex, primary auditory cortex**, and medial frontal cortex. And finally, responding to a printed noun by saying a related verb produced additional activity in the **lateral prefrontal cortex** of the left hemisphere just in front of Broca's area and in the *medial prefrontal cortex* of both hemispheres. Depicted in the accompanying diagram are the results that were observed in the lateral cortex of the left hemisphere.

The results of Petersen et al. challenge the Wernicke-Geschwind model in several respects. For example, each of the three experimental conditions added activity to both hemispheres, not just to the left; none of the three conditions added activity to Wernicke's area, Broca's area, or the angular gyrus; and areas of cortex not included in the Wernicke-Geschwind model were activated (e.g., the medial cortex).

**Primary visual cortex**
The area of cortex that receives direct visual input from the thalamus; it constitutes much of the occipital lobe.

**Primary motor cortex**
The area of cortex from which motor signals descend into the motor circuits of the brain stem and spinal cord; it constitutes most of the precentral gyrus.

**Primary somatosensory cortex**
The area of cortex that receives direct somatosensory input from the thalamus; it constitutes most of the postcentral gyrus.

**Primary auditory cortex**
The area of cortex that receives direct auditory input from the thalamus; it is located in the superior temporal lobe largely hidden from view in the lateral fissure.

**Lateral prefrontal cortex**
The cortex of the lateral prefrontal lobe, the left lateral prefrontal cortex seems to play a role in forming word associations.

### Coloring notes

*In this learning unit, do not color the spaces between the dashed lines; color only the geometric shapes within the labeled areas— they indicate exactly where increased activity was observed.  First, using the same color, color the three squares in the lateral prefrontal area. Then, using a different color, color the triangle in the primary visual cortex. Finally, using three different colors, color the two circles in primary motor cortex, the one in primary somatosensory cortex, and the one in primary auditory cortex.*

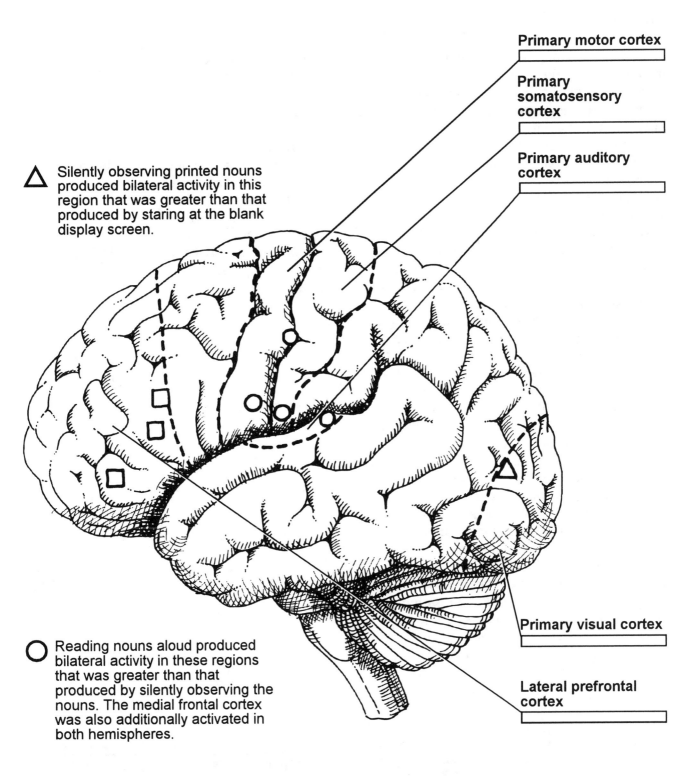

**Primary motor cortex**

**Primary somatosensory cortex**

**Primary auditory cortex**

△ Silently observing printed nouns produced bilateral activity in this region that was greater than that produced by staring at the blank display screen.

**Primary visual cortex**

**Lateral prefrontal cortex**

○ Reading nouns aloud produced bilateral activity in these regions that was greater than that produced by silently observing the nouns. The medial frontal cortex was also additionally activated in both hemispheres.

☐ Responding to printed nouns with a related verb produced activity in these regions that was greater than that produced by reading the nouns. The medial prefrontal cortex was additionally activated in both hemispheres.

## 12.3 Cortical Areas Involved in Naming Objects: Mapped by Stimulation

One of the weaknesses of the PET scan as a method of studying localization of brain function is its low power of spatial resolution. It can locate general areas of increased neural activity, but it cannot pinpoint them. This is not a problem with the electrical stimulation procedure. In several studies, specific points on the cortical surface of conscious patients have been stimulated during neurosurgery, and the speech deficits associated with the stimulation of various sites have been documented.

Such studies have led to two important findings. First, the cortical tissue that performs a particular language function is not distributed uniformly throughout a particular area of cortex; the tissue that performs a particular language function is localized in islands of tissue that are scattered throughout a large area. Second, the area of cortex that participates in a particular language function varies greatly from subject to subject. Thus, methods that either lack spatial resolution or are based on group averages are unlikely to provide a great deal of insight into the detailed cortical organization of language processes in individuals.

In one study, Ojeman and his colleagues (*Journal of Neurosurgery, 1989, 71:316-326*) assessed the ability of electrical stimulation to disrupt the naming of common objects in 117 neurosurgery patients. Most of the active sites were located in **posterior frontal cortex**, **inferior parietal cortex**, and **superior temporal cortex**. However, many patients had no active sites at all in the classic Wernicke and Broca areas. The accompanying drawings illustrate the general location of sites where stimulation did (o) and did not (●) disrupt the naming of common objects in two particular patients.

**Posterior frontal cortex**
The cortex of the posterior frontal lobe; the region of frontal cortex adjacent to the central fissure.

**Inferior parietal cortex**
The cortex of the inferior parietal lobe; the region of parietal cortex just superior to the lateral fissure.

**Superior temporal cortex**
The cortex of the superior temporal lobe; the region of temporal cortex just inferior to the lateral fissure.

*Coloring notes*

*First, color the areas of cortex in the top illustration by staying within the dashed lines. Then, color the positive stimulation sites in the bottom two illustrations—color each positive site with the color of its cortical area in the top illustration.*

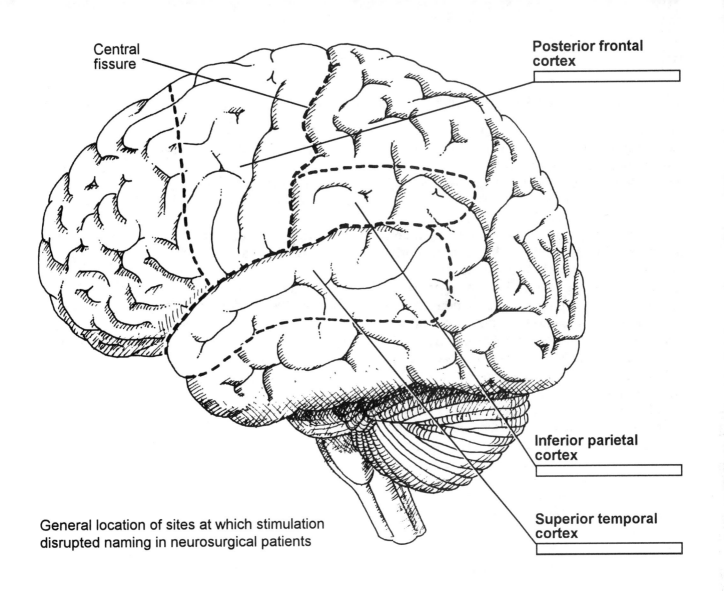

Central fissure

Posterior frontal cortex

Inferior parietal cortex

Superior temporal cortex

General location of sites at which stimulation disrupted naming in neurosurgical patients

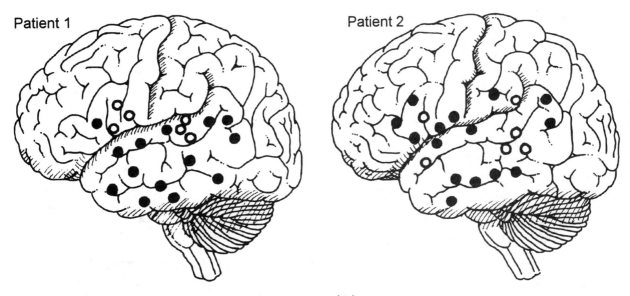

Patient 1

Patient 2

Specific locations of sites at which stimulation did (O)
and did not (●) disrupt naming in two particular patients

## 12.4  Cortical Areas Involved in Thinking:  Mapped by Blood Flow Measurement

The flow of blood into an area of the brain increases when the area is active. Thus, one method of measuring the brain activity associated with a particular psychological process (e.g., thinking) is to measure the distribution of blood in the brain while the subject engages in that process. One method of measuring the distribution of blood in the cortex of one hemisphere is to inject a slightly radioactive substance into the *carotid artery* feeding that hemisphere and then measure the distribution of radioactivity in the cortex with a bank of radioactivity detectors placed next to the skull. This technique was used by Roland and Friberg (*Journal of Neurophysiology*, 1985, *53*:1219-1243) in a study of thinking.

In Roland and Friberg's study, subjects were instructed to engage in three kinds of thinking while the distribution of blood in their cerebral cortices was measured. In one condition, they thought about numbers in a sequence starting at 50 and counting backwards by 3s; in a second, they thought about every second word in a well known jingle; and in a third, they thought about walking out their front door and turning alternately left and right at each corner that they encountered. Each type of thinking produced increases in cortical blood flow above those measured in a resting control condition.

All three types of thinking produced significant bilateral increases in activity in **superior prefrontal cortex**; none produced increases in primary motor or sensory areas. In addition, each of the three types of thinking produced increases in activity in areas not influenced by the other types of thinking. For example, route thinking produced selective bilateral increases in the activity of **inferior prefrontal cortex**, **posterior parietal cortex**, and **inferior temporal cortex**.

**Superior prefrontal cortex**
Cortex of the superior anterior frontal lobes..

**Inferior prefrontal cortex**
Cortex of the inferior anterior frontal lobes.

**Posterior parietal cortex**
Cortex of the posterior parietal lobes.

**Inferior temporal cortex**
Cortex of the inferior temporal lobes.

*Coloring notes*

*First, color the superior prefrontal cortex, an area that seems to be involved in many kinds of thinking. Then, color the three areas that seem to be specifically involved in route thinking.*

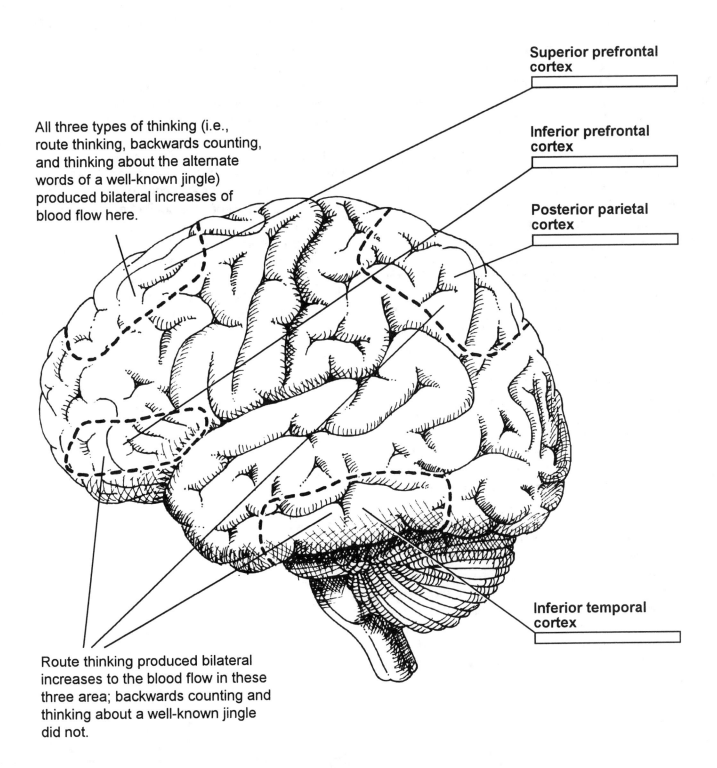

**Superior prefrontal cortex**

**Inferior prefrontal cortex**

**Posterior parietal cortex**

**Inferior temporal cortex**

All three types of thinking (i.e., route thinking, backwards counting, and thinking about the alternate words of a well-known jingle) produced bilateral increases of blood flow here.

Route thinking produced bilateral increases to the blood flow in these three area; backwards counting and thinking about a well-known jingle did not.

211

## 12. 5   Cognitive, Social, and Emotional Effects of Prefrontal Cortex Lesions

The large area of the frontal cortex anterior to the primary and secondary motor cortex is the *prefrontal cortex*. Although the prefrontal cortex has often been assumed to be the seat of intelligence, large prefrontal lesions have little or no adverse effect on the ability to perform conventional tests of intelligence. However, appropriately designed tests reveal several major deficits, which depend to a large degree on the particular area of the prefrontal cortex that has been damaged.

The prefrontal cortex contains three large areas: the **dorsolateral prefrontal cortex**, which is on the lateral surface of the prefrontal cortex just in front of the *premotor cortex*, the **orbitofrontal cortex**, which is on the *frontal pole* (i.e., on the anterior tip of the brain) and inferior surface of the prefrontal lobes just next to the orbits (i.e., eye sockets), and the **medial prefrontal cortex**, which includes anterior portions of the *cingulate gyrus*.

Damage to the dorsolateral cortex often results in deficits in creative thinking, in remembering the temporal sequence of events but not the events themselves, in inhibiting incorrect but previously correct responses, and in developing and following plans of action. Damage to the orbitofrontal cortex often results in marked personality changes, particularly in the ability to inhibit inappropriate behaviors consistently behave in socially acceptable ways. Damage to the medial prefrontal cortex often results in emotional blunting; patients with damage to medial prefrontal cortex react only slightly to positive or negative emotion-inducing events that induce extreme positive or negative emotions in most people.

**Dorsolateral prefrontal cortex**
The large area on the lateral surface of the prefrontal lobes, which plays a role in memory for temporal order, response sequencing, response inhibition, and creative thinking.

**Orbitofrontal cortex**
The large area of prefrontal cortex on its anterior pole and inferior surface; lesions of this area often lead to inappropriate social behaviors.

**Medial prefrontal cortex**
The area of prefrontal cortex on the medial surface of the prefrontal lobes; lesions to this area produce a blunting of affect.

---

***Coloring notes***

*First, color the orbitofrontal cortex shown in both the top (medial orbitofrontal) and bottom (lateral orbitofrontal) illustrations. Then, color the medial prefrontal cortex in the top illustration and the dorsolateral prefrontal cortex in the bottom.*

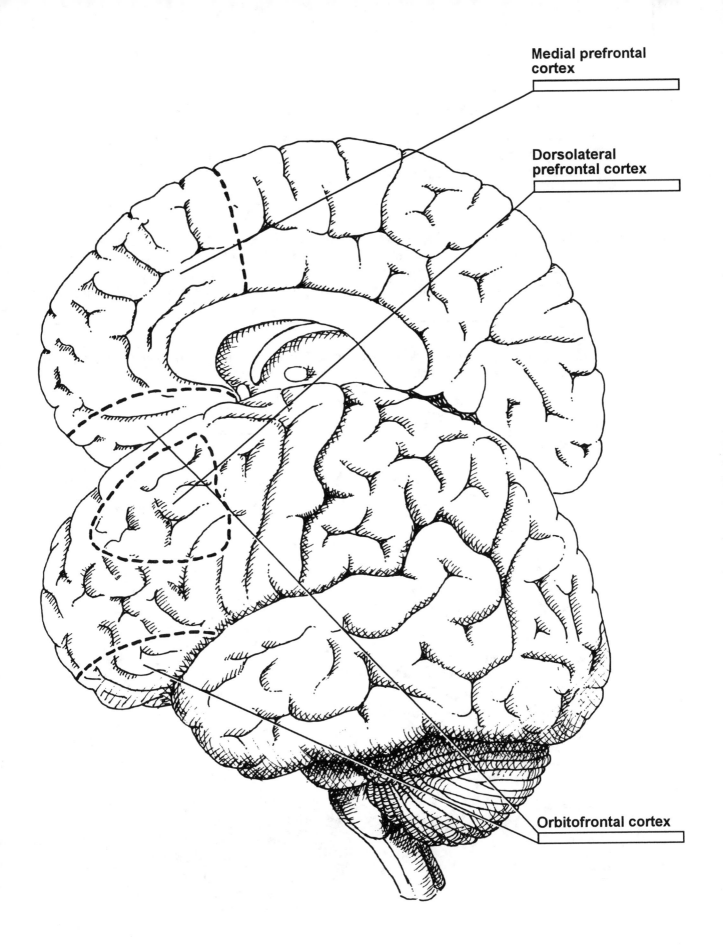

**Medial prefrontal cortex**

**Dorsolateral prefrontal cortex**

**Orbitofrontal cortex**

# Review Exercises: Cortical Localization of Language and Thinking

Now it is time for you to pause and consolidate the terms and ideas that you have learned in the five learning units of Chapter 12. It is important that you overlearn them so that they do not quickly fade from your memory.

## Review Exercise 12.1

Turn to the illustrations in the five learning units of Chapter 12, and use the cover flap at the back of the book to cover the terms that run down the right-hand edge of each illustration page. Study the five illustrations in sequence until you can identify each labeled structure. Once you have worked through all five illustrations twice in a row without making an error, advance to Review Exercise 12.2.

## Review Exercise 12.2

Fill in the missing terms in the following illustration. The answers are provided at the back of the book. Carefully review the material related to your incorrect answers.

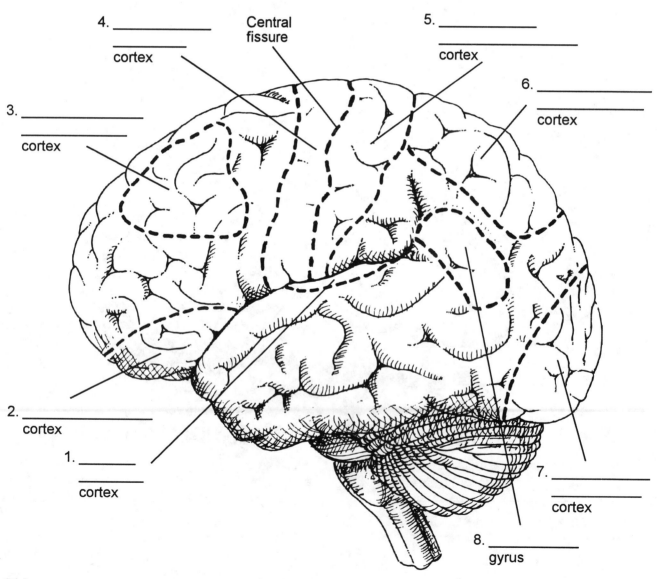

4. _____ _____ cortex

Central fissure

3. _____ _____ cortex

2. _____ cortex

1. _____ _____ cortex

5. _____ _____ cortex

6. _____ _____ cortex

7. _____ _____ cortex

8. _____ gyrus

## Review Exercise 12.3

Without referring to Chapter 12, fill in each of the following blanks with the correct term from the chapter. The correct answers are provided at the back of the book. Carefully review the material related to your incorrect answers.

1. The Wernicke-Geschwind model of language was proposed in the mid 19__s.

2. Language-related abilities are seldom disrupted by lesions of the _____ hemisphere.

3. According to the Wernicke-Geschwind model, the _____ gyrus translates read words into the auditory code.

4. The _____ fasciculus connects Wernicke's and Broca's areas.

5. Primary _____ cortex is located in the precentral gyrus.

6. Primary _____ cortex is located in the postcentral gyrus.

7. Although not predicted by the Wernicke-Geschwind model, reading activates the _____ prefrontal cortex (i.e., the frontal cortex in the longitudinal fissure).

8. In the following three regions of the surface of the left hemisphere, electrical stimulation often disrupts the naming of common objects: posterior frontal cortex, _____ parietal cortex, _____ temporal cortex.

9. Superior to the angular gyrus is _____ parietal cortex.

10. The angular gyrus is in the _____ lobe at its boundary with the temporal lobe.

11. Thinking about going for a walk along a particular route produced activity in the superior prefrontal cortex, the posterior parietal cortex, inferior prefrontal cortex and the inferior _____ cortex of both hemispheres.

12. The precentral gyrus is in the _____ lobe.

13. According to the Wernicke-Geschwind model, _____ area is the center of language comprehension.

14. According to the Wernicke-Geschwind model, _____ area contains the programs of speech production.

15. The mouth area of the left motor homunculus is adjacent to _____ area.

16. The Wernicke-Geschwind model was originally based on the study of brain-damaged patients suffering from _____.

17. According to the Wernicke-Geschwind model, language-related visual signals are relayed from primary visual cortex to Wernicke's area via the _____.

18. The main advantage of electrical stimulation in the study of cortical localization of function is its power of _____ resolution.

19. _____ cortex is at the anterior pole of the brain on the inferior surface of the frontal lobes.

20. The _____ prefrontal cortex plays a role in emotional expression; lesions to it produce emotional blunting.

## Review Exercise 12.4

Below in alphabetical order is a list of all the terms and definitions that you learned in Chapter 12. Cover the definitions with a sheet of paper, and work your way down the list of terms, defining them to yourself as you go. Repeat this process until you have gone through the list twice without an error. Then, cover the terms and work your way down the list of definitions, providing the correct terms as you go. Repeat this second process until you have gone through the list twice without an error.

| | |
|---|---|
| Angular gyrus | The parietal lobe gyrus that is located on its boundary with the temporal lobe; according to the Wernicke-Geschwind model, the angular gyrus of the left hemisphere translates images of written words into an auditory code. |
| Arcuate fasciculus | The large tract that connects Wernicke's area with Broca's area. |
| Broca's area | The area of the left frontal cortex, just anterior to the mouth region of the primary motor cortex; according to the Wernicke-Geschwind model, it contains the motor programs for speech. |
| Dorsolateral prefrontal cortex | The large area on the lateral surface of the prefrontal lobes, which plays a role in memory for temporal order, response sequencing, response inhibition, and creative thinking. |
| Inferior parietal cortex | The cortex of the inferior parietal lobe; the region of parietal cortex just superior to the lateral fissure. |
| Inferior prefrontal cortex | Cortex of the inferior anterior frontal lobes. |
| Inferior temporal cortex | Cortex of the inferior temporal lobes. |
| Lateral prefrontal cortex | The cortex of the lateral prefrontal lobe, the left lateral prefrontal cortex seems to play a role in forming word associations. |
| Medial prefrontal cortex | The large area of prefrontal cortex on the medial surface of the prefrontal lobes; lesions to this area produce a blunting of affect. |
| Orbitofrontal cortex | The area of prefrontal cortex on its anterior pole and inferior surface; lesions of this area often lead to inappropriate social behaviors. |
| Posterior frontal cortex | The cortex of the posterior cortex frontal lobe; the region of frontal cortex adjacent to the central fissure. |
| Posterior parietal cortex | Cortex of the posterior parietal lobes. |
| Primary auditory cortex | The area of cortex that receives direct auditory input from the thalamus; it is located in the superior temporal lobe, largely hidden from view in the lateral fissure. |
| Primary motor cortex | The area of cortex from which motor signals descend into the motor circuits of the brain stem and spinal cord; it constitutes most of the precentral gyrus. |

| | |
|---|---|
| Primary somatosensory cortex | The area of cortex that receives direct somatosensory input from the thalamus; it constitutes most of the postcentral gyrus. |
| Primary visual cortex | The area of cortex that receives direct visual input from the thalamus; it constitutes much of the occipital lobe. |
| Superior prefrontal cortex | Cortex of the superior anterior frontal lobes. |
| Superior temporal cortex | The cortex of the superior temporal lobe; the region of the temporal cortex inferior to the lateral fissure. |
| Wernicke's area | The area in the superior temporal cortex of the left hemisphere just posterior to primary auditory cortex; according to the Wernicke-Geschwind model, it is the center of language comprehension. |

## Chapter 1

### Exercise 1.2
1. Spinal cord
2. Autonomic
3. Somatic
4. Motor
5. Parasympathetic

### Exercise 1.3
1. gonads
2. cervical, thoracic, lumbar, sacral
3. sympathetic
4. cortex
5. hypothalamus
6. autonomic
7. gray
8. 2, 2
9. pituitary
10. afferent
11. sympathetic
12. central
13. parasympathetic
14. pituitary, hypothalamus
15. somatic
16. dorsal, ventral
17. endocrine
18. medulla
19. spinal cord
20. motor

## Chapter 2

### Exercise 2.2
1. Sagittal
2. Midsagittal
3. Horizontal
4. Coronal
5. Cross

### Exercise 2.3
1. planes
2. ipsilateral
3. coronal
4. coronal
5. horizontal
6. sagittal
7. cross
8. decussate
9. dorsal
10. posterior
11. posterior
12. medial
13. lateral
14. anterior
15. anterior
16. inferior
17. anterior
18. superior
19. midsagittal
20. bilateral
21. contralateral
22. caudal
23. rostral

## Chapter 3

### Exercise 3.2
1. Button
2. Nodes of Ranvier
3. Dendrites
4. Nucleus
5. Cell body
6. Axon hillock
7. Golgi apparatus
8. Synaptic vesicle
9. Mitochondrion
10. Microtubules

### Exercise 3.3
1. all-or-none
2. axon, dendrites
3. buttons
4. nucleus
5. Action
6. Golgi
7. exocytosis
8. vesicles
9. receptive
10. hillock
11. presynaptic, postsynaptic
12. synapse
13. endoplasmic reticulum
14. receptors
15. axon hillock
16. ribosomes
17. decrementally
18. cell body
19. saltatory
20. Ranvier
21. Golgi apparatus
22. Oligodendrocytes
23. Metabotropic
24. Ion channels

## Chapter 4

### Exercise 4.2
1. Forebrain
2. Midbrain
3. Hindbrain
4. Spinal cord
5. Telencephalon
6. Diencephalon
7. Mesencephalon
8. Metencephalon
9. Myelencephalon

### Exercise 4.3
1. dorsal, plate
2. hindbrain, midbrain, forebrain
3. groove
4. aggregation
5. diencephalon
6. 18
7. metencephalon
8. radial
9. anterior
10. growth cone
11. death
12. myelinated, glial
13. 3
14. crest
15. telencephalon, myelencephalon
16. totipotential
17. Proliferation
18. mesencephalon
19. pioneer
20. chemoaffinity
21. blueprint

## Chapter 5

### Exercise 5.2
1. Corpus
2. Anterior
3. Massa
4. Mes
5. Met
6. Myel
7. Fourth
8. aqueduct
9. Third

### Exercise 5.3
1. brain stem
2. vagus
3. brain stem
4. dura mater
5. aqueduct
6. subarachnoid
7. central
8. central canal
9. massa intermedia
10. lateral
11. pia mater
12. hydrocephalus
13. myelencephalon
14. ganglia
15. 12
16. commissure
17. longitudinal
18. sensory
19. parasympathetic
20. telencephalon
21. trigeminal
22. axons
23. third, fourth
24. meninges

## Chapter 6

### Exercise 6.2
1. Medulla or Myelencephalon
2. Pons
3. Posterior pituitary
4. Anterior pituitary
5. Mammillary body
6. Hypothalamus
7. Thalamus
8. Massa intermedia
9. Superior colliculus
10. Inferior colliculus
11. Tegmentum
12. Cerebellum

### Exercise 6.3
1. medulla
2. pons
3. red, periaqueductal, nigra
4. contralateral
5. reticular formation
6. superior, inferior
7. pons
8. massa intermedia, third
9. pons
10. white
11. peduncles, olives
12. pyramidal
13. anterior
14. metencephalon
15. hypothalamus, posterior
16. thalamus
17. cerebellum
18. hypothalamus
19. anterior
20. mesencephalon
21. tectum

## Chapter 7

### Exercise 7.2
1. Frontal
2. Middle frontal
3. Precentral
4. Central
5. Postcentral
6. Parietal
7. Angular
8. Occipital
9. Middle temporal
10. Inferior temporal
11. Lateral

### Exercise 7.3
1. longitudinal
2. hippocampus
3. cingulate
4. occipital
5. allocortex
6. basal ganglia
7. secondary
8. secondary
9. striatum
10. occipital
11. striatum
12. precentral, postcentral
13. primary
14. lateral
15. limbic
16. frontal
17. temporal
18. hippocampus
19. globus pallidus
20. central
21. 3
22. superior

## Chapter 8

### Exercise 8.2
1. Secondary somatosensory
2. Primary somatosensory
3. Posterior parietal
4. Prestriate
5. Primary visual
6. Inferotemporal
7. Secondary auditory
8. Primary auditory

### Exercise 8.3
1. ganglion
2. auditory
3. decussate
4. postcentral, parietal
5. right, right
6. dorsolateral
7. inferotemporal
8. optic tracts
9. colliculi
10. geniculate
11. temporal
12. Heschl's, lateral
13. occipital
14. medulla
15. aqueduct
16. trigeminal
17. retinotopically, tonotopically, somatotopically

18. homunculus
19. parietal
20. periqueductal
21. raphé

---

## Chapter 9

### Exercise 9.2
1. auditory
2. Supplementary
3. Premotor
4. Primary
5. Dorsolateral
6. corticorubrospinal
7. corticospinal
8. Ventromedial

### Exercise 9.3
1. dorsolateral prefrontal
2. proximal, distal
3. nigrostriatal
4. at rest
5. corticospinal
6. L-DOPA
7. corticospinal
8. caudate
9. striatum
10. balance
11. thalamus
12. ventromedial
13. globus pallidus
14. substantia nigra
15. somatotopic
16. corticospinal
17. primary
18. internal
19. cingulate
20. primary, precentral
21. putamen, caudate

---

## Chapter 10

### Exercise 10.2
1. Mediodorsal
2. Hippocampus
3. Subicular
4. Perirhinal
5. Rhinal

6. Entorhinal
7. Dentate gyrus
8. Fimbria

### Exercise 10.3
1. temporal
2. hippocampus
3. acetylcholine
4. consolidation
5. dentate
6. subicular
7. forebrain
8. amygdala
9. entorhinal
10. mediodorsal
11. 4
12. anterior
13. place
14. pyramidal
15. explicit
16. diencephalon
17. rhinal
18. amyloid
19. hippocampus, dentate, subicular
20. hippocampus
21. short-term, implicit
22. rhinal

---

## Chapter 11

### Exercise 11.2
1. Suprachiasmatic
2. preoptic
3. Lateral
4. Paraventricular
5. Dorsomedial
6. Ventromedial

### Exercise 11.3
1. ventromedial, lateral
2. retinohypothalamic
3. raphé, coeruleus
4. subfornical
5. raphé
6. substantia nigra, tegmental
7. suprachiasmatic
8. orbitofrontal
9. pontine

10. amygdala
11. preoptic
12. lateral
13. REM
14. sympathetic
15. paraventricular
16. Mesotelencephalic
17. ventromedial
18. angiotensin II
19. periaqueductal gray, lateral tegmental
20. tegmentum
21. hypothalamus

---

## Chapter 12

### Exercise 12.2
1. Primary auditory
2. Orbitofrontal
3. Dorsolateral prefrontal
4. Primary motor
5. Primary somatosensory
6. Posterior parietal
7. Primary visual
8. Angular

### Exercise 12.3
1. 60
2. right
3. angular
4. arcuate
5. motor
6. somatosensory
7. medial
8. inferior, superior
9. posterior
10. parietal
11. temporal
12. frontal
13. Wernicke's
14. Broca's
15. Broca's
16. aphasia
17. angular gyrus
18. spatial
19. Orbitofrontal
20. medial

# Index

## A

Abducens nerve 81
Accessory nerve 81
Acetylcholine 176, 192
Action potentials 40, 42, 76
Adrenal cortex 14, 15
Adrenal glands 14, 15
Adrenal medulla 14, 15
Adrenaline 14
Afferent 10, 80
Aggregation 54, 55
Allocortex 112, 113, 118, 168
Alzheimer's disease 176
Amygdala 118-121, 158, 159, 169, 170, 188-191
Amyloid plaques 176
Analgesia 196
Angiotensin II 186
Angular gyrus 110, 111, 204, 205
Anterior 24, 25
Anterior commissure 78, 79, 97, 99, 176, 177, 187
Anterior pituitary 98, 99
Anxiety 190
Aphasia 204
Apical dendrite 112, 113
Arachnoid membrane 72, 73
Arcuate fasciculus 204, 205
Association area 114, 115
Ataxia 90
Auditory nerve 134, 135
Auditory radiations 134, 135
Autonomic nervous system 8, 9, 10, 12, 13
Axon 32, 33, 35, 40, 42, 76
Axon branches 32, 33
Axon growth 60, 61
Axon hillock 38-40
Axonal conduction 40
Axonal regeneration 42

## B

Basal forebrain 176, 177
Basal ganglia 120, 121, 158, 159
Bilateral 26, 27
Blueprint theory 60, 61
Brain 6, 7
Brain stem 68-71
Broca's area 204, 205
Buttons 32, 33, 36, 37, 40, 41

## C

Carotid artery 210
Caudal 24
Caudate 120, 121, 152, 153, 158, 177

Cell body 32-35, 38, 39, 76
Cell membrane 32, 33, 44, 45
Central canal 74, 75
Central fissure 106-109, 111, 117, 133, 141, 151, 153, 209
Central nervous system 4, 5, 6, 7
Centrifugal pathways 142
Cerebellar peduncles 90, 91
Cerebellum 88, 90, 91, 158, 159
Cerebral aqueduct 74, 75, 92, 142, 143
Cerebral commissures 78, 79
Cerebral cortex 94, 106, 107, 112, 114
Cerebral hemispheres 68, 69, 106, 108, 110
Cerebral ventricles 74, 75
Cerebrospinal fluid 72, 73, 74
Chemoaffinity theory 60, 61
Cingulate cortex 118, 119, 188, 189
Cingulate gyrus 212
Cingulate motor areas 150, 151
Circadian clock 194
Cochlea 134, 135
Cochlear nuclei 134, 135
Contralateral 26, 27
Convolutions 106
Cornu ammonis 171, 172
Coronal section 22, 23
Corpus callosum 78, 79, 97, 118, 175
Cranial nerves 80, 81, 88, 90
Cross section 22, 23
Cytoplasm 32, 33

## D

Decussation 27
Dendrites 32, 33, 38, 39
Dentate gyrus 168, 169
Diagonal band of Broca 176, 177
Diencephalon 58, 59, 70, 71, 74, 84, 94, 96
Dopamine 120
Dorsal 24, 25
Dorsal column 138, 139, 142, 143
Dorsal column nuclei 138, 139
Dorsal root 10, 11, 138
Dorsal route 132, 133
Dorsal-column medial-lemniscus system 138
Dorsolateral corticorubrospinal tract 154, 155
Dorsolateral corticospinal tract 154, 155

Dorsolateral prefrontal cortex 150, 151, 212, 213
Dura mater 72, 73

**E**
Efferent 10, 80
Endocrine glands 14, 15
Endorphins 142
Entorhinal cortex 170, 171, 173
Excitatory postsynaptic potentials 38, 40
Exocrine glands 14
Exocytosis 40
Explicit memory 168
Exteroceptive system 138

**F**
Facial nerve 81
Fasciculation 60
Fear 190
Fimbria 168, 169
Fissure 106, 107
Forebrain 56-59, 70, 71
Fornix 118, 119, 168, 175, 177, 185-187
Fourth ventricle 74, 75, 89, 90, 143
Frontal cortex 188, 189
Frontal lobe 108, 109
Frontal section 22

**G**
G-protein 44, 45, 48
Ganglia 76, 77
Glial cells 42, 43
Globus pallidus 120, 121, 152, 153, 158, 177
Glossopharyngeal nerve 81
Golgi apparatus 34-37
Gonads 14, 15
Granule cells 112
Gray matter 42, 106
Growth cone 54, 55
Gyrus 106, 107, 110, 111

**H**
Heschl's gyrus 136, 137
Hindbrain 56-71
Hippocampal commissure 79
Hippocampal formation 168, 169, 171, 172
Hippocampus 118, 119, 168, 169, 172, 173
Horizontal sections 22, 23
Hydrocephalus 74

Hypoglossal nerve 81
Hypothalamopituitary portal system 98, 99
Hypothalamus 14, 15, 94-99, 121, 130, 131, 174-176, 184, 190-196
   lateral hypothalamus 184, 185
   lateral preoptic area 96, 97, 186, 187
   mammillary body 96, 97, 99
   medial preoptic area 96, 97, 187, 196, 197
   paraventricular nucleus 99, 184, 185
   preoptic area 96, 97, 195
   supraoptic nucleus 99
   ventromedial nucleus 96, 97, 184, 185, 196, 197
Hypovolemia 186

**I**
Implicit memory 168
Inferior 24, 25
Inferior colliculus 92, 93, 95, 134, 135
Inferior frontal gyrus 110, 111
Inferior parietal cortex 208, 209
Inferior prefrontal cortex 210, 211, 216
Inferior temporal cortex 210, 211
Inferior temporal gyrus 110, 111, 132, 137
Inferotemporal cortex 132, 133
Inhibitory postsynaptic potentials 38, 40
Internal capsule 152-154
Interneurons 154
Interoceptive system 138
Intracranial self-stimulation 188
Ion channels 44, 45
   chemical-gated 44
   voltage-gated 44
Ionotropic receptors 44
Ions 44
Ipsilateral 26, 27

**K**
Kidneys 186
Korsakoff's amnesia 174

**L**
L-DOPA 160
Lateral 24, 25
Lateral fissure 106-109, 111, 117, 133, 141, 169

Lateral geniculate nucleus 94, 95, 130, 131
Lateral hypothalamus 184, 185
Lateral prefrontal cortex 206, 207, 216
Lateral preoptic area 96, 97, 186, 187
Lateral tegmental field 196, 197
Lateral ventricles 74, 75, 79, 153, 175, 177, 187
Limbic system 118, 119
Locus coeruleus 192, 193
Longitudinal fissure 78, 79, 106, 107, 109, 132, 150

**M**
Mammillary body 96, 97, 99, 118, 119, 131, 175
Massa intermedia 78, 79, 94, 95, 97, 177
Medial 24, 25
Medial diencephalon 174, 175
Medial geniculate nucleus 94, 95, 134, 135
Medial lemniscus 138, 139
Medial prefrontal cortex 206, 212, 213
Medial preoptic area 96, 97, 187, 196, 197
Medial septum 176, 177
Medial temporal cortex 170
Mediodorsal nucleus 174, 175
Medulla 13, 88, 89, 139
Memory consolidation 168
Meninges 72, 73
Mesencephalon 56-59, 70, 71, 74, 92, 93
Mesotelencephalic dopamine system 188, 189
Metabotropic receptors 44
Metencephalon 58, 59, 70, 71, 90, 91
Microtubules 34, 35
Midbrain 56-59, 70, 71
Middle frontal gyrus 110, 111
Middle temporal gyrus 110, 111, 137
Midsagittal section 22, 23
Migration 54, 55
Mitochondria 34-37
Motor homunculus 152, 153
Motor nerves 10, 11
Myelencephalon 58, 59, 70, 71, 88, 89
Myelin 42
Myelination 54, 55

**N**

Naughty bits 14

Neocortex 112, 113, 169, 171
  cingulate cortex 118, 119, 188, 189
  dorsolateral prefrontal cortex 150, 151, 212, 213
  entorhinal cortex 170, 171, 173
  frontal cortex 188, 189
  inferior parietal cortex 208, 209
  inferior prefrontal cortex 210, 211
  inferiorotemporal cortex 210, 211
  inferotemporal cortex 132, 133
  lateral prefrontal cortex 206, 207
  medial prefrontal cortex 206, 212, 213
  medial temporal cortex 170
  orbitofrontal cortex 190, 191, 212, 213
  perirhinal cortex 170, 171
  posterior frontal cortex 208, 209
  posterior parietal cortex 132, 133, 136, 137, 141, 150, 151, 210, 211
  prefrontal cortex 212
  premotor cortex 150, 151, 212
  prestriate cortex 132, 133
  primary auditory cortex 116, 117, 134-137, 204-207
  primary gustatory cortex 116, 117
  primary motor cortex 116, 117, 151-153, 204-207
  primary olfactory cortex 116, 117
  primary somatosensory cortex 116, 117, 138-141, 206, 207
  primary visual cortex 116, 117, 130-133, 204, 205-207
  rhinal cortex 170
  secondary auditory cortex 136, 137
  secondary motor cortex 150, 151
  secondary somatosensory cortex 140, 141
  striate cortex 132
  superior prefrontal cortex 210, 211
  superior temporal cortex 208, 209

supplementary motor cortex 150, 151

Nerves 76, 77
Neural crest 52, 53
Neural groove 52, 53
Neural plate 52, 53
Neural tube 52-55
Neurofilaments 34, 35
Neuroglia 42, 43
Neuron 32, 36
Neuron death 54, 55
Neurons 32-37
Neurotransmitters 36, 37, 40, 41, 44, 45
Nigrostriatal pathway 160, 161, 188
Nodes of Ranvier 42, 43
Noradrenalin 192
Nuclei 76, 77
Nucleus 34, 35
Nucleus accumbens 188, 189
Nucleus basilis of Meynert 176, 177
Nucleus cuneatus 138, 139
Nucleus gracilis 138, 139

**O**

Object-recognition memory 170
Occipital lobe 108, 109, 131
Oculomotor nerve 81
Olfactory nerve 80, 81
Olfactory nerves 116, 118, 119
Oligodendrocytes 42, 43
Olive 88, 89
Opiate analgesics 142
Optic chiasm 79, 96, 97, 99, 130, 131, 177, 187, 194, 195
Optic nerve 80, 81, 130, 131, 194, 195
Optic radiations 130, 131
Optic tract 130, 131
Orbitofrontal cortex 190, 191, 212, 213
Osmoreceptors 186
Ovaries 14, 15

**P**

Pancreas 15
Parasympathetic nervous system 12, 13, 80
Parathyroids 15
Paraventricular nucleus 99, 184, 185
Parietal lobe 108, 109
Parkinson's disease 120, 160

Periaqueductal gray 92, 93, 143, 196, 197
Peripheral nervous system 4, 9
Perirhinal cortex 170, 171
Pia mater 72, 73
Pioneer growth cones 60
Pituitary
  anterior 98, 99
  posterior 98, 99
Pituitary gland 14, 15, 95-99, 177
Pituitary stalk 99
Place fields 172
Pons 90, 91, 159, 193
Positron emission tomograph 206
Postcentral gyrus 110, 111, 1 140, 141
Posterior 24, 25
Posterior commissure 79
Posterior frontal cortex 208,
Posterior parietal cortex 132 136, 137, 141, 150, 151 211, 216
Posterior pituitary 98, 99, 18
Postsynaptic membrane 40,
Precentral gyrus 110, 111, 1 150
Prefrontal cortex 212
Premotor cortex 150, 151, 2
Preoptic area 96, 97, 195
Prestriate cortex 132, 133
Presynaptic membrane 40,
Primary auditory cortex 116 134-137, 204-207
Primary gustatory cortex 11
Primary motor area 114, 11
Primary motor cortex 116, 1 151-153, 204-207
Primary olfactory cortex 116
Primary sensory area 114, 1
Primary somatosensory cor 116, 117, 138-141, 206
Primary visual cortex 116, 1 130-133, 204, 205, 206
Process growth 54, 55
Proliferation 54, 55
Proprioceptive system 138
Prosencephalon 56, 57
Putamen 120, 121, 152, 15 159, 161, 177
Pyramidal cell 112, 113, 17
Pyramids 88, 89, 154, 155

## R

Radial glial cells 54, 55
Raphé nuclei 142, 143, 190, 191, 192, 193
Rapid eye movement 192
Receptive area 38, 39
Receptors 40, 41, 44, 45
    ionotropic 44, 45
    metatropic 44, 45
Red nucleus 92, 93, 154, 155
Releasing factors 14
Renin 186
Reticular formation 88-93, 142, 156, 191-193
Retina 130, 131
Retinal ganglion cells 130
Retinohypothalamic tract 194, 195
Retinotopic 130, 132, 136
Rhinal cortex 170-172
Rhinal fissure 170, 171
Rhombencephalon 56, 57
Ribosomes 34, 35
Rostral 24
Rough endoplasmic reticulum 34, 35

## S

Sagittal section 22, 23
Saltatory conduction 42
Schwann cells 42, 43
Secondary auditory cortex 136, 137
Secondary motor area 114, 115
Secondary motor cortex 150, 151
Secondary sensory area 114, 115
Secondary somatosensory cortex 140, 141
Sensory nerves 10, 11
Septum 118, 119, 188, 189
Serotonin 142, 192
Sexually dimorphic nucleus 196, 197
Short-term memory 168
Signal proteins 44, 45, 49
Slow-wave sleep 192
Soma 32, 33
Somatic nervous system 8, 9
Somatosensory homunculus 140, 141
Somatotopic 140, 152
Spinal cord 6, 7, 10-13
    cervical region 4, 5, 12, 13
    lumbar region 4, 5, 12, 13
    sacral region 4, 5, 12, 13
    thoracic region 4, 5, 12, 13

Spinal gray matter 10, 11
Spinal white matter 10, 11
Spinocerebellar tract 158
Stellate cell 112, 113
Striate cortex 132
Striatum 120, 121, 158, 160, 161, 188, 189
Subarachnoid space 72, 73, 74
Subfornical organ 186, 187
Subicular cortex 168, 169, 173
Substantia nigra 92, 93, 160, 161, 188, 189
Sulcus 106, 107
Superior 24, 25
Superior colliculus 92, 93, 95
Superior frontal gyrus 110, 111
Superior olivary nucleus 134, 135
Superior prefrontal cortex 210, 211
Superior temporal cortex 208, 209
Superior temporal gyrus 110, 111, 137
Supplementary motor area 150, 151
Suprachiasmatic nucleus 96, 97, 99, 187, 194, 195
Supraoptic nucleus 99
Sympathetic nervous system 12, 13, 190
Synapse 38-41
Synapse formation 54, 55
Synaptic transmission 40, 41
Synaptic vesicles 36, 37, 40, 41

## T

Tectum 92, 93, 156
Tegmentum 92, 93
Telencephalon 58, 59, 70, 71
Temporal lobe 108, 109, 169
Temporal lobes 78, 79
Testes 14, 15
Testosterone 196
Thalamus 94, 95, 115, 119, 121, 152, 153, 159, 174, 175, 177, 185
    internal lamina 94, 95
    lateral geniculate nucleus 94, 95
    medial geniculate nucleus 94, 95
    ventral posterior nucleus 94, 95
Third ventricle 74, 75, 78, 143, 153, 174, 175, 185-187
Threshold of excitation 38, 40
Thymus 15
Thyroid 15
Tonotopic 136
Totipotential 52
Tracts 76, 77

Trigeminal nerve 80, 81, 138, 139
Trigeminal nucleus 138, 139
Trochlear nerve 81
Tropic hormones 14

## U

Unilateral 26, 27

## V

Vagus nerve 80, 81
Ventral 24, 25
Ventral posterior nucleus 94, 95, 138, 139
Ventral roots 10, 11
Ventral route 132, 133
Ventral tegmental area 188, 189
Ventromedial cortico-brainstem spinal tract 156, 157
Ventromedial corticospinal tract 156, 157
Ventromedial nucleus 96, 97, 184, 185, 196, 197
Vertebrae 4, 5
Vestibular nerve 134
Vestibular nucleus 156
Vestibulocochlear nerve 80, 81, 134

## W

Wernicke-Geschwind model 204, 206
Wernicke's area 204, 205
White matter 42, 106

## Z

Zeitgeber 194